My Baseball Journey
A Sportscaster's Story

My Baseball Journey
A Sportscaster's Story

Bill Brown and Tim Gregg

Foreword by Craig Biggio

*To my good friend Zach—May you continue to inspire
the best in others as well as yourself.*

Former Houston Astros All-Star and St. Thomas High School
Baseball Coach Craig Biggio with Zach Hamm

CONTENTS

To

Myrna

My Baseball Journey
A Sportscaster's Story

Thanks For Supporting NFED!

Bill
Brown

Zach
Hamm

Myrna~
Hope you enjoy the book!

Romans 5:3-4

FOREWORD

Players know when they stink.

And in the minds of most players, at least when it comes to the media which covers their games, there's a good way you can talk about or write about a poor performance and then there's the "other" way you can describe it.

Bill Brown has always been respectful in letting fans know when a player stinks. For me, that's class.

I feel fortunate to have worn Houston's baseball colors for twenty seasons. During my career, the things that stuck with me were the bad times: the slumps, the heartbreaking defeats, the disappointment of a season ending short of the goal. True competitors hate that kind of stuff. Now, since I've been retired for a while, what I remember most about my playing days are the good times: the 3,000th-hit game, getting to the World Series, and the camaraderie which is a little hard to find in the outside world.

While much of my baseball life played out on television, as a kid I found it painful watching the game on TV. I loved to play—I could do that all day—but watching someone else play wasn't really my thing. Growing up on Long Island, I would go to a Yankees' game maybe once a year. Thurman Munson was my favorite player. When I got to the big leagues myself, that's when I really started paying attention to what I saw on television. The guys I watched were the guys I played against. I frequently tuned in just to try to pick up an edge.

Television also helped educate me on the history of baseball. I have a lot of respect for the players who came before me and for the sacrifices and the commitments they made. Now, I'm trying to help pass on that legacy to the next generation. That's where the game's great storytellers—people like Bill—become so important. Personally, I don't think I'm cut out for a spot in the broadcast booth. I've enjoyed coaching my sons' high school baseball team in Houston. The game still seems to suit me best from field level.

Bill got to Houston a year before I did. He'd already been around baseball for a while by the time our paths crossed. Whether in the dugout for an interview or on a team flight over a beer, Bill helped me understand as a young ballplayer what it meant to be in the big leagues. The players knew Bill could be trusted. You could let down your guard with him in a private moment and be assured what you had to say wouldn't wind up on the air the next day. As I grew older, I gained more and more respect for Bill as a man. Today I feel fortunate to call him a friend.

Bill Brown and I share a common bond. We got to the top of our professions, and then we stayed there to have a pretty good run. And we did it, in a sense, side by side.

What does it take to be the best? Dedication, perseverance, and humility are qualities that come to mind. And so is loyalty: to the organization, to the fans, and to the game. Both on the field and behind a microphone, the commitment to excellence is pretty much the same.

This is a different kind of baseball book. I'm glad Bill has taken the time to look back on his life and it's a privilege to have been a part of his story.

But, Bill's motivation to write this book goes beyond wins, losses, averages, and spinning a few good yarns. People matter a lot to Bill, and some of the stories about people you'll find in the pages to follow will inspire you.

One of those stories is about a youngster I've spent a lot of time with in the last couple of years. His name is Zach Hamm. That's him with Bill on the front cover of the book, and with me in the photo on the dedication page. Zach has overcome a lot to get to where he is today. He's an inspiration to both Bill and me. Proceeds from the sales of this book will go toward helping make Zach's life—and the lives of those who also suffer from a pretty crummy disease called ectodermal dysplasia—better in the years ahead.

Whether or not you're a baseball fan, I think you'll enjoy Bill's book. I encourage you to tell your friends about it. From beginning to end, Bill writes from a position of humility and integrity. As he's done for more than twenty-five years as the television voice of the Astros, Bill tells it like he's seen it, and he does so in a fair and honest way.

Like I said before, in my book that's class.

Craig Biggio
Houston, Texas

PREFACE

Hope springs eternal in the human breast;
Man never Is, but always to be blest:
The soul, uneasy and confin'd from home,
Rests and expatiates in a life to come.

Alexander Pope
An Essay on Man, Epistle I

Pope probably didn't have baseball in mind when he famously wrote about the origins of optimism. After all, the English poet expressed his sentiment more than a hundred years before New York City volunteer firefighter Alexander Cartwright invented the game he called "town ball."

Long-suffering Brooklyn Dodger fans expressed predilection for their 20th-century team in more colloquial terms. "Wait 'til next year!" became the perennial September battle cry, echoing from the rafters of stately Ebbets Field. Then, one day, next year never came. The team moved west to California and the landscape of baseball was forever changed.

Soon, the Astros will be making their own move "West," across league boundaries and into a new division. Thus, "next year"—the 2013 season—will bring considerable change to the baseball landscape in Houston.

Perhaps change will be a good thing for the Astros and their fans. The 2011 campaign was a tough one as the team lost a club-record 106 games. It was also a year of transition, first on the field and later in the front office. By season's end, nearly a dozen first-year players dotted the Houston roster and by year's end a new owner had taken over the reins of the franchise.

It appears Jim Crane is approaching the business of baseball with a different mindset than has been seen around the club in recent years. His stated aim is to build a foundation on which success can be achieved for years to come.

Hope does spring eternal. I've seen it with my own eyes.

The 1991 Astros, much like the team of today, featured a youth movement in progress. Only one regular was older than 28. Despite tying a then club-record for losses in a year—ninety-seven—that season was not without its highlights: 23-year-old first baseman Jeff Bagwell won the NL Rookie of the Year award and 25-year-old catcher Craig Biggio was named an All-Star for the first time. Also that season, rookies Luis Gonzalez and Darryl Kile showed flashes of the brilliance which would make them future big league standouts, as did 24-year-old reliever Curt Schilling, later to become a mainstay on World Series championship teams in Phoenix and Boston.

As the television voice of the Astros for 25 years, I've had the best seat in the house to witness the rise and fall of Houston's baseball fortunes, from the lean years of '91 and '11 to six of the nine playoff appearances the team has made. I've seen milestones achieved and records broken, been privy to behind-the-scenes decisions which have changed the face of the franchise, and have personally witnessed the on- and off-field heartache and triumph which comes with a life lived as a big league ballplayer.

Some broadcasters—Vin Scully, Jack Buck, and our own Milo Hamilton immediately spring to mind—also become household names, even sporting institutions. Prodigious egos sit behind a few of the big league microphones, just as inflated opinions of self-worth can be found among those who perform on the field of play.

But, there are many more good, honest, and humble people who both play and cover the game.

Those who achieve success in their life's calling, even those of us who make our living "making the calls," usually learn the importance of a grounded existence. I was fortunate to be nurtured into manhood by caring parents, and to have found a loving wife, my bride of more than forty years Dianne, who has stood with me in the face of all manner of challenges. Jesus Christ is also, for me, a rock in a sometimes weary land.

When it came to choosing a title for this book, two finalists emerged from a long list of suggestions. The first was *Descriptions and Accounts*. Baseball fans—sports fans in general—are familiar with the copyright disclaimer read or shown during almost every professional and collegiate broadcast. It goes something like this:

"Any publication, rebroadcast, or other use of the pictures, descriptions, and accounts of this game without the express written consent of the (team name here) is strictly prohibited."

The title seemed fitting because the book contains descriptions of my life story as well as accounts of the lives of those who have influenced and inspired me. Some of those are individuals you know well. Others are people you may be meeting for the first time.

Ultimately, though, my life—like yours—has been a journey, with twists and turns and triumphs and tribulations. At the heart of that journey, baseball has been the constant.

My decision to write this book was inspired by one of the most influential and memorable people I've had the privilege to meet in recent years. Zach Hamm is a go-getter and a do-gooder. Any room he walks into instantly becomes his own through his combination of charm, personality, and spirit. He's the founder of and driving force behind the aptly named "Don't Sweat It Golf Classic" played each year on his home course at Gleannloch Pines Golf Club in far northwest Houston. The event benefits the National Foundation for Ectodermal Dysplasias.

Did I mention Zach is twelve years old? You'll meet him and learn more about his worthy cause later in the book.

The past twelve months have been quite a year for those of us who follow the Houston Astros. During the 2011 campaign I was regularly reminded of the words of Hall-of-Fame manager Sparky Anderson, one of the most interesting and charismatic people I've encountered during my time in baseball. I grew to become friends with Sparky during his tenure at the helm of Cincinnati's "Big Red Machine."

Those Reds teams didn't lose a lot—in fact, they won back-to-back World Series championships during my time as a Cincinnati broadcaster. When they did lose, Anderson had a strong conviction about the best way to cope with defeat:

> **"I cannot get rid of the hurt from losing, but after the last out of every loss, I must accept that there will be a tomorrow. In fact, it's more than there'll be a tomorrow, it's that I want there to be a tomorrow. That's the big difference, I want tomorrow to come."**

For Sparky Anderson, waiting until next year was never an option. He looked ahead to tomorrows and in doing so became one of only two managers to win the World Series in both leagues. As for me, this book is a collection of the tomorrows which became my most memorable yesterdays. My desire is that the descriptions and accounts of the life I've lived will be of interest, and that you, the reader, will discover inspiration and instruction from the tales on the pages to come.

May hope spring eternal in all your seasons to come.

INTRODUCTION

Like many men of his generation, my father wasn't much for offering advice. He grew up under modest circumstances, came of age during the Great Depression, and served his country with honor in World War II. For the duration of his professional life he practiced law in the small central Missouri town of Sedalia, where he married and raised two children. Upon retirement, my father and mother moved to Arizona and it was there, in the autumn of 1992, that he died.

His influence on me was immense.

William Forrest Brown was born on June 10, 1910, in Roger Mills County, Oklahoma. When my father was just two, his mother died, and his father abandoned the family. Relatives took in the four children as best they could. Ultimately, young Billy wound up with his maternal grandmother in the small Iowa town of Lamoni, which derived its name from a pacifist king in the Book of Mormon. Lamoni remains a significant historic site for the Community of Christ, previously known as the Reorganized Church of Jesus Christ of Latter Day Saints.

Eddie Watt, who wrapped up a ten-year major league career in Chicago just as I was getting my start as a big league broadcaster in Cincinnati, also hails from Lamoni.

From an early age, my father set his sights on becoming a lawyer. He was a good student and a good athlete in high school. He was the first in his family to attend college, but that effort was derailed for a time by the onset of the Great Depression. Still, Dad persevered, ultimately working his way to a degree from the Kansas City School of Law.

Seeking to establish a practice in a small town, he moved to Sedalia, about 90 miles southeast of Kansas City. Life there suited Dad's nature, but building a business takes time, especially when law is your trade. Thanks to Uncle Sam, Dad found steady employment in service to his country following the full-scale outbreak of World War II.

Dad joined the U.S. Army and was sent to the Pacific theater. He advanced quickly in rank and became a supply sergeant. He spent two-and-a-half years in the military before the atomic bombs were dropped on Japan. Upon his return to the States, the first thing he did was seek out the biggest, greenest head of lettuce he could find and eat the whole thing like an apple. Fresh produce had been in short supply during the war—even for a supply sergeant.

Although my father was fortunate not to see heavy combat, he met and befriended many soldiers who did. Over the course of the war, he heard stories of terrifying battles and heinous atrocities. He felt great sadness when casualty lists included the names of men he knew. Throughout most of the rest of his life, he talked little about his military experience. Almost always, he deflected questions to the story about that single head of lettuce.

***

Dad returned to Sedalia after the war and resumed his practice in a modest office on the second floor of a building across the street from the county courthouse. Soon, business began to pick up, due in part to his tending to the legal matters of other returning veterans. As his caseload grew, he found the need for an assistant and hired a bright, young, and attractive secretary by the name of Hazel Colvin. Soon, Dad developed an interest in Ms. Colvin beyond her typing and filing skills. They eloped on December 28, 1946.

Shortly after my birth on September 20, 1947, Mom and Dad moved into their first home. While the original structure was small—a tiny kitchen, two bedrooms, one bathroom, a living room and a garage—the lot on which it stood was huge. Over the years, the house grew in size as my father's legal practice and his family, with the addition of my sister Jessica, both flourished.

Dad always had a keen mind, legal and otherwise. He was known for his large vocabulary and lighthearted use of polysyllabic words. He frequently counseled my sister and me—almost always with a smile on his face—to "conduct ourselves with dignity and decorum." His way of asking about our day at school tended toward the obtuse. "Did they teach you The Rosicrucian Theory of Cosmo-Conception?" he'd inquire. When our puzzlement finally gave way to curiosity, he explained Rosicrucianism was a philosophical "secret society." Today membership in the Rosicrucian Order is open to all and a mere click away on the organization's Web site.

Throughout his life, it wasn't uncommon for my father to suddenly burst into extemporaneous conjugation of random Latin verbs. Dad rarely met a circumstance he couldn't convolute, at least for those of us with less than an advanced degree in English literature. For instance, when a man found trouble of his own making, Dad proclaimed the individual had received a "hoist with his own petard." Jessica later discovered the line was from Shakespeare's *Hamlet*.

My father also liked to say, "It's erysipelas with me." He'd just chuckle when we asked what that meant. It wasn't until many years later that Jessica ran across the word in James Herriot's book *All Creatures Great and Small*. It turns out erysipelas is an acute bacterial infection common to both humans and pigs. Jessica was quite proud when she called

Dad to alert him of her discovery. She says she can still hear his laughter on the other end of the line.

I distinctly remember the first time Mom called me with concerns about my dad's well-being, years after their move to the giant retirement enclave of Sun City, Arizona, on the northwest side of the Greater Phoenix area. As he grew older, Dad's memory began to fail him and increasingly his attempts at word play came up short of the mark. While my father grew more and more frustrated with his memory lapses, no one really gave it too much thought as those were the days when senility was a word used much more than dementia and few people had a very good understanding of "Old-Timer's Disease."

Eventually, the situation grew worse.

"He keeps getting up in the middle of the night and sometimes he leaves the house," Mom told me on the phone in 1991. Alarmed with her revelation, I asked if she knew why he would do such a thing. "He says he's going to work," she replied, "and sometimes he leaves wearing only his pajamas and bathrobe. I'm afraid he'll get lost or something bad will happen to him."

My parents were always vivacious and self-reliant people. I was caught off guard with my mother's intimation. There had been signs for some time something wasn't quite right with Dad, but this new turn of events was disturbing.

"At first I thought he was just confused," she continued, "but I think it could be more serious than that."

Soon after, Dad was diagnosed with Alzheimer's disease.

***

Among my most enduring childhood memories are the times I found my father up before the crack of dawn preparing for his work day at our kitchen table. Many were the mornings I would shuffle into the kitchen for breakfast to find him immersed in a case file or making notes on his legal pad. When asked, he invariably described his labors in the simplest of terms. Not wanting to disturb him, I carefully made room at the table for both my bowl of cold cereal and the sports section of the morning newspaper.

My dad was an immensely likable man and he was a good husband and father. He was, by all accounts, a dynamo in front of a judge and jury, a man of great charm and complete conviction. As Alzheimer's ravaged his brain, silence became his ever-more constant and unwelcome companion.

On a visit to Arizona to see my parents after his diagnosis, Dad and I again found ourselves alone together at the kitchen table. It was there my father offered the only piece of advice he ever shared with me. "Whatever you do, son," he said in a somber tone, "don't let this happen to you."

Less than a year later he was gone.

My sister Jessica—"Jebby" as our family historian is better known—has compiled a list of Dad's favorite sayings. When a business entity seemed in disarray, he would observe, "You can't run a circus without a few clowns." He called his good friends "gentlemen of rare perspicacity and discernment," and if they were well dressed, they were a "picture of sartorial splendor."

Of bad news he would lament, "What a revolting development." Anyone who has lost a loved one to Alzheimer's understands what a revolting development the disease truly is.

Our daughter Allison adored her grandfather and as a child she loved to sit on his lap. Any time he was about to pinch her nose, he would say, "I'm going to tweak your proboscis." She'd look with wonderment into his eyes, scrunch her face, and giggle.

I'd like to think my father was proud of my accomplishments, personal as well as professional. After retirement, when he and Mom visited us in Houston, I would sometimes bring Dad to the ballpark. He usually didn't have much to say. In hindsight, that might have been an early sign of the disease which claimed his life. I know he enjoyed those times and I enjoyed having him with me.

And in many respects, he's still with me today.

CHAPTER 1
"What a Time for Houston Baseball"

One of life's great pleasures is simply sitting around and talking. Anyone can do it. Everyone *does* do it. Some of the time, some of us—the lucky ones—actually get paid to do it. Such is my life as one of the fortunate few to earn a livelihood as a play-by-play announcer for a big league baseball team. With a turn of phrase to describe just the right moment in just the right way, a sportscaster's words can become immortal. With a slip of the tongue, the man behind the microphone can be "hoisted by his own petard."

Same holds true for the women in the broadcast business.

My job may seem "glamorous" to some, but during a baseball season, I'm sort of a working stiff like most Americans. Granted, I really love my job—I'm one of the fortunate few in that regard, too—but, on average, I put in eight-hour days, have a boss who demands my best, and occasionally I'll make a mistake. Frequently I eat at my desk and stay late at the office, and sometimes I'll question—at least to myself—management's decisions. I mean, who among us hasn't second-guessed whether or not to pitch to Albert Pujols with runners on and first base open.

A baseball broadcaster's biggest job is to fill the steady downtime between pitches with pertinent and pithy remarks. In the 2012 Astros booth, I specialize in the pertinent details,

1

while my partner Jim Deshaies gets to handle the "pithy" side of things. That's the way we've tried to do it—for the most part—since 1997.

On the afternoon of June 27, 2007, JD and I did our best to keep things interesting and lively over the course of a three-hour, twenty-minute ballgame in Milwaukee. The Astros lost that Wednesday afternoon contest 6-3 in eleven innings. The defeat dropped the team's record to 32-46, fourteen games out of first place in the National League Central Division.

Despite yet another lackluster start to an Astros season, ratings for our television broadcasts remained high and fans continued to flock to home games at Minute Maid Park. Team icon Craig Biggio was on his way to becoming the first Astro to total 3,000 career base hits and the milestone mattered a lot to everyone. A fixture at the top of the Houston batting order for 20 seasons, Biggio was seeking to achieve a distinction only a handful of big league players had ever attained.

With the extra-inning loss at Miller Park, the veteran second baseman completed the team's nine-game road trip with eight hits, three short of the milestone. Wanting to ensure his career-crowning achievement took place in front of the home fans, the club gave Biggio the day off in the series finale with the Brewers. He did pinch hit in the eleventh, fouling out to first. That hitless at-bat lowered his season batting average to .238, almost forty-five points below his career mark. Age seemed to have caught up with the perennial All-Star.

Good things can be a long time coming, and standout athletes accustomed to performing for the good of a team can occasionally experience a sort of emotional meltdown when chasing individual achievement. Roger Maris lost clumps of hair in his pursuit of Babe Ruth's single-season home run record. No one may hit .400 in a season again simply because the pressure over the long haul is just too great.

The strain of reaching 3,000 hits weighed so heavily on Yankee Derek Jeter that after finally achieving the milestone and becoming the twenty-eighth player to join the esteemed club, he bowed out of the 2011 All-Star game due to mental fatigue. Jeter missing the Mid-Summer Classic was like swallows failing to return to Capistrano.

Even entire countries can be affected by malaise. Recently, the nation of Belgium went 461 days without an official government.

But what about the pressures facing the *broadcaster* destined to make the historic call? Nobody thinks about him, but if he's worth his salt, he gives the matter ample consideration—most of the time.

On the flight from Milwaukee home to Houston and with Biggio's 3,000th hit an impending certainty, I pondered my responsibility in the scheme of things. My call of Biggio's historic moment would matter, although it took a friend to help me reach that obvious conclusion.

Wayne Hagin was the voice of the Colorado Rockies for the first decade of the team's baseball existence. He still makes Denver his off-season home. With almost as many years of big league service as I, Wayne is a trusted ally. When I saw him for lunch while the Astros were at Coors Field to face the Rockies early in the '07 season, Wayne seemed relaxed and in good spirits. He had been forced to sit out the year after his contract was not renewed in St. Louis.

"Have you thought about what you're going to say when Biggio gets the hit," Hagin asked in one of the trendy restaurants populating Denver's LoDo district near the ballpark. "You must be excited about the prospect of being involved in that."

"Honestly, Wayne, I haven't given it too much thought," I said. "I guess I figure I'll be spontaneous and try to stay in the moment when it comes."

3

Hagin smiled and put down his fork. "This isn't about just the moment, Bill. This is going to be one of the handful of achievements which will define your own career. You might think about having something prepared to say when it happens. "That can take off a lot of the pressure if something unpredictable takes place."

Unpredictable? I hadn't thought about the event in those terms. I nodded my head in agreement as I sliced off another bite of key lime pie.

"It's baseball," Hagin added. "You never know."

Scripting a moment during a live broadcast—other than live spots, sponsor mentions, or the copyright disclaimer— was almost unthinkable to me, just not part of how I chose to do my job. And then, strangely, I thought of how my Dad had been stripped of his command of the language by an insidious disease. Wayne was right. I couldn't be left with nothing to say.

Not until I pulled into my driveway after the Milwaukee trip did I come up with a flicker of an idea as to how I might frame Biggio's big moment. With Dianne already asleep—she gave up waiting on me a long time ago—I entered the house as quietly as possible and sat my bags on the floor. I found a pad of paper in a kitchen drawer and sat down at the breakfast table to make a few notes. Relieved I finally had the beginnings of a plan in place, I headed off to bed.

I figured I probably had a couple more days to sort things out.

The next morning while preparing my scorebook for that evening's broadcast, I took another look at the note from the night before. I mulled over the idea for a time and then, on a clean sheet of paper, I wrote words I thought might be appropriate to say. I spent probably 30 minutes on the matter. Once done, I folded the sheet of paper into my scorebook and breathed a sigh of relief. The words would be there if I needed them, but then another thought popped into my head.

Sometimes, what you don't say can have as powerful an impact as what you do say.

For decades, play-by-play men have avoided dead air like the plague. Russ Hodges' 1951 call of the "Shot Heard Round the World," Bobby Thomson's dramatic pennant-clinching home run for the New York Giants, is a classic example of an announcer's instinctive need to keep talking.

As Thomson's fly ball sailed into the left field bleachers of the Polo Grounds, Hodges screamed to his listeners "The Giants win the pennant!" He repeated the exclamation five times before twice adding, "They're going crazy!" and remarking aloud "I don't believe it!" three consecutive times. Finally, with a "Heyyyyy-ooohhhhh!" Hodges ran out of things to say, and took a deep breath.

A 23-year-old Vin Scully would have been behind the microphone for the Brooklyn Dodgers that day, but the winners write—and announce—history. Compared with today's sensibilities, Hodges probably got a little carried away with his call, but the moment did culminate a dramatic final six weeks of the season in which the Giants erased a thirteen-and-a-half-game deficit to force the best-of-three playoff which Thomson's home run ended.

Scully is still going strong in his seventh decade as the Voice of the Dodgers. He was among the first in the television sportscasting business to realize how effective silence can be in telling a story on the air.

In the pantheon of greatest moments in sports broadcasting history, the one Al Michaels got to call at the 1980 Winter Olympics ranks near the top. Al and I were colleagues in Cincinnati in the early 1970s. I was a new kid in town while Al was doing radio play-by-play for the Reds. Michaels was friendly and approachable, just three years older than I. His "one-of-the-guys" demeanor belied his amazing talent.

Rarely does a sportscaster's work become a culture touchstone, but Michaels' call during the waning seconds of the "Miracle on Ice" was truly one for the ages. In the final moments of the U.S. hockey team's historic Winter Olympics win over the Soviet Union, Michaels posed a rhetorical question: "Do you believe in miracles?" He later said the word "miraculous" popped into his head as he described the Soviets' furious last-minute efforts to tie the game. The Russians failed, but Michaels succeeded in defining one of the greatest moments in American sports history by answering his own question as the game came to an end.

"Yes!"

Michaels then fell silent for more than a minute as the pictures and sounds of the ensuing celebration, both on the ice and throughout the arena, told the story in a way spoken words could not. Michaels put aside both his instincts and ego to let the camera shots draw his viewers into the emotion of the occasion—a once-in-a-generation experience on both sides of the cathode-ray tube.

***

Anticipation filled the air upon Biggio's return home to continue his pursuit of 3,000 hits. I arrived at Minute Maid Park the afternoon of June 28 shortly before three o'clock for the 7:05 p.m. game. And like the fans who packed the house that evening, all of us on the Fox Sports Southwest crew were eager to see history in the making.

Biggio needed three hits. In just the last sixteen days, he'd cranked out three three-hit games. Anything was possible.

Roy Oswalt got the nod as the starting pitcher for the Astros against Colorado right-hander Aaron Cook. A standing-room-only crowd of 42,537 took their seats a little early. The stage was set.

In the home half of the first inning, a standing-room only crowd of 42,537 greeted Biggio as he led off for Houston. Cook coaxed him into grounding out to third. Colorado broke a scoreless tie in the top of the third on a solo home run by catcher Chris Iannetta. In the bottom of the third, after Oswalt singled with one away, Biggio batted again. By then, former Astros great Jeff Bagwell—linked to Biggio like Lewis is to Clark, Hall is to Oates, and Bartles is to Jaymes—joined us in the broadcast booth.

Houston's all-time home run leader had cut short a trip to Colorado to be home for Biggio's big moment. Just about the time the Astros' second-baseman approached the batter's box, Bagwell got a little sidetracked. While golfing on his recent vacation, Bagwell recorded a hole in one. As Biggio dug in to face Cook, viewers learned way more about Bagwell's ace than they probably wanted to know. When it appeared the story might run deep into the Biggio's at-bat, I gave Jeff a nervous look. He picked up the cue and circled the conversation back to the moment at hand.

"It would have been a little bit nicer if he had gotten one or two more (hits in Milwaukee)," Bagwell told viewers, "just to get this thing over with and get this monkey off his back."

Deshaies and Bagwell agreed it would be fitting if hit number 3,000 turned out to be a double since Biggio was one of baseball's all-time leaders in that offensive category. With what sounded like insider information, Bagwell observed, "Second base is the plan, I promise you that."

As had been the case with his lead-off appearance in the first, flashbulbs exploded throughout the ball park in a dizzying array as Biggio took his cuts. On a 2-2 offering, he lined a Cook fastball to left center for a base hit. Oswalt stopped at second base.

A recent re-examination of the broadcast of that game revealed my call of that single to be simple and straightforward, "Line drive and there's one of them. Two-nine-nine-eight." Both Houston runners were stranded as the inning came to an end.

The Rockies still led by a run when Biggio batted again in the fifth, this time with one out and nobody on. Our Fox Sports cameras caught wife Patty and daughter Quinn watching the game from the Diamond-level seats behind home plate as their man of the house adjusted his pine-tar-laden batting helmet at home plate. On an 0-1 delivery from Cook, Biggio hit a smash toward third. Garrett Atkins backhanded the ball, but his hurried throw was wild, landing in the seats behind first base. The play was scored a hit and an error.

In the booth, Deshaies breathed a sigh of relief, happy such a messy play hadn't marked the historic occasion. The infield hit left Biggio just one hit short of immortality. Again, he was stranded on base as the inning ended.

The Rockies continued to cling to their 1-0 lead when Biggio batted in the seventh with two outs and Brad Ausmus on second base. Home plate umpire Larry Poncino accepted a supply of specially authenticated baseballs to ensure that if history was made in Houston, the right ball would find its place at Cooperstown.

"You know you've got it going on when they use special baseballs for you," Deshaies crowed on the air. A few seconds later, JD further threw decorum to the wind.

"Double down the line, how about it!" he cheered as Hilry Thornal, our director for the telecast, began a sequence of crowd shots.

"Look at Patty!" Deshaies laughed peering at his monitor in the booth. "There's something exciting going on here." He looked at me and we both took a deep breath.

Then, as if on cue, fans throughout the stadium and in one accord took up the chant which had become so familiar over the years.

"BIJ-EE-OH! BIJ-EE-OH!" The noise was extreme.

"Important memories for these kids," said Deshaies, speaking not only of the rest of Craig's family—sons Conor and Cavan in the Houston dugout—but also to the kid in each of us who was there that night, either in person or watching the telecast.

Here's how Biggio's seventh-inning at bat played out on television:

> Bill Brown (BB): *"He singled in the third, a line drive over shortstop. Ground ball behind third in the fifth.*
>
> (Pause as the "Bij-ee-oh" chant continues in the background)
>
> Jim Deshaies (JD): *"Get your cameras ready!"*
>
> BB: *"Flashbulbs popping. (Cook throws the first pitch). Ball one. With his two-for-three night, he's now five for twelve against Aaron Cook, who was complimentary in his pregame interview. But he would just as soon not be the guy to give up 3,000, he said."*
>
> (More crowd noise for the next five seconds; a sequence of great shots from the camera crew.)
>
> JD: *"Good action on that sinker. Of course, Cook trying to preserve a shutout and a 1-0 lead. (Pause) Not a whole lot of room between Atkins and the line."*

Cook's next pitch missed the strike zone and another great roar came from the crowd. Biggio stepped out of the box. Nervously, he adjusted his helmet and batting gloves, took his own deep breath, and looked to third base coach Doug Mansolino—as if there was any doubt what he would be trying to do with a 2-0 pitch.

Biggio moved back into the batter's box. From the mound, Cook looked in for the sign from Iannetta, nodded agreement, and went into his stretch with Ausmus taking a conservative lead off second base. Cook lifted his front leg and delivered the pitch toward home.

> BB: *"Line drive, right center field - that's number 3,000 and he drives in a run and he's going for second! Taveras with the throw. He's...out, but that's 3,000 hits for Craig Biggio! It ties the ball game!"*

Jeff Bagwell's insider information had been dead on. Biggio clearly wanted a double to be his 3,000th hit and took a gamble he wouldn't have normally made. Somewhat awkwardly, the milestone achievement resulted in the third out of the inning.

Who would have imagined something like that? Completely unexpected.

Fortunately, I knew what I wanted to say. My plan from the night before was to frame the moment with a brief summation of Biggio's career. So, I looked down to my scorebook, found my note, and began to read, improvising jut a little along the way.

> BB: *"He arrived twenty years ago from Smithtown, New York, with Texas-sized dreams and now, as he's mobbed by his teammates, those dreams have become reality, and they'll be recognized some day in another town in New York - Cooperstown. 3,000 hits for Craig Biggio, the 27th man to reach that figure."*

> JD: *"Here comes Patty and Quinn, Conor and Cavan. The boys have been on the last two road trips and they're in the dugout."*

> (Crowd noise for approximately six seconds.)

> BB: *"What a time for Houston baseball; one of the few*

players to get all of his 3,000 hits for one team."

JD: *"He's loving it with the boys and Patty and Quinn. Just nine now. Craig Biggio becomes the ninth player in Major League Baseball history to get 3,000 hits all with just one team. And he is overwhelmed. He was bound and determined to get to second base. He wanted that double in the worst way."*

BB: *"Pitching coach Dave Wallace, Lance Berkman as the teammates come one by one now to get their moment with Craig Biggio. 1988 - the day it started with the first hit of his career, June 29. Now on June 28, 2007, number 3,000.*

JD: *"When he first came to the big leagues I don't think he was shaving yet. They could knock the bat out of his hands. But they haven't been able to take the bat out of his hands for the next twenty years."*

BB: *"He's the all-time right-handed doubles leader and he tried for one more double. This would have been his 659th, but Willy Taveras threw him out."*

JD: *"Willy apparently failed to read the script."*

With history firmly secured, the two teams got down to the business of playing the rest of what turned out to be one heck of a baseball game!

The Rockies scored three times in the eighth to take a 4-1 lead. Houston answered with three in the home half of the inning on home runs by Lance Berkman and Mike Lamb. The game was knotted at 4-4 in the bottom of the 9th when Biggio led off with a single for his fourth hit of the night. But, he was stranded at first and the contest went into extra innings.

In the 11th, Colorado pushed across a run to take a 5-4 lead. Rockies' closer Brian Fuentes retired the first two Houston hitters he faced, which brought up Biggio with the outcome of the game—not his own personal achievement—on the line. Quickly, Fuentes got ahead on the count, no balls and two strikes. On the next pitch and with the pressure of 3,000 hits no longer a consideration, Biggio hit a slow roller to short, beat the throw to first, and upped his career hit total to 3,002. It was the second five-hit game of his career.

After a Hunter Pence double and a hit batsman, Carlos Lee came to the plate with the bases loaded.

> BB: *"Fly ball, left field, this could be a game winning grand slam... and Carlos Lee has done it! An unbelievable night in Houston, Texas! Carlos Lee with his second walk-off homer of the season."*
>
> JD: *"Wow, you have gotta be kidding me!"*
>
> BB: *"He is the all-time Panamanian home run leader and he has provided one of the most exciting nights in Houston, Texas, the capper on a Biggio night. And Biggio kept it going."*
>
> JD: *"Yeah, he did. With his hustle."*

Years later, after re-watching the telecast of that game, I came to a couple of interesting conclusions. I still feel good about my call of Biggio's 3,000[th] hit, but I sort of blew the aftermath of Lee's game-ending grand slam. The way I made it sound, being the all-time Panamanian leader in home runs topped 3,000 big league hits. That definitely was not and is not the case.

I mean, who could have scripted a moment like *that*?

CHAPTER 2
Wiffleball

If my life story ever makes the silver screen, it would begin with a flashback to the late 1950s.

Picture a beautiful, sunny, summer day on a residential street in Middletown, America. Elm and oak trees stand majestically in the front yards of comfortable middle-class homes. Here and there cars, bold in their palette of colors and oversized tail fins, sit parked in driveways or along the curb. Birds sing, dogs bark, and children play...wiffleball.

The humble beginnings of a broadcaster.

"There's a high fly ball to deep right field! Brown really got hold of that one! It's got a chance to go. It's going. It's going. It's..."

"Out! You're out, Billy Boy! Side retired!"

I, or my character, stand dumbfounded. As the cackle of my nemesis' laughter rings in my ears, I am flushed with embarrassment. The towering shot, with home run seemingly written all over it, lands well short of the Silverman's petunia bed across the street from my home near downtown Sedalia, Missouri. The corner of New England and 11th street is as famous for its wiffleball games—at least among my circle of friends—as the intersections of Grand and Dodier in St. Louis or Clark and Addison in Chicago are to big league baseball fans.

The ground rules of front-yard wiffleball at Brown Field are clear: any fly ball which fails to clear the street is an automatic out. Anything which caroms off the front of the houses or plops amidst the flowerbeds of the homes across the street is a double. Anything landing on the near side of our neighbors' roofs is a triple; and anything that clears the houses all together gives new meaning to the term "home" run.

I pound my thin plastic bat in frustration before slowly making my way to retrieve the white plastic ball with the peculiarly-elongated holes. This small sphere fills a disproportionate amount of summer for my friends and me, and keeps the passion strong for our ever-growing love of baseball.

Fade to black.

Today, as it was when I grew up there, Sedalia, Missouri, is a town of about 20,000 people, the Pettis County seat and home to the Missouri State Fair. Each year, Sedalia also hosts the Scott Joplin Ragtime Festival to honor the city's most famous musical son. In 1974, well after I had departed, more than 300,000 people descended on the fairgrounds in Sedalia for the Ozark Music Festival, a worthy successor, nearly equal in size, to the more famous three-day "Aquarian Exposition" held on the Yasgur farm near the hamlet of Woodstock, New York, in the summer of 1969.

During the Civil War, sentiments in town were split. Sedalia was a key rail terminus for Union forces, which at least made half the citizenry happy. During the Cold War, nearby Whiteman Air Force Base, home to the 351st Missile Wing, controlled scores of nuclear-armed missiles contained in underground silos around the Sedalia area. Among my most vivid early memories were the "duck-and-cover" Civil Defense drills held at my grade school. Hard to believe the prevailing sentiment of those bygone days was that a school desk could provide adequate protection from the immense destruction of an atomic bomb.

In the 1983 made-for-television movie *The Day After*, Sedalia was destroyed in a fictional limited nuclear war. Nothing was mentioned about whether grade-school children survived the annihilation.

One of the first Boy Scout troops in America was founded in Sedalia in 1909. And more than one hundred years later, on May 25, 2011, a tornado ripped through the town destroying homes and damaging businesses not too far from where I was raised.

Disasters, natural or otherwise, weren't on the minds of most young boys growing up in the heartland of America in the 1950s. My father provided well for his family and may have worried about disease, pestilence, and the Soviet threat, but he never talked about those things. My mother set the tone for our family. She was always a source of optimism and encouragement for anyone with whom she came in contact. Rarely did she have anything other than a smile on her face.

Hazel Colvin grew up a farm girl on the outskirts of Sedalia. Her father Harry was a milk man who lived in the country but didn't take much to raising livestock or crops. I remember seeing a few chickens when we paid him a visit, but that was about the extent of my grandfather's pursuit of farm living.

After he died, his widow Mildred moved in with my family and slept in my sister Jessica's room for a time. Our grandmother was crippled and at times confined to a wheelchair, but she was a welcome addition to our family unit.

Mom was a dutiful parent. She never approached raising her children as merely a job. She was upbeat and could be the life of the party. She loved working in the yard and eagerly endorsed my father's desire for our family to join the local country club. In fact, Mom enjoyed golf more than Dad. She took lessons, practiced, and immersed herself in the sport as much as a young mother with two children could do. She wound up winning upwards of a dozen club championships.

After my father died, Mom became an avid Astros fan and religiously watched the team's games on satellite television. It was not uncommon for her to call me with commentary and occasional criticism about player performance. She was always complimentary of the job I'd done, which, given her grasp of the sport, was no small praise. She died in 2009.

Mom was definitely the jock in the family and I did not inherit those genes. While not much of an athlete myself, from the beginning I was always a pretty good student. I paid attention in class and made good grades. Given Dad's keen intellect, both my sister and I were eager to emulate his worldly wisdom, if for no other reason than to figure out what the heck he was talking about so much of the time.

By the time I reached high school, I had sort of come into my own as a person. I was a better-than-average trumpet player, sitting first chair in both marching band and symphony orchestra. I even won a top rating at the state music festival one year.

Our music teacher, Gerry Schrader, was devoted to both her job and her students. One year our school musical was *South Pacific* and I played in the small orchestra which accompanied the production. Mrs. Schrader served as the conductor and at one point, I noticed she began to cry. Fearful our performance had been sub-standard, I approached her after the final curtain and asked if everything was okay.

"Oh, Bill, it was just wonderful," she exclaimed, her eyes still red. "*South Pacific* was my late husband's favorite musical and 'Some Enchanted Evening' was always our favorite song. Tonight reminded me of him."

Just a few years ago, Dianne and I had the opportunity to see a Broadway revival of the famous Rodgers and

Hammerstein musical and "Some Enchanted Evening" touched my heart that night, too.

Without question my favorite class in high school was Latin. If Deshaies catches wind of this piece of trivia, he's going to suspect I was a bit of a nerd growing up.

My Latin teacher at Sedalia's Smith-Cotton High School was John Allen. If one were to pick a Latin instructor out of a police lineup, Mr. Allen would have been the oh-so-obvious choice with his neatly pressed dark slacks, propensity toward sweater vests, and horned-rim glasses. Latin is a difficult language to learn and Mr. Allen was a stickler for details. He taught in a strict and no-nonsense manner. He was a widower and his students, particularly those who showed a passion for language, meant the world to him.

Even though Latin is no longer spoken in common usage, Mr. Allen made his courses come alive. I took three semesters of Latin in high school, which later made my required foreign language in college—Spanish—an absolute breeze. I'd like to think Mr. Allen and I became friends during my time in his classes. He lived into his 90s, and after he retired he wrote and published a volume of poetry which is one of my most prized possessions.

Another educator I'll never forget was my English teacher Susan Callis. On the other end of the age spectrum from Mr. Allen, Mrs. Callis was a former Smith-Cotton student herself. Fresh out of college, she seemed a bit overwhelmed with her job when she signed on to teach in her hometown.

One day she made the rookie mistake of stepping out of the class as her fifth-hour students filed in. Upon her return, she immediately took to writing instructions on the chalk board. When she turned to begin the period, her eye caught something amiss on her desk. Since I usually sat in the first couple rows, I followed her gaze to see what appeared to be a pile of vomit atop a stack of essays she was set to return and discuss.

Quickly, I determined the vomit wasn't real, although it was the first time I'd seen the newly-minted novelty item. Classroom discipline wasn't Mrs. Callis' strong point yet and when I saw her facial expression change, I feared either she or the class was in for the worst. As I eyed her closely, it appeared she might have stifled a shriek. To her credit, she quickly regained her composure and managed to ignore the practical joke.

After class, I waited for the rest of the students to leave before approaching Mrs. Callis at her desk.

"That was a dirty trick," I said, referring to the fake spew which Mrs. Callis had casually tossed into the trash can before handing us back our essays.

"Do you know who put it there?" she asked.

"No, ma'am. I didn't notice it until after class began. Maybe it was someone from fourth-hour?"

"Perhaps, Bill. I guess it's okay if it's all in good fun, but discipline must be maintained, wouldn't you agree?"

"Yes, ma'am," I said.

I began to walk away when Mrs. Callis called out.

"Oh, Bill, that was an excellent paper you turned in yesterday. You received one of the highest marks in the class."

"Thank you, ma'am. It was an easy paper to write. I've thought a lot about what I want to be when I grow up."

"So, you want to be a baseball announcer?" She paused as if looking for something more to say.

"That sounds exciting! I know you'll be a good one, if that's what you want to do."

***

The front-yard wiffleball field wasn't the only venue where I learned the meaning of diminishing expectations. From Little League and Babe Ruth play to ventures on the Connie Mack and Ban Johnson diamonds, I kept pushing

18

toward becoming an accomplished ballplayer, but the game kept pushing back. Each summer I began a new season with conviction: this would be the year my body and my God-given talent would finally equal my desire for the game. Instead, I learned a .150 batting average doesn't cut it at any level of play. Defensively, I was a weak-armed second baseman and as the years progressed, stiffer and stiffer competition nudged me further and further to the far reaches of the dugout bench.

Alas, if only my physical skills had been the match for my intellectual prowess as an APBA enthusiast, I, too might have someday become a "Killer B."

APBA, pronounced "APP-buh" was and is today a baseball simulation table game. The acronym stands for "American Professional Baseball Association," but no one ever called it that when I was a kid. Today, the game is available on Amazon.com, but hurry, only 14 remain at a retail price of $21.99.

For something approaching four times that amount, a computer-based version of the game is available via the APBA Web site.

As a youngster, particularly one who couldn't seem to play the game a lick, APBA was the next best thing to the real deal. The game, created in 1931, featured player-performance cards, from which a roll of the dice triggered life-like "action." There was a card for almost every big league player—each year a new set of cards was created—and the game was designed so the table play would closely resemble what might take place in a major league ballpark.

I became an APBA whiz because I played a lot and became familiar with how the numbers on the cards translated to results. And, I was not alone as an APBA aficionado. Not only did many of my friends play the game, but so, too, over the years have the likes of Presidents George H. W. Bush and his son George W., actor Jeff Daniels, sportswriter Frank Deford, and a quartet of fairly well-known baseball guys by the names of Torre, Kaat, Killebrew, and Schilling.

There is little doubt the game advances baseball knowledge, but who would have guessed it also hones critical leadership skills, too. Bet you never found a future president or MVP wasting time as a kid playing something as inane as Parcheesi. Actually, now that I think about it, Parcheesi was one of my sister's favorite games and since, as a librarian, she's a good bit brighter than me, I'll withhold judgment on her recreational past.

While I was among the league leaders at the APBA board, my father wasn't quite ready to give up the dream of my becoming—if not the next Nellie Fox—at least an average ballplayer. His hope for me continued to spring, if not eternal, at least into the beginning of each summer, which was how I wound up at the Mickey Owen Baseball School. It was there, near the small southwest Missouri town of Miller, my playing career effectively ended—at the ripe old age of 14.

Mickey Owen was a four-time major league All-Star catcher, but he was more well-known as one of the biggest World Series goats of his time. In fact, if not for Bill Buckner, people would still talk poorly of Owen—and undeservedly so.

With the Brooklyn Dodgers on the verge of leveling the 1941 World Series at two games apiece, Owen mishandled what would have been the final pitch of Game Four against the New York Yankees. When Tommy Heinrich's swinging strike three got away from him, allowing the Yankee to reach base, Owen unexpectedly opened the floodgates for the one of the Fall Classics most unexpected comebacks.

The Yankees rallied for five ninth-inning runs to win the game and then closed out the Series with a victory the following day. Owen took the blame with class and only years later was it revealed pitcher Hugh Casey may have crossed him up by unexpectedly throwing a spitball.

In 1942, Owen rebounded to become the first player to hit a pinch-hit home run in the All-Star Game. Prior to the 1946 season, after being unable to reach a new deal with the Dodgers, Owen, along with several other big league stars, signed a controversial-but-lucrative contract to play in the Mexican League. He was threatened with a lifetime ban from Major League Baseball, but instead served a three-year suspension, after which he spent three years as a backup catcher with the Chicago Cubs before ending his playing career.

In 1959, he founded the Mickey Owen Baseball School.

Campers at the Owen School stayed in cabins labeled with the nicknames of big league teams. Everyone ate together in a large cafeteria, but otherwise attendees were mostly divided into groups on a per-cabin basis.

My most vivid memory of the Owen School came during one of the many practice games played at the camp. Our catcher accidentally interfered with the swing of an opposing hitter and before anyone knew it, the two parties involved started swinging at each other. Unfortunately for all of us, Owen was monitoring our game. He immediately called a halt to the proceedings and sent the opposing team, made up of players from nearby Springfield, home. As for those of us who were full-time campers, we ran laps until we collapsed.

Sadly, the experience didn't raise my game to a new level and the most important lesson I learned at the Mickey Owen Baseball School was the importance of fair play and good sportsmanship. After selling the school in 1963, Owen got into law enforcement and became the county sheriff. In 1980, he made an unsuccessful run to become lieutenant governor of Missouri.

Meanwhile, I became a teen-aged baseball has-been.

***

In 1960, my father was a delegate to the Democratic National Convention supporting Missouri Senator Stuart Symington for the party's presidential nomination. Symington was an Ivy League-educated business executive from St. Louis who served four terms in the U.S. Senate, and was also the first Secretary of the Air Force during the presidency of fellow Missourian Harry Truman.

Although Symington did not receive the Democratic nomination, he and my dad became friends.

I joined Dad on a business trip to Washington in the summer of 1961 and we met with Symington in his office on Capitol Hill. The senator was a gracious host and kind enough to provide us with tickets for that night's game at Griffith Stadium, a matchup of baseball's two new expansion franchises—the Washington Senators and the Los Angeles Angels.

Growing up, I'd gone with Dad on a few outings to Municipal Stadium near downtown Kansas City to see the Athletics play, but the Senators-Angels game still left a big impression, thanks to the biggest man on the field, Angel first baseman Ted Kluszewski.

The strapping slugger from Argo, Illinois, was concluding his 15-year career that season. As was his fashion, he cut off the sleeves of his uniform shirt to reveal the most massive biceps in baseball. Over a three-year stretch with the Reds in the early '50s, Kluszewski hit 136 home runs, nearly half his career total.

Kluszewski looked even larger playing pre-game catch in front of the Angels' dugout with diminutive teammate Albie Pearson. At just 5 '5" and 140 pounds, Pearson was one of the smallest players in the game not named Gaedel or Keeler—although according to some accounts, "Wee Willie" Keeler may not have been as "wee" as his nickname suggested.

Perhaps in my incubating dreams of becoming a broadcaster I might have imagined getting acquainted with someone like "Big Klu" at some point of my professional life. In fact, we became friends after he took over as hitting coach for the Reds in Cincinnati. Later, as a roving minor league hitting instructor for the club, Kluszewski filled in as my partner on a few television broadcasts. He was always a welcome—albeit it oversized—presence in the booth.

By the time I turned 15—and with hopes of a baseball playing future extinguished—Dad decided I needed to find a job, which is how I came to work one summer in a bowling alley.

Broadway Lanes were about three blocks from my house, and the proprietor there, Charley Thompson, was kind enough to hire me part-time. Rather than employing me to play trumpet, conjugate Latin verbs, or excel at sports-themed board games, Mr. Thompson wanted me to do maintenance work. My "training" amounted to following around the chief maintenance man and watching him repair and adjust the automatic pinsetting machines. He wasn't the talkative sort and I wasn't the kind of person to ask questions, so we got along just fine.

In no time—or so I thought—I had mastered my new trade. Clearing pin jams became a snap and the pinsetters themselves rarely malfunctioned. Plus, I discovered the bowling alley was a popular Friday and Saturday night hangout for kids from the high school. And that meant girls.

I didn't actually meet any girls in the job, but I always took notice. *Something* distracted me one evening when, standing atop one of the pinsetter machines to ensure it functionality, my foot slipped and my leg fell into the slot where the 5-pin would normally go. Luckily, an eagle-eyed—and mostly sober—customer noticed a black loafer and khaki pant at the far end of the lane and thought better of trying to knock down that turkey.

I was fortunate my academic advancement at school took me out of the bowling business before I could do real damage to either the equipment or one of my appendages. All things considered though, it wasn't the worst summer of my life. After all, I got to meet an active big leaguer for the first time.

For years Charley Thompson made frequent visits to Kansas City to watch the Athletics play. Originally from New York, Charley was a big baseball fan who enjoyed seeing the Yankees when they were in town. Many A's fans did, too, as many of Kansas City's promising stars of the past eventually wore the Yankee uniform.

The Athletics moved from Philadelphia to Kansas City when Arnold Johnson bought the franchise after the 1954 season. In doing so, Johnson had to give up one of his most prized real estate holdings: Yankee Stadium. For the rest of the decade, the A's were awful and the Yankees were perennial pennant winners, thanks in part to some suspect deals between the two clubs.

The shenanigans between Athletic and Yankee management, coupled with the fact Kansas City never won much, limited my enthusiasm for the A's. I never really adopted them, or any other club, as my favorite team.

Dorrell Norman Herzog—more commonly called "Whitey"—was a former Yankee prospect who wound up in Kansas City. Somehow my boss at Broadway Lanes and Herzog became friends. Even after Whitey was traded from the Athletics to the Baltimore Orioles in 1960, he and Thompson still saw each other socially when the Orioles visited Kansas City to play. During an off day in the summer of '62, Herzog drove to Sedalia and had the good fortune to meet the young Bill Brown.

As I recall, one of us came away with an autographed photo.

Herzog finished his playing career with a .257 average and 25 home runs in eight seasons as a part-time player. But it wasn't as a player that Whitey made his mark. His stellar managerial career, which included a stay in Kansas City as skipper of the Royals and three National League pennants in St. Louis, is what ultimately earned him enshrinement into the National Baseball Hall of Fame.

I can't say meeting Herzog and Owen, or watching Kluszewski and Pearson play, inspired me to become a broadcaster. Perhaps the most important event which shaped my future career was the purchase of a cassette tape recorder with the money earned from my job at Broadway Lanes. For the next couple summers, whenever a friend happened to be at my house on a Saturday afternoon, we'd tune in the *Game of the Week*, turn down the sound on the television, and call the action ourselves. Since I was never going to become the next Nellie Fox, I set my sights on emulating some of the great broadcasters of the day, men like Merle Harmon and Monte Moore in Kansas City, and Harry Caray and Jack Buck in St. Louis.

Our audiences for those pretend affairs was meager, anywhere from no one to a maximum of three if my father, mother, and sister were willing to humor me, which wasn't usually the case. My friends also grew bored quickly since I had a tendency not to let my partner get a word in edge-wise.

After all, the microphone *did* belong to me.

CHAPTER 3
Mrs. Fox's Letter

Cornelius McGillicuddy was the Jerry Jones of his day.

Better known as Connie Mack, he managed the Philadelphia Athletics for fifty years, winning five World Series championships to the Dallas Cowboys owner's three Super Bowl titles. Mack managed, won, and lost more games than anyone in baseball history. Even though his teams finished in last place seventeen times, he was never at risk for being fired.

Mack owned the ball club.

And Jerry Jones' Cowboys have won exactly one NFL playoff game since 1996.

The moral of the story? It's good to be the boss.

Connie Mack was no fool, although his A's teams in the early 1940s were abysmal, finishing in the American League cellar four consecutive seasons. These were the war years and most teams' talent stock was severely depleted. So, when Mack received a letter from a woman in St. Thomas, Pennsylvania, asking if he could give her 16-year-old son a tryout, he took notice.

"My boy is baseball crazy," Mae Fox wrote. "He won't study in school. All he talks about is you and the Athletics.

"He worries me to death."

Mack wrote back, expressing his appreciation for Mrs. Fox's letter. He told her it was possible to make a living playing baseball. "I may one day be able to help (your son)," he replied.

Someday came quickly. Limited by wartime travel restrictions, the Athletics held their spring training camp in Frederick, Maryland, about 150 miles from Philadelphia. Mae Fox's boy got his tryout, though finding a uniform small enough to fit his frame was difficult. He impressed team officials and earned a contract offer. The young Fox spent his first year in professional baseball splitting time between Class D and B leagues.

As a teenager, Jacob Nelson Fox went by his boyhood nickname, "Pug." Not until he spent a year or two in the minors did teammates begin calling him "Nellie."

Nellie Fox played parts of three seasons in Philadelphia and hit .255 as a utility player in 1949. That off-season, Mack approved the trade of Fox to the Chicago White Sox. Quickly, Fox earned his new team's starting second base job. He batted .247 for the year, and saw his new club finish eight full games ahead of the Athletics, who once again occupied the league basement.

At season's end, Connie Mack retired as A's manager.

Fox played nineteen summers in the big leagues. He appeared in twelve All-Star games, and won the American League Most Valuable Player award in 1959, the year he led the White Sox to their first World Series since the infamous Black Sox betting scandal of 1919.

By the time I was seven years old, the Philadelphia Athletics had moved to Kansas City, just a couple hours from where I lived. They continued to be awful and failed to capture the imagination. Many of my pals were fans of the St. Louis Cardinals. But, despite the Redbirds' storied past and the presence of such standouts as Stan Musial, Red Schoendienst, and Wally Moon, the Cardinals really weren't anything to write home about in the '50s, either.

In fact, I never really had a favorite team growing up, but I certainly had a favorite player, and he was Nellie Fox.

What I liked about Fox was his enthusiasm for the game. Ogden Nash, one of America's most beloved humorists, once wrote, "Nellie so lives to play that every day's a hollerday." As much as any player of his era, Fox put gusto into the great game of baseball.

Despite his reputation as a sparkplug-type player, Fox did not possess great speed. Nor did he have much of an arm. What he had in abundance was grit and determination. He was intelligent and smart enough to know his limitations. His batting stance looked like something a grandmother might employ at the family picnic. He may have swung one of the ugliest bats ever, but he almost always made contact with the ball.

If you discount his first three years in Philadelphia, Fox averaged 627 plate appearances per season. He struck out, on average, less than thirteen times a year. Yankee pitching great Whitey Ford said, "Nellie was the toughest out for me. In twelve years I struck him out once, and I think the umpire blew the call."

That's what appealed to me most about Nellie Fox. He did everything in his power to get the most out of his talent and more times than not, he got the best of guys considered far better players than he.

Fox spent the last two years of his playing career in Houston. He was traded to the Colt .45s prior to the 1964 season and batted a respectable .265 as the club's regular second baseman. In spring training the next year, with the club sporting a new nickname, Astros, and preparing to move into a new stadium, the Astrodome, Fox lost his infield job to a prodigiously talented young man from Oakland, California. Joe Morgan would finish the season as the runner-up for the National League Rookie of the Year award and in 1975 with the Cincinnati Reds, he would follow in Fox's footsteps as a

Most Valuable Player. In fact, Morgan would become the first second baseman since Fox to be named MVP.

When Morgan was inducted into the Baseball Hall of Fame in 1990, he paid tribute to Fox. "I played with him, and I wouldn't be standing here today if it wasn't for what I learned from him. Nellie Fox was my idol." Fox was a player-coach with the Astros for the first half of the 1965 season. He retired mid-year and was a full-time coach for the ball club through the 1967 campaign.

During my time in Cincinnati, I talked with Morgan about Nellie Fox on more than one occasion. Later, upon my arrival in Houston, I had the opportunity to hear more Fox stories from Milo Hamilton, who had worked White Sox games during Fox's last two years with the Chicago club.

No one ever had an unkind thing to say about Nellie. Even if he drove you crazy as an opponent, he earned universal respect for his dedication to the game. It's good when your heroes live up to expectations.

Fox died of lymphatic cancer at the age of 47. Throughout his career, he was famous for his large wad of chewing tobacco, always tucked in his left cheek. He preferred a brand called "Favorite." In the end, it killed him.

I remember the day Nellie Fox died: December 1, 1975. Joe Morgan had led the Big Red Machine to the World Series championship that year and I was a part of the Cincinnati broadcast team although a year shy of assuming play-by-play responsibilities. When I learned about Fox's death from a report on the Associated Press wire machine, I decided to put together a small tribute for on-air use at WLW Radio and WLWT-TV.

Fox was born on Christmas Day, 1927. His first date with his future wife Joanne was on Christmas Day 1943. They got engaged on Christmas Day three years later, but Joanne refused a Christmas Day wedding. They got married in June

1948 and stayed married for the remaining 27 years of Nellie's life.

No doubt Nellie Fox battled hard to see one more Christmas Day. Former teammate Jim Lemon observed, "The cancer had to be incurable, otherwise, Nellie would have beat it." In my tribute, I called Fox an inspiration for the "little guy" and someone who got as much out of his talent as any ballplayer ever. I told my audiences I could definitely identify with the scrappy second sacker.

In 1985, Fox came up two votes shy of enshrinement into the Baseball Hall of Fame and was dropped from the regular ballot. Another twelve years passed before the Hall's Veterans Committee finally voted him into Cooperstown.

Joanne Fox gave her late husband's induction speech and said, "He played the game with all his heart, all his passion, and with every ounce of his being."

Nellie Fox played the game the way it ought to be played.

CHAPTER 4
New Horizons

Biggio. Fox. Morgan. While on the subject of great Astros second basemen of the past, let's talk briefly about another.

When the 2004 All-Star game was held at Minute Maid Park in Houston, there were two Houston players in the National League starting lineup. Roger Clemens was named starting pitcher by NL skipper Jack McKeon. Jeff Kent was voted by fans as the team's starting second baseman.

Kent spent only two years in Houston, but certainly earned his laurels. After signing with the club as a prized free agent, Kent tied the team record in 2003 for most home runs in a season by a second baseman. He also set a new club standard for most RBIs at his position. He broke both marks the next year in a season which saw the Astros come within a game of the World Series.

Houston marked a much-needed change of scenery for Kent. He and Barry Bonds formed one of the National League's most dynamic offensive duos in San Francisco, but the two stars hated each other. While it was easy to place the blame squarely on Bonds' shoulders given his surly and arrogant nature, Kent, as I was to learn, was no picnic to be around, either.

On road trips as an Astro, Kent was one of the few players to ride the team bus from the hotel to the ballpark.

Most players caught or shared cabs, but that wasn't Kent's style. Since saving a buck is never a bad idea when you're *not* a millionaire ballplayer—or sharing a taxi ride with one—I usually rode the team bus, too.

The first road games of the 2003 season were in St. Louis, and thus the first time I saw Kent step onto a bus was a Friday afternoon heading from the team hotel to Busch Stadium. Always leery to be the last one aboard, I usually found a seat somewhere in the middle and if someone happened to sit next to me, I'd usually strike up a conversation to pass the time. When Kent came aboard the bus in St. Louis, I figured it was a good opportunity to get better acquainted with the team's talented new infielder.

We made eye contact and I offered a cordial greeting. Kent looked right through me, didn't say a word, and walked on to the back of the bus. I knew his reputation, but couldn't fathom his indifference to common civility. I concluded he must not have seen or heard me.

The next day I was determined to get Kent's attention. I cleared my voice and began the process of extending an invitation for him to join me. I don't think I got past "Hello" when Kent flashed a look my way which cut me to the core. Obviously he wanted nothing to do with me. It was hard not to take a slight like that personally.

I interviewed Jeff a few times during his two years in Houston and he did just fine, but I never really figured out what made him tick. Some players turn inward in an attempt to eliminate all distractions from their game-day routine. Others are just plain indifferent, seemingly incapable or uncomfortable in dealing with the social vagaries of the game. I think Kent fell somewhere in the middle of that continuum. As a ballplayer, he simply wasn't intent on making friends.

Jeff Kent broke baseball's career home run record for second basemen in 2004, playing in what turned out to be his final regular season game in an Astros' uniform. He nearly willed the team into the World Series that year, but, in the end, the club fell just short of the pennant and Kent moved on, concluding his playing days in Los Angeles. As a Dodger, he was forced to co-exist with the tempestuous Manny Ramirez and "Manny being Manny" must have driven Kent crazy.

When Kent signed with the Astros, Craig Biggio lost his accustomed starting spot at second base. Certainly the move was a bitter pill for Biggio to swallow, but publicly he spoke of Kent's acquisition only in the most positive of terms. The two years Biggio roamed the Houston outfield, he committed just one error. Offensively, he scored at least one hundred runs in both seasons.

I had a keen sense of the kind of adjustment Biggio was asked to make. I'd been there and done that myself.

***

"Bill, how would you like to have a brother?" my father said from the doorway of my room with my mother standing at his side sporting a nervous smile on her face.

With the remark, Mom punched Dad in the arm and my father broke out in a laugh. "Not a brother," said Mom. "More like a roommate."

Since the impending year was my last in high school and I had grown set and comfortable in my ways, sharing *my* room wasn't at or near the top of my wish list.

"Share with who?" I asked incredulously. "'Whom'," Dad corrected.

My parents looked at each other as if they'd both swallowed canaries.

"We're thinking about sponsoring an exchange student for the upcoming school year," my father told me. "Frankly, we're a little disappointed with the kids we have now."

"*WILL-YUM!*" My mother put her foot down, literally, on top of my dad's shoe, which caused him to flinch. "Hey, I was just *KIDD-ING!*"

"We're very proud of you, Bill," Mom assured me, "ss we are of Jessica. We believe this could be a wonderful learning experience for you and your sister."

"How long have you been thinking about this?" I asked. Suddenly, it seemed I couldn't trust my own parents.

Mother threw an elbow into dad's ribcage before he could continue his stand-up comedy routine. "For a while," she said. "We still have time before we have to commit to anything. We've talked about it, but wanted to make sure you don't have any objections."

"Shouldn't you ask Jebby, too?" I said flippantly. Three years my sister's senior, she and I had developed a strong bond and I felt certain she would never go along with having an interloper in our home.

"We wanted to talk to you first," Dad said.

"I appreciate that," I countered mockingly. The apron strings between us were already straining. "I really appreciate that."

I turned my attention back to the book I was reading. My parents stood in silence in the doorway. When I finally noticed they hadn't left I said, "I'll think about it. Now if you'll excuse me..." The rest of that thought went unspoken. Later that evening Dad held a family meeting to address the matter. Surprisingly, Jebby was all for the idea. She swayed my opinion and the Brown family reached a consensus.

Thus, did Michel Dizin, the heartthrob of Smith-Cotton High School's senior class of 1965, enter my life. He was tall, blonde, *French*, handsome, polite, *French*, and he had this bad habit of making every female with whom he came into contact swoon at the sound of his *French* accent, my own sister and *mother* included!

He won me over pretty quickly, too.

Michel and I had a decidedly better relationship than Jeff Kent and Barry Bonds. Michel was, literally, the nicest person I'd ever met. He also was an attentive listener, eager to assimilate as much of our American way of life as he could. I helped him learn a passable form of English. He added a little French to my vocabulary.

Having a Frenchman as a friend, roommate, and classmate certainly spiced up the beginning of my senior year. Other changes were in the offing, too.

Two months before the beginning of my senior year, Congress passed the Civil Rights Act of 1964, outlawing major forms of discrimination against both African Americans and women, including racial segregation.

In Sedalia, my father, as well as other community leaders, had been working on a plan to integrate the local school district in advance of the federal mandate. Thumbing through the pages of my high school yearbook recently, I counted twenty-five black students as members of my senior class of more than three hundred people.

Like many places in America, Sedalia schools had been racially segregated for generations. Hubbard was the name of the predominantly-black high school in town. As president of the Smith-Cotton senior class, I became acquainted with Walter Bell, my counterpart at Hubbard High. We attended several civic events together and became friends. I also enjoyed the company of A.C. Byrd and Anthony Buckner, former Hubbard students who chose to ride the bus to Smith-Cotton in order to complete their secondary education. Both were standouts on our Tiger football team. Buckner also ran track and was the fastest runner in school.

A year and a half after graduation, Tony Buckner was drafted into the Army. He was sent to Vietnam in August 1967 and two months later he was killed in action. He died less than a month shy of his 20th birthday. In his short time of active duty, he earned the Purple Heart, Bronze Star, National

Defense Service Medal, Vietnam Service Medal, and Vietnam Campaign Medal. A public housing project and child care center in Sedalia today bear his name.

I would eventually see the war, too, but didn't arrive in Southeast Asia until Tony was already gone.

***

After graduation from high school, the Brown family took a European vacation. That trip is still one of the highlights of my life. We visited several countries, including France, and that meant a reunion with Michel. Returning home from Sedalia, he insisted everyone—including his own family—call him "Mike."

Mike was particularly excited to show me the ski resort of Grenoble which was near the small village where he lived in the French Alps. "The Olympics are coming in just three years," he proudly proclaimed, "and the world will learn of our great champion, Jean Claude Killy." Like most Americans, I had never heard of Killy, but it seemed every ski shop in Grenoble had a picture of him. He was a dead ringer for Michel.

Killy became a worldwide celebrity when he swept the three alpine events contested at the '68 Winter Games.

Upon returning from the trip, I began preparation for college. I seriously considered attending the University of Oklahoma to study journalism. After spending nine months with Michel, I figured it might be a good idea to get away from home and go to school someplace "exotic." Norman, Oklahoma, wasn't quite exotic enough and eventually, I went with the obvious choice: the University of Missouri in Columbia, an easy 70 mile drive from Sedalia.

"Mizzou" had and still has one of the top journalism schools in the country and my sights were set on getting a degree in broadcasting. In the '60s, the first two years of

36

college were filled with general studies courses, which, in theory, prepared undergraduates for both a major field of study as well as entry into the real world.

My Freshman year was a bit of a blur to me as I'm sure the first year of school is to most people. Coming from a small town, I was initially intimidated by the size of the campus and the location of classes: here, there, and everywhere. I had achieved a good grade-point average in high school, finishing in the top ten of my class, so the pressure was on—mostly self-inflicted—for me to continue making good grades in college. As I recall, my first semester GPA was in the neighborhood of 3.7. That mark was to be the scholastic high point of my college years.

I could blame my less-than-stellar marks on my membership in Phi Kappa Psi fraternity, but I'll take personal responsibility for my academic shortcomings. I pledged Phi Psi soon after arriving on campus and to the credit of the chapter, mandatory study hall for pledges did make my academic life easier that first semester. As a member of the Greek system, I opted out of living in a dormitory my freshman year, residing in the fraternity house instead. Existence there was reasonably serene most weekdays.

Friday nights were a different story. "Hazing" was a popular pastime throughout the Greek system at Missouri.

The party scene at Mizzou was mostly off campus. Downtown Columbia was a popular destination and when members returned to the Phi Psi house late on a Friday or Saturday night, pledges could count on more than a little abuse from the upperclassmen. This sort of behavior "built character," or so I was told numerous times. They never quite convinced me.

Saturday mornings—at least during the football season—offered a welcome reprieve for my pledge brothers and me. Missouri Tiger football captured the imagination of the entire state, but there was nothing like attending games at Memorial Stadium to bring out one's collegial nature.

Under the direction of head coach Dan Devine, and led by All-Americans Johnny Roland and Francis Peay, Mizzou went 8-2-1 my freshman year of 1965. The biggest home victory was a 30-0 thrashing of perennially-powerful Oklahoma. The Tigers then capped off the season with a dramatic 20-18 win over Florida in the Sugar Bowl. I loved the games and paid special attention when the band performed at halftime. I had considered trying out to become a member of "Marching Mizzou," but our family's six-week trip to Europe didn't give me enough time to prepare for an audition. Maybe that was just an excuse. For whatever reason, I joined a fraternity and not the band.

My fraternity experience lasted just two years. After my initiation, the house was placed on academic probation. There were other issues which came to the surface and in time, I moved out.

Fortunately, I soon fell in with another group of students whose interests and passions were much more in line with my own. We shared a common purpose and a common dream. We attended many of the same classes and spent time away from school pursuing the same goals. We had one collective ambition in life: We wanted to be broadcasters.

***

My first experience "on the air" came in high school as part of a class project. Small groups of English students put together five-minute programs centered around "topical subjects of interest to the local community." The program deemed the best on paper would be produced and aired on Sedalia radio station KDRO.

With a chance to make my radio debut, I took control of my group's project. We chose to do a piece on the Smith-

Cotton marching band, of which I was a member. Working an ample amount of natural sound into the project script, my group earned the highest marks in the class. During the ensuing week, my team worked busily with station personnel to prepare the show for broadcast. I suggested including a trumpet solo into the mix, but settled for the role of program narrator. We recorded the show on a Friday afternoon for playback the following Sunday morning. The project helped me get my foot in the door at the station.

During the spring semester of my senior year, two events came into convergence which impacted the rest of my life. Our Smith-Cotton Tigers baseball team was outstanding that year and qualified for the state final in St. Louis. KDRO sports director Jimmy Glenn asked if I wanted to assist him with the broadcast of the game—an offer I couldn't refuse even though our school's junior-senior prom was the preceding night.

My prom date was Dianne Dugan. Her father owned the biggest paint store in town. I had known Dianne throughout high school, but prom night marked our first date. I picked her up at her house, obligatory corsage in hand. Her parents were great people, and after they snapped a number of photographs, Dianne and I were on our way. In the car, nary a word was said between us. Finally, I broke the silence.

"Look, I'm really happy to be with you tonight. I've wanted to ask you out for a while. And, yes, I'm a little nervous about the prom and all, but there's something you should know."

Dianne looked at me curiously. I can only imagine what must have crossed her mind.

"I'm going to have to cut the evening a little short," I said. "I have a job at one of the radio stations in town." That stretched the truth of my employment situation since my duties at the station were all volunteer. "I'm going to be in St.

Louis tomorrow to help broadcast the state baseball final. You know our team is playing in that game, right?"

All this time my hands had been planted firmly on the steering wheel and my attention had been focused on the road ahead. When I stopped talking, I turned to look at Dianne, uncertain as to her reaction. I took it as a good sign she was smiling.

Relieved, I finished, "I have to catch the 2:30 train tomorrow morning, so that's why I'm going to have to have you home a little early tonight."

Dianne's smile wilted like a time-lapse image of her corsage. She was silent for a few moments lost in thought. When she finally spoke, she looked at me like I was a complete stranger.

"How early?" she asked.

My plan was to have her home by nine, but when I told her that, the look on her face made me realize I was being completely unreasonable. Even if I was home and in bed by ten, I still would get only about three hours of sleep before heading to the train station. Seeing her sadness, I quickly changed my mind.

"Okay, what if I get you back home about 12:30?" That brought a big smile to her face which, I discovered, gave me a surprisingly warm feeling. Plus, I realized, I could always sleep on the train!

Relieved, Dianne leaned over and planted a kiss on my cheek. I've never forgotten that moment.

I had a really good time that night, but probably talked too much about the next day's game. To her credit, Dianne was a good sport, but after I took her home, arriving just a little after midnight, another kiss on the cheek was all I got. We wouldn't see each other again socially for some time.

From the Dugan house I drove home. Pulling into the driveway, I could see the light still on in the kitchen. As I entered the house, a note on the refrigerator door—in my

40

father's handwriting—said, *"Make sure I'm up by 1:30. Don't want you to be late for the train."* He knew how important the next day was to me.

When Jimmy Glenn asked if I would be interested in joining him at the state baseball tournament, I couldn't believe my good fortune. While he didn't openly offer me a spot in front of the microphone, I just assumed he wanted me there as his expert analyst. After all, I knew all the guys on the team and nobody was as nuts about baseball as I was.

During the week preceding the big game, I worked feverishly to put together notes for the contest. I figured once Glenn saw my vast store of facts, figures, anecdotes, and asides, he'd welcome me as his broadcast partner. At school, I perused team scorebooks and spent time in the coaches' office.

I was as prepared as I'd ever been for a final exam.

Before leaving to pick up Dianne for the prom, I had offered myself up for final inspection to my parents. Upon seeing me in my tuxedo, Mom gasped and Dad beamed. They made a big fuss while Jebby stood off to the side rolling her eyes.

"Son, I'm proud of you, *we're* proud of you," my father told me, reaching his arm around Mom's shoulders and pulling her to his side. "I've got something for you. Let's go to the study."

Since Dad had already explained the "birds-and-bees" to me and the prom marked my first date with Dianne, I wasn't certain why my father wanted to meet with me in private. Perhaps he was going to give me money. An extra five or even ten dollars wouldn't be a bad thing considering most of my work at the radio station was of the volunteer kind. Instead, when we reached the study, he walked behind his desk and lifted up a briefcase. He turned and handed it to me.

"Bill, I used this to start my law practice," he said. I retired it a few years ago, but I've been saving it to give to you.

I know tomorrow's game is a big deal and I just thought you might want to look the part of a professional."

I couldn't have been happier or more honored. The five-dollar bill he slipped into my hand as I headed out the door also put a smile on my face.

Before I got home from the prom, Dad had placed the briefcase on the desk in my room and left it open with a crisp twenty-dollar bill inside. "Just in case you need it," he had written on yet another note. An apple and a small sleeve of cookies sat next to the money, no doubt courtesy of Mom. The radio station was picking up the tab for my one-way train ticket. Glenn had driven his car to St. Louis on Friday and was spending the night with family who lived there. I'd make the six-hour train trip in the early hours on Saturday, do the broadcast with Glenn that afternoon, and then he and I would drive back to Sedalia together that night.

I stacked my game notes into a neat pile, slid them inside one of my dad's legal-sized envelopes, and placed the fruits of my labor into the briefcase. I closed the lid and fastened the latches with a confident-sounding click.

The state tournament was played at Busch Stadium, home of the St. Louis Cardinals. Originally called Sportsman's Park, the facility was long past its prime. In fact, a new stadium was being built in downtown St. Louis as part of a massive civic renovation endeavor. After my train's arrival at the city's Union Station, Glenn met me along Market Street. As I climbed into the front seat of his car, he told me to look to the east. There we could see the Gateway Arch still under construction, its two giant legs curving into the sky but not yet joined.

We arrived at the ballpark about ten o'clock for the twelve o'clock game. Once there, Glenn handed me my very first press pass. There was no elevator to the press box, so by the time we'd trudged up the stairs—with his equipment and my briefcase—and found our broadcast position, I was sweating profusely in the suit I'd worn to the game.

As Glenn set up the gear, I grew more excited about my impending moment in the radio spotlight. Below us, the two teams began warming up on the field. Our train had been packed with fans and many of them were beginning to find their way into the ballpark. I had placed my briefcase on an extra folding chair in the booth and while Glenn was busy, I leaned over, affixed my hands at the two near corners of the case, and with my thumbs pressed the latch mechanisms to reveal the contents inside.

A star was about to be born.

But, nothing happened.

I tried a second and third time, but the latches wouldn't budge. Then a notion hit me square between the eyes: Dad had forgotten to give me the key.

My heart sank. I tried to hide my despair from Glenn, which wasn't difficult since he was engrossed in solving the electronic puzzle of patch cords and headsets which constituted the tools of his broadcasting trade. I saw he had set up microphones on *two* separate stands.

Back in those days, games were transmitted via telephone lines, and we had an actual rotary-dial phone in the booth. I thought if I called my father, maybe he could share the secret to springing the latches on the briefcase.

"Mr. Glenn, I told my parents I would try to contact them after I got to town," I said in all honesty. "Would it be okay if I used the phone here to call them? I can call collect."

"Sure," Glenn said, busy as he checked vacuum-tube connections in the mixing-board unit.

The phone cord enabled me to step into the hallway behind our booth and make the call. I inserted my finger into the zero slot and twisted the dial to the right. I waited until a voice came on the line. "Operator, I'd like to make a collect call."

"One moment please."

One moment seemed an eternity until my mom answered the phone back home.

"Mom, I've got to talk with Dad, it's an emergency."

'Bill, are you all right?" Mom had worry in her voice to match my own.

"No!" I said. "Just get Dad!"

"He's right here, honey, just a second." Mom handed my father the phone.

"Bill, did you make it okay?" Dad asked nonchalantly.

"Dad, you forgot to give me the key to the briefcase!" I exclaimed in as low a voice as I could manage between gritted teeth. A stage whisper it could have been called.

There was a pause on the other end of the line. "Bill, there *isn't* a key."

Now, it was my turn to pause. I could feel my face flush with raw emotion.

"But, Dad, it's locked! I can't get it to open!" A lump caught in my throat. "I've got all my stuff inside. I don't think Mr. Glenn will let me on the air if I don't have my notes!"

"Son, in all the years I've had that briefcase, I think I probably only locked it a half dozen times. After I lost the key, I never *could* lock it. Are you sure it's locked? Maybe if you gave it a good nudge…"

I interrupted him. "Dad, I've tried everything short of throwing it out the press box window." I was beginning to panic. I hadn't considered taking such a drastic measure, although as soon as I said it, I imagined a good heave-ho might be worth a shot.

"Bill, I don't know what to say. Maybe there's a maintenance worker there you can ask for help."

Dad's idea wasn't a bad one, but I probably wasn't going to make that big a fuss, which meant I also wouldn't be giving the briefcase a toss out the window.

"I'm sorry, Bill,' Dad said. "Maybe I should have put some 3-in-One oil on the latches before I gave it to you. I wish I would have thought to do that. Oh, my consternation is considerable." I knew he was serious.

The briefcase latches never budged. I knew Glenn kept some tools in his equipment bag, but I was too embarrassed to borrow any. Just about the time I was ready to break down and cry, Glenn asked me to go down to the field and get the starting lineups. I did so, which made me feel a little better. By the time I returned, Glenn had his equipment set up and arranged. The second microphone was pointed toward the field of play—to pick up crowd noise.

He had never intended for me to be a part of the broadcast, at least not on the air.

Between innings Glenn did quiz me about the team and the game and I had most of the answers. It turned out I really didn't need my note cards. The preparation in creating them—just like studying for a test—seared the information into my mind.

Glenn and I wound up making a pretty good team although he did all the talking. After the game—which Smith-Cotton lost—he concluded his broadcast thanking me by name. Before heading back to Sedalia, Glenn took me to an Italian restaurant on the St. Louis Hill, and regaled me with stories of Yogi Berra and Joe Garagiola who had grown up in that part of town. Over the course of the entire trip, he didn't ask me once why I had carried around a locked briefcase.

The next day at home, Dad and I never said a word about my missed opportunity to be on the radio. He also popped the latches on the briefcase with ease. Good thing I never needed that twenty-dollar bill.

CHAPTER 5
Lincoln's Shadow

For anyone who sees journalism as a reputable pursuit—and of course I say this with tongue planted *somewhat* firmly in cheek—the University of Missouri, my alma mater, played a pivotal role in bringing credibility to the profession.

Walter Williams, who later became university president, established the world's first school of journalism at Mizzou in 1908. Since then, Columbia has been the foundry in which a number of stellar careers have been cast. And, I don't use that analogy lightly. The "Missouri Method" of hands-on training can truly be a journalism "trial by fire"—particularly on the radio and television side of things.

KOMU-TV is the NBC affiliate in Columbia, owned by the University of Missouri. In my day, students served as interns, offering behind-the-scenes support to the station's full-time news and sports professionals. Select and capable seniors ultimately were rewarded with anchor-desk opportunities during the station's five-minute morning news blocks aired as part of the NBC *Today Show* feed. Albert Brooks' one-and-done turn as a profusely-sweating "wannabe" network anchorman in the movie *Broadcast News* could have been taken right from the annals of the KOMU-TV newsroom, circa 1969.

The year after I graduated, station officials decided to turn over virtually the entire news operations to students and it's remained that way ever since.

The station has churned out some truly talented broadcasters.

On ESPN, anchors John Alexander and Michael Kim are Mizzou grads. The winner of the network's initial *Dream Job* series, Mike Hall, was still an undergrad at Missouri when he earned a spot behind the anchor desk in Bristol, Connecticut. Joel Meyers, one of the most versatile play-by-play men in the business and former voice of the Los Angeles Lakers got his start in Columbia.

Mizzou grad Jim Lehrer, anchored the evening news on PBS for more than 35 years. Chuck Roberts, who was two years behind me in school, served as a news anchor at the CNN networks in Atlanta from day one—January 1, 1982—to his retirement in 2010. The *CBS Evening News* is capably anchored on weekends by St. Louis native and Missouri grad Russ Mitchell. Elizabeth Vargas, class of '84, does outstanding work on ABC's news magazine show *20/20*.

And, let's not forget another giant of journalism with ties to Ol' Mizzou: James Jackson Kilpatrick.

A native Oklahoman, Kilpatrick graduated from the Missouri school of journalism in 1941, and became one of the nation's leading conservative voices. While a print journalist for much of his career, Kilpatrick earned greater notoriety during the 1970s on CBS's acclaimed *60 Minutes* television news program. He was featured on a segment called "Point-Counterpoint," paired regularly with *Life* magazine columnist Shana Alexander.

Comedian Dan Akroyd found Kilpatrick's curmudgeonly nature ripe for parody on *Saturday Night Live*. During *SNL's* "Weekend News Update" segments in '77 and '78, Akroyd and fellow cast member Jane Curtain created their own brand of debate. Akroyd always began his rebuttal to Curtain's lead-off commentary with what became one of the classic lines in television comedy: "Jane, you ignorant slut."

Kilpatrick, who died in 2010, once said of writing, "Be clear, be clear, be clear! Your image or idea may be murky, but do not write murkily about it."

Jim, I'm trying.

In addition to my TV work in college, I also spent time at Columbia radio station KFRU, the longtime flagship of the Missouri Tiger football and basketball networks. KFRU had no affiliation with the university, but drew heavily on students and recent grads to populate its music, news, and sports programming. I quickly discovered the station's plum sports assignments all went to one person: my classmate Chris Lincoln.

What impressed me most about Lincoln in our days together at Mizzou was his affable nature combined with a level of self-confidence that made him also seem aloof. His was a somewhat discombobulating personality mix, at least for those of us below him on the station's broadcasting totem pole.

Lincoln grew up in Warren, Michigan, and by the time he arrived as a student in Columbia, he had already amassed an impressive and well-rounded resume. In college, he was a student assistant in the athletic department's sports information office; a sportswriter for the local newspaper, the *Columbia Daily Tribune*; and the lead sports voice at KFRU. *Plus*, he carried a full-time class load as an undergraduate student. His energy level was prodigious and everywhere I went, either as a journalism student on campus or a young sportscaster covering games, chances were good I'd run into Chris Lincoln. Small wonder it took him an extra year to get his degree.

He was the standard by which I measured myself at the time. After all, in addition to holding the coveted title as "Voice of the Kewpies"—more on that in a moment—Lincoln hosted the pre- and post-game portions of the Missouri Tigers' network broadcasts. I was one of several underlings who did the grunt work enabling Lincoln to reap on-air acclaim. I found myself also spending considerable time muttering under my breath about his good fortune.

As for Kewpies, that's the nickname associated with Columbia's David H. Hickman High School. According to Wikipedia, no other academic institution or organized sporting entity goes by that name. As legend has it, a member of the school's faculty once sat a kewpie doll—popular a century ago—along the home sideline of a basketball game to serve as a good-luck charm. Columbia High School, as it was known then, won the game and the Kewpie soon was adopted as the official mascot.

To extricate myself from Chris Lincoln's sizable—and somewhat Kewpie-shaped—shadow, I sought out "other opportunities," that famous destination for those with nowhere else to turn.

***

While Chris Lincoln was dominating the airwaves on KFRU, I broke into the play-by-play ranks following the fortunes of the Hickman Kewpies' biggest athletic rivals: the Jefferson City High School Jays.

Landing the job on KWOS radio in Jefferson City was a nice break for me. My wage demands certainly made me an attractive candidate. I was paid $25 per game plus gas money.

In truth, I would have paid *them* for the experience.

That job brought me in contact with one of the great high school football coaches of all time. Pete Adkins directed the Jays' football fortunes for forty-four years, amassing a record of 405-60-4. Before my arrival, Adkins' teams won a then-national-record seventy-one games in a row between 1958 and 1966. State championships weren't contested in

Missouri until 1968, and beginning in 1976, well after my departure, Adkins led the Jays to nine titles, including three in a row from 1976-1978 and back to back repeats in 1990-1991 and 1993-1994.

My KWOS duties also included broadcasting Lincoln University basketball. Under Coach John Staggers, the Blue Tigers were a small college powerhouse, usually averaging more than one hundred points a game. The team's tempo and raw athleticism were unlike anything I had seen. For that matter, I was unlike anything many Blue Tiger fans had seen gracing their home court. Lincoln University was a predominantly black institution of higher learning, while I came from the historically white Brown family of Sedalia. I learned quickly skin color meant little in comparison to wins and losses and the team eventually considered me somewhat of a good-luck charm in the manner of the Hickman Kewpie.

In broadcasting, nothing beats the "University of Experience," but as a Mizzou student, nothing quite compared academically to my Broadcast News and Film course, taught by Professor Robert Canon. I fail to recall what Canon's real-world experience was before he turned to teaching, but I do remember, as if it were yesterday, his first-day-of-class instruction on the art of shooting clouds from an airplane.

Perhaps Canon took pride in his "eccentricity." The final exam in his class had students split into teams, write collaborative scripts, and then shoot film to cover their stories. Since most of his lessons for the semester had dealt with abject broadcast theory, few in the class actually learned anything about the functionality of a news camera. One group managed to shoot the entire final project with its camera turned upside down!

***

Over the course of my last three years at Missouri, my social life was turned upside down—in a good way—by the return of Dianne Dugan, not that she had ever completely disappeared.

After our prom date, Dianne and I headed in different directions. While I went off to Mizzou, she enrolled in a private girls' school, William Woods College, located in Fulton, Missouri. A girlfriend of one of my best friends also attended school there and whenever I tagged along with my buddy on a road trip to Fulton, I seemed to always bump into Dianne there.

After her freshman year, Dianne transferred to Mizzou, but not because of me. Over time we started seeing each socially. By our junior year, we were in an exclusive dating relationship.

Then, as if to trump our prom experience, I wound up leaving Dianne again—this time for an entire summer—when I landed an internship at a television station in San Antonio before my senior year.

Let me note here that it was thanks to that internship at WOAI-TV—and not Professor Canon's class—I learned the right way to operate a news camera.

Miraculously, Dianne stuck with me despite my walkabout ways. Early in the fall semester of our senior year, we became engaged with plans for a summer wedding in Sedalia.

Leading up to the nuptials, I joked with friends that part of my reason for wanting to get married was to alter my draft status. The war in Vietnam was not going well from a U.S. perspective. The enemy was proving formidable and under Richard Nixon, who entered the White House at the beginning of my final semester of college, the conflict began coming apart at the seams. In a tiny village called My Lai, American soldiers killed more than four hundred unarmed civilians.

Still, nothing on foreign soil did as much damage to the war effort in Southeast Asia as the actions of a few American soldiers on the campus of a college in Ohio.

By the time of the Kent State tragedy, I already knew there was a good chance I would be drafted. The first-ever Selective Service lottery was held December 1, 1969, determining in random sequence by date of birth those who would be called into the military. That first lottery was applicable for young men born between the years 1944 and 1950 and that included me. The lower the lottery number, the greater the likelihood a young man would see active duty.

Here's a list of the lottery numbers for birth dates leading up to my own:

Sept. 12	242
Sept. 13	175
Sept. 14	1
Sept. 15	113
Sept. 16	207
Sept. 17	255
Sept. 18	246
Sept. 19	177
Sept. 20	63

Despite the fact I was a college graduate, had married Dianne on June 14, 1969, and found a full-time job after graduation, my lottery number virtually guaranteed I would be drafted. I wasn't the kind of person to consider burning my draft card or defecting to another country, so despite the fact I was concerned and a little scared, I knew circumstances were beyond my control. So, I decided to try to stay focused on my new job and my new marriage until I got my call from Uncle Sam.

***

Unless you're a Chris Lincoln, Bob Costas, or Charles Barkley, paying one's dues in the business of broadcasting— especially when sports is the ultimate goal—almost always means starting out professionally in news because there are a lot more news jobs than sports positions. I entered the workforce with boatloads of real-world experience as a sportscaster—and probably could have landed a small- or medium-market job in radio somewhere—but, I had my sights set on a career in television.

The staff at WOAI-TV had been patient in teaching me the tricks of the trade during my college internship in San Antonio, so, after graduation, it made sense for me to apply for a full-time position there. I wound up landing a job as a news photographer.

One of my first assignments involved a drowning. The story took me to the outskirts of Bexar County and by the time I got there, the sun was already beginning to set. In the darkening conditions, I was out of my element and beyond my level of experience with a camera. I did the best I could shooting in the available light.

Upon returning to the station, I handed my film canister to our processor and told him he would need to "push" the footage because of the poor lighting conditions. I stood behind him the entire time he developed the film, curious to see if anything useful would come of my labors that evening. Fortunately, the footage was good. I certainly wasn't the best shooter around and now, almost 40 years removed from my work as a cameraman, I still have the occasional nightmare about blowing an assignment.

One night, I had the opportunity to produce the ten o'clock news. On weekends, particularly at 10 p.m. on Sundays, the news was basically a rehash of the earlier 6 o'clock broadcast. Other than late sports scores, there was rarely anything new about which the producer needed to worry.

I can't recall now why I was asked to produce the newscast, but under my watch—and in textbook fashion, I thought—the scripts, slides, and film were all ready by the appointed hour of 9 p.m. In our pre-production meeting, director Tom Maguire went through the materials, seemed satisfied, and departed. Everything seemed to be in order until a minute before the newscast was scheduled to begin. Over the studio intercom Maguire cried out frantically, "I need news film NOW!"

Without thinking, I began a mad scramble to find the missing footage, failing to remember that Maguire had taken the reels with him. When our weekend anchor Gene Lively went live—I always thought his was a great name for a TV news man—he got an awful lot of face time, a circumstance for which he was both unaccustomed and uncomfortable. But, with no film footage available, Maguire had no choice but to keep Lively on camera. Soon, everyone at the station not on-camera or working one—basically the janitor and I—was desperately looking for the misplaced reels. I took the lead in digging through trash cans.

Nothing.

With no stone left unturned, I admitted failure and trudged toward the control booth ready to accept the consequences of my dereliction of duty. Then, miraculously, film started to appear on the newscast and the rest of the night went off without a hitch.

After the show, Maguire casually strolled through the newsroom, his arms loaded with food containers. Somehow, he had earned the privilege of emptying the staff refrigerator and assuming ownership of any uneaten leftovers. He was a man seemingly without a care in the world, while I was in the pits of despair. When he caught me out of the corner of his eye, Maguire said, "Hey, kid, don't worry. Turns out the reels were in the booth the whole time."

He laughed as if it was no big deal, but it was to me. This was long before pop psychologists proclaimed the uselessness of "sweating the small stuff," or fretting about "who moved the cheese."

"It was kind of funny watching Lively be stuck on camera so long," Maguire continued as he neared the back exit. "I'll bet our viewers got tired of seeing his ugly mug."

He paused as he hip-checked the door open. "What few viewers we have on a Sunday night."

He then disappeared into the dark.

***

During our time in San Antonio, Dianne and I shared a small one-bedroom apartment. She worked in an accounting job getting back and forth to work was tricky at times since we owned only one car. Somehow we managed. But, as the days passed, prospect of military service—mine—grew to be an ever-more frequent topic of conversation between us.

My station manager Ed Cheviot had been a Marine in the Korean War. He was doing his best to get me into a reserve unit so I could remain stateside for as long as possible. My application for reserve duty was rejected because of poor eyesight, which I thought might be a good sign. If I couldn't see well enough to be a warrior-in-waiting, then surely I couldn't pass the grade for full-time service. That logic turned out to be flawed.

On one of my late-night crime-reporting escapades, someone with the San Antonio police department got the novel notion that I would be a perfect candidate to go undercover in one of the toughest high schools in town. Admittedly, I did look young for my age, but I couldn't imagine the authorities were serious about the possibility. Undercover *reporting* maybe, but undercover *police work*???

To my surprise and chagrin, the station's news director and assignment editor actually gave serious thought to the idea. In the end, negotiations broke down because the station wanted to do a story on my experience.

Thank goodness my draft papers finally arrived.

CHAPTER 6
AFVN

Entertaining a contingent of active military personnel has become a Sunday tradition at Minute Maid Park. Astros pitching coach Doug Brocail, since his arrival in the middle of the 2011 season, is the unofficial host for most of these events.

At 6'5," Brocail has a somewhat fearsome countenance, but his heart is as big as all outdoors. In fact, he's a regular on the cable television series *Veteran Outdoors* in which veterans wounded in the line of duty receive all-expenses-paid hunting or fishing experiences. Any chance he gets, Doug talks at length about the impact the Sportsman Channel series and the non-profit venture it's spawned have made in his life.

Well before the first pitch on those special Sundays, Brocail leads a group of Astros' players, coaches, and front-office personnel to welcome the "Home Sweet Home" project guests of honor. The club typically hosts the groups in the media auditorium directly across the hall from the team locker room. Lunch and refreshments are served there.

I try to get downstairs and say hello as often as possible. As a veteran myself, I appreciate the sacrifice these young men and women make for our country. I'm pleased the ball club arranges these visits and I'm certain our soldiers enjoy the warm reception they're given by fans when introduced before the game.

One individual made a particularly strong impression on me a couple years ago. He was from San Antonio, Hispanic, and married with two small children. When we met, he was on leave from his third tour of duty in Iraq. While the rest of his counterparts were being regaled by the Brocail bunch, he was seated alone near the back of the room picking at his food. I walked over to this lone soldier, introduced myself, and asked if I could sit down with him.

To break the ice, I posed the usual questions about hometown, family, and length of service. He was a master sergeant in the U.S. Army, overseeing a cadre of mechanics in a maintenance pool. His company was stationed inside the Green Zone in Baghdad.

I could tell something was bothering him, so I shared a little about my own military experience. That seemed to relax him some and our conversation picked up steam. Finally, he took a deep breath as if there was something important he wanted to say.

"I really feel bad about being here."

"Why?" I asked.

"I should be home with my family."

I knew it was an honor for him to be tabbed for recognition at the game. The soldiers are chosen in large part based on merit. But as he explained, the day also took precious time away from his wife and kids. They had been unable to make the trip because one of his children was sick.

"It's hard being away from them when I'm *away*," he confided in a voice softened by emotion. "I mean away, over there in Iraq. But it's even harder being away when I'm supposed to be home."

How do you respond to something like that? I searched for a reply.

"I remember leaving for induction a year out of college," I finally told him. "I had a new wife and a new job in a new town, San Antonio, in fact." He smiled at that part of my story.

"Keep in mind I was drafted and, admittedly, I had some misgivings about that war. But once I got to Vietnam, I was fully committed to 'duty, honor, country,' just like you are."

"Don't get me wrong," he replied, "I appreciate being here. It seems like people care. Flying home to San Antonio last week, I got stopped in airports a dozen times, people wanting to shake my hand and tell me how much they appreciate what I'm doing for our country."

I sat quietly and listened.

"*Do* people really care?" he asked me, his pleading look expressing uncertainty. "Do they really understand how hard this is? Not the work or the danger. I'm okay with that. Honestly, this is probably the most exciting job I'll ever have. But, man, it's tough being away from the people you love."

"You bet people care," I quickly assured him, then leaned in closer to continue. "Listen, when I came home from Vietnam, I really didn't know what to expect. Our country was in a completely different place with that war. In fact, to be honest with you—and I'm a little ashamed to admit this—when I got back I was glad to have the chance to put on civilian clothes again and just blend in with the crowd.

"It's different now," I continued. "You should never doubt how much your nation appreciates and values you, and not just for the uniform you wear. You're being honored today as a representative of the United States Army, but it's obvious to me you're a good husband and a great father."

Running late for my return to the press box, I got up from my seat. "Sergeant, I am honored to know you." I reached out to shake his hand. He stood. An idea came to my mind.

"Give me your wife and daughter's names and I'll be sure and say hello to them on today's broadcast."

His face instantly lit up. "Would you really? That would mean a lot. I'll call and tell them to listen."

"'Watch'," I corrected. "I'm the guy on TV."

"I've got a picture of them in my wallet. Would you like to see it?"

"You bet!"

There's nothing better than making someone's day, unless someone else is making yours.

***

My draft notice arrived via certified mail almost one year to the day after the Selective Service lottery had sealed my fate. Induction took place three months later in Kansas City. Dianne and I spent my last week as a "free man" home with our parents in Sedalia. Spring was in the air. The year was 1970.

At the induction station in downtown Kansas City—formerly the old Foremost Dairy building—we were relieved of our civilian attire and marched into a large conference room where a battery of medical personnel awaited. Standing in single file with several others, I noticed a tall, gangly young man—the epitome of a "country boy"—standing at attention in front of a doctor.

"Son, you can relax," I heard the doctor say. I couldn't help but notice the doctor was staring down at the recruit's feet. They were enormous and the soles hugged the floor from heel to toe.

"Soldier," the doctor said his gaze still turned downward, "those are the flattest feet I've ever seen." Still rigid in his best approximation of attention, the young man lowered his chin ever so slightly as he tried to get a better look at the subject of concern.

"If you say so, sir."

"Do they ever give you problems?" The doctor picked up a clipboard and began rifling through pages in an obvious search for something.

"You mean my feet?"

The doctor paused and looked up incredulously. "Yes, your *feet.*" He resumed flipping through forms—the Army is all about forms—until he found what he was looking for. He pulled a pen from his pocket, clicked it into the ready position, and held it poised in his right hand.

I thought: "This guy's going to get his ticket punched right out of here." I'd heard the military didn't take anyone with flat feet. "Son of a gun!" I mumbled to myself.

"No, sir, my feet feel fine. Never give me any problems." I did a double take at the reply. The doctor indeed seemed poised to send the young man home to Momma.

"Well then," the physician said looking earnestly into the young man's face. He never finished the thought. The doctor shook his head, returned the pen into the pocket of his lab coat, and sat the clipboard back on the table behind him.

"Welcome to the United States Army. Head out the door and follow the arrows down the hall.

"Next!" he said, turning to look directly at me.

***

I expected to do my basic combat training in close proximity to home. Fort Leonard Wood is located in the northern reaches of the Ozark Mountains and was, in its days as a training encampment, known for its challenging mountainous terrain. "Fort Lost in the Woods of Misery"—a play on Fort Leonard Wood, Missouri—came by its nickname honestly.

My misery though, would come elsewhere.

An outbreak of meningitis at Fort Leonard Wood quarantined the installation. So, the Army sent me west to California for basic training at Fort Ord, hard by the Pacific Ocean and considered the most scenic of military outposts.

My second excursion to California bore little resemblance to the first. My parents had taken Jebby and me to Disneyland when I was young. Boot camp at Fort Ord was definitely no "walk in the park," amusement or otherwise. While the sparkling waters of the Pacific offered an inviting vista from camp, the ocean could have been a mirage for all the good it offered. The only time recruits spent near the water was at the camp's rifle range, and the five-mile run to and from target practice removed any notion the experience would be a "day at the beach."

Forgive my abundant use of idioms here. The recollection of boot camp is a little unnerving, even today.

NCOs—non-commissioned officers—at Ford Ord were experts at torture. From the third day of basic until about the third week, immense pain radiated from every muscle in my body. My legs were particularly victimized given our runs through the sandy dunes which sequestered the rifle range. I had been assigned a top bunk in the barracks and can still recall the agony of getting out of that bed and my feet onto the floor to start my day.

I was not alone in this regard. As bad as I felt for myself, I felt even worse for a fellow Sedalian. Let's call him "Roger."

Other than our hometown and a fervent desire to survive the demands of basic training, Roger and I shared little else in common. He had been a senior in high school when I was a sophomore and I didn't recall our paths ever crossing. Roger was 25—the upper age limit of the draft—and was in terrible physical shape; maybe not so much for a used-car salesman, but he was a long way from becoming a competent soldier.

One of the most important aspects of military training is the instilling of an "all-for-one" mentality into the minds of new recruits. "No soldier left behind" is a dictum which is constantly reinforced. Call it brainwashing if you will, but the attitude is critical in enabling the military to achieve its overarching strategic objectives while keeping its fighting forces as safe as possible.

No drill or exercise at boot camp was completed until everyone finished, and that included Roger. Invariably, two or three of us were at his side, imploring, encouraging, or, if need be, dragging him to the finish line. Our drill instructor, a short, stocky man with ebony skin and a steely determination, didn't ride Roger any harder than the rest of us. Instead, he used our weakest link to teach valuable lessons which would be of benefit on the battlefield.

By the time boot camp was over, Roger had shed more than 20 pounds. He became a dervish on the obstacle course, and transformed into a soldier alongside whom anyone would have been confident to serve. He made Sedalia proud.

Before leaving Fort Ord, the company commander called me into his office. Because the war was becoming increasingly unpopular at home, college ROTC programs were seeing a significant decline in numbers. Young officers were in short supply.

"Brown," the commander said with a big smile on his face during our brief but memorable encounter, "I'm impressed with your marks here. As a college graduate, you qualify to become an officer in the United States Army. I'd like to recommend you for Officer Candidate School."

He continued with his pitch the wattage of his smile diminishing. "Admittedly, I have a quota to fill, so, I'll be blunt. If you choose not to take advantage of my largesse"—a word I knew thanks to my father—"there's a total certainty you will get a guided tour of the jungles of Southeast Asia with enemy fire thrown in at no additional cost.

"Frankly, I'm not looking for soldiers who are going to tell me 'no'."

As I pondered how to frame my response, I remembered my flat-footed compatriot. Honesty would have to do.

"With all respect, sir, I think Vietnam is an inevitable part of my future. In fact, I think my chances of seeing serious action would increase as a platoon commander. I just don't think being an officer is what I'm cut out to be. No disrespect meant, sir."

The commander stared at me for a moment. "No disrespect taken, solider. In fact, I appreciate your candor." His demeanor changed once again.

"Usually I can scare up candidates with my 'guided tour of the jungle' bit," he laughed, "but not you. Fair enough."

With a long line of additional prospects sitting outside his office, the commander stood and called me to attention. We saluted and shook hands. "One last piece of advice, soldier," he said. "Regardless of how nasty and smelly the Army's bug repellant might be, never, ever go anywhere in the jungle without it. Truth be told, we're fighting two sets of enemies over there and one's just as damned bad as the other."

I spent the remainder of that year at Fort Sill, near Lawton, Oklahoma. While I had bypassed becoming an officer, my broadcast experience made me a natural for the Army Public Information Office. First and foremost I was an infantryman-in-waiting, but in the lead-up to overseas deployment, soldiers with particular aptitudes were groomed for the junior enlisted ranks.

My training at Fort Sill reminded me of my days at KFRU. I was given the responsibility to produce and host daily reports on camp activities. Dianne moved to Lawton and for the next several months we lived a somewhat normal life in an off-base apartment. Then, in January 1971, I received new orders.

Next stop: Long Binh and the U.S. Army's major command headquarters for the war in Vietnam.

***

Upon arrival "in country"—what Vietnam was called by most soldiers serving there—I assumed I would report to a fire base near the front lines. I had little reason to believe my combat training at Fort Ord wouldn't be put to an immediate life-and-death test.

Instead, I wound up getting my own air-conditioned office.

Simply stated, I caught a huge break upon arrival at Long Binh. There was a Public Information Office—PIO—position available for which I was qualified and quickly assigned. The Army had plenty of foot soldiers, but few who knew how to handle a microphone and a tape deck. I was designated an audio specialist and my air-conditioned office doubled as a recording studio. I wouldn't have to be ducking mortar rounds, at least for a while.

In response to the ever-increasing number of anti-war protests back home, the Army made a great effort to work on the hearts and minds of the American taxpayers. PR is a critical part of any wartime effort. According to an unclassified document describing the Army's Public Affairs mission in the year 2000, the program "fulfills the Army's obligation to keep the American people and the Army informed and helps to establish the conditions that lead to confidence in America's Army and its readiness to conduct operations."

That was pretty much the business case for operation "Hometown Heroes." After getting my figurative feet wet—a major cause of trench foot in the literal sense—I was assigned to go into the field and give infantrymen a chance to tell their stories to the folks back home.

I conducted more than 200 interviews in places like Da Nang, Qui Nhon, and Song Be. I roved through encampments looking for troops willing to talk. Since mine was an official Army operation, I had the support of commanding officers in the field, which meant soldiers were more or less obligated to participate, but not everyone did.

The interviews were not unlike those I've done with athletes throughout my broadcasting career. Then, as now, my job was to humanize the efforts of those in uniform and bring their lives into personal perspective. The outcomes—whether soldier or jock—usually amounted to nothing more than a lot of *clichés*.

There were strict parameters on what could be covered in the "Hometown Heroes" project. Since the interviews were taped, I was never in danger of inadvertently revealing classified information unless a shout-out to friends and family was of strategic importance to the enemy. Many of my subjects fell into rehashing letters from home. Maybe it wasn't always great radio, but it was an invaluable experience for me. The project was a sizable undertaking and brought me close to the nature of war.

Throughout my military service—except at boot camp—I never fired a weapon. I also never encountered the enemy face-to-face, at least not to my knowledge. But, thanks to my series of interviews with our fighting force, I did get a strong sense of the effect war can have on the individual. It turned out to be a much more personal and even intimate experience than I ever imagined. I came to think of war like a tsunami: Individuals are powerless against its current and with its strong tide comes massive anguish, devastation, and loss of life.

Every time I returned to the command staff at Long Binh, I thanked God for keeping me on the periphery of harm's way. I'd like to think I took my job as seriously as any soldier, but I did have the luxuries of an air-conditioned workplace, regular meals, and—most importantly—the opportunity for a good night's sleep.

Ernie Williamson, news editor for the *Houston Chronicle* served with me at command headquarters. Ernie is an outstanding newspaper man today and remains a good friend. At Long Binh, the two of us, along with about 40 other staff specialists, lived in what we called a "hooch". That word has many connotations, but in the case of the military—circa Vietnam—hooch was slang for a thatched hut, which, of course, many of the natives actually called their home.

The hooch Ernie and I shared was more than a hut. Unlike the majority of office buildings in camp, our barracks was not air-conditioned, but did have fans hanging from the ceiling which circulated the air and made sleeping at night more comfortable. For recreation, Ernie and I played a lot of volleyball. Music was also a popular diversion, as was correspondence to and from loved ones far away.

During the war, Long Binh was a city unto itself with a population of more than 50,000 men and women. The area surrounding the command center was mostly countryside and bereft of the moral and financial temptations to be found in the heart of nearby Saigon. Today, Long Binh is home to one of Vietnam's most bustling shopping malls.

As a result of my work on the "Hometown Heroes" series, I received both a commendation and promotion, thus paving the way for another new assignment.

I was transferred to the American Forces Vietnam Network in Saigon. At AFVN, I was part of a broadcast operation which rivaled that of any major-market back home. Programming featured news, weather, sports, information, and entertainment. Every day—on the radio side of the house—began with a morning show called "Dawn Buster." And every morning "Dawn Buster" kicked off with a simple three-word opening which served as a spoken Reveille for the American men and women who listened.

"Goooood Morning, Vietnam."

I did not know Adrian Cronauer, the AFVN disk jockey made famous by the movie based on both his life and his famous radio catchphrase, but I was aware of his reputation. He wasn't as manic as Robin Williams' cinematic portrayal. In fact, Cronauer was a member of Mensa, the famous society of the super intelligent. He was also a bit of a rock star, and in some ways he reminded me a lot of another *enfant terrible*: Chris Lincoln.

Before my arrival, AFVN headquarters was nearly destroyed in a car-bomb attack. By the time I got there, operations were contained in a much more secure location, albeit, still near the center of the city, where almost anything could happen. My "barracks" was a nearby hotel, commandeered to house American military personnel, and I was shuttled to work each day in a bus.

The AFVN radio network was heard throughout southeast Asia, its signal beamed from the skies by Navy planes. AFVN television aired locally in Saigon. I split my time working in both media.

My assignment, believe it or not, was sports. The Army gave me my first big career break.

Our sports department consisted of three individuals: myself, bumped up in rank to Specialist Fourth Class with a pay grade commensurate to that of a corporal, and two military "lifers:" U.S. Army Staff Sergeant Preston Cluff and U.S. Air Force Technical Sergeant Arthur Burnett. Although both outranked me, they treated me as an equal and were two of the finest men I met in the military.

Sports mattered to the military as a means of boosting morale. Many soldiers owned transistor radios and listened when they could. From our studios, we offered a measure of sanity in an otherwise crazy and chaotic world. Wagering on the outcome of games, regardless of sport, duty station, or rank, was a popular military pastime.

Before satellite communications became a common television staple or a high-speed Internet connection could stream video directly to a soldier's laptop computer, the Armed Forces Network—which picked up feeds of a wide range of play-by-play broadcasts—was a popular source of AFVN radio programming. A college or pro football game which kicked off at noon Central Standard Time in the States got underway at 1 a.m. the next day in Saigon. Thus, most of the games on the Armed Forces Network were broadcast to the troops on a tape-delayed basis.

Sergeant Burnett was the technical expert among us. If equipment needed repair, he was the man for the job. He was also a night owl. Thus, the midnight to noon shift was perfect for him. Since AFVN operations were downsized at night, with no television programming from 2200 to 0600—10 p.m. to 6 a.m. local time—Art spent much of his time tinkering with faulty equipment and recording Armed Forces Network transmissions on oversized reels of tape.

The 1971 Alabama-Auburn game was one of the biggest of the year in college football. I looked forward to the showdown, not only for its sporting significance, but also because it marked the end of my active duty. I was originally slated to serve two years in the Army, but thanks to the downsizing of American forces in Southeast Asia, I had more than five months knocked off my tour. My discharge was set for the end of November. I truly had something for which to be thankful at Thanksgiving.

Beginning with the 2012 school year, my *alma mater* Missouri will play Alabama and Auburn on a regular basis as a new member of the Southeastern Conference. Alabama, of course, is coming off the 2011 National Championship—Auburn won in 2010—and forty years ago, both schools were also national powerhouses. Entering the '71 Iron Bowl—as the Auburn-Alabama football game is called, the Tide was ranked third in the country, while the Tigers were rated number five. AFVN Sports spent a good bit of our programming week building up the matchup and the more we hyped the game, the more we created the unintended consequence of soldiers wagering more of their money. Even locals got in on the action, and that group included, no doubt, at least a few enemy combatants. Ask anyone who served in

Southeast Asia and they'll tell you no one is more eager to gamble on the outcome of almost anything than the Vietnamese male. They are a daring, resourceful, and tenacious people as was proven by the outcome of the war.

At the duly-appointed time in the wee hours of a Sunday morning in Saigon, Sergeant Burnett hit the record button as the Auburn-Alabama game kicked off at Birmingham's Legion Field. In order to shorten the duration of the broadcast and avoid commercial mentions, Art stopped the tape during breaks. He had to be on his toes for the entirety of the game.

Burnett was the consummate multi-tasker. While recording games, he also routinely cleaned playback heads on tape machines and made other repairs as needed. He was a real professional and rarely made a mistake, either on or off the air.

The next day, I found the tapes labeled and ready to go. I cued the first reel and began airing the game broadcast roughly twelve hours after the contest had been played. To give me one last "night on the town"—during which nothing untoward happened, I can assure you—Sergeant Cluff had switched shifts with me. When I arrived for work on Sunday, I made sure to steer clear of the teletype machines. I wanted to listen to the game as if it were happening live.

From the outset of the contest, Auburn had great difficulty moving the ball against Coach Bear Bryant's stifling Alabama defense. The Crimson Tide, meanwhile, ran its wishbone offense to perfection. Bama took a quick 14-0 lead and was up 14-7 at halftime. The score remained the same heading into the fourth quarter of play.

Then something strange happened, something which brought back an eerie sense of *déjà vu.*

Suddenly, the score was no longer Alabama14, Auburn 7; but Dallas 10, Washington 0.

In the comfort of an easy chair at home, one might have been prompted to say, "Who changed the channel?" But in my AFVN control booth, there were no other channels. The reel continued to turn and the tape continued to play, but the game was not the same. My palms suddenly grew sweaty and I half expected to hear a voice from the past in my headsets—WOAI's Tom Maguire—proclaiming, "I need some *Alabama football.* NOW!"

Soon phone calls—real and not imagined—started pouring in. There was only one line into the studio and that number was never given out on the air. The calls—much to my chagrin—weren't from Sergeants Cluff or Burnett with a quick fix to my dilemma. Instead, the inquiries were much higher up the chain of command, officers and brass with access to the PIO phone directory who were used to getting their way.

"What's going ON up there?" "What the HELL happened to the game?" "Soldier, you WILL get that game back on the air and that's an ORDER!" These were just a few of the calls I took in the ensuing minutes.

Finally, as Tom Landry's Cowboys added a field goal to increase their lead, I decided to drop out of the game and, with no other recourse, found a record to play. This musical interlude bought me time to consider my options. I ignored the phone to concentrate on a course of action: If I couldn't deliver the rest of the game broadcast, the least I could do was pass along the final score.

I looked through the rack of taped actualities to see if Sergeant Cluff had put together a recap of the game before concluding his Saturday shift. Fortunately, he had. I finally switched on my microphone to apologize for "technical difficulties" and introduced Cluff's report. Along with everyone else tuned in, I learned Alabama had scored seventeen unanswered points in the final period to coast to a 31-7 blowout win.

The next day, in a staff meeting which included more khaki and service ribbons than normally graced such gatherings, group consensus determined Sergeant Burnett had failed to depress the record button adequately after a commercial break. Upon learning of the matter when he reported for duty after my ill-fated Sunday shift, Burnett scanned through the second-half reel to figure out the problem. What he discovered—to his horror and mine—was that only about four minutes of the college game was missing. At the next commercial break, he successfully engaged the record mechanism to pick up the rest of the contest. The Cowboys-Redskins game had been a remnant of an earlier broadcast. The someone who had failed to bulk-erase the tape turned out to be me.

No one was court-martialed or even reprimanded over the matter and my discharge was not put on hold. I managed to serve out the remaining days of my tour avoiding car bombs, pickpockets, and any further on-air snafus.

The day I left the war, as the troop transport plane ascended from Tan Son Nhut Air Base, I took one last look at the city of Saigon, rapidly fading into the distance below. Unlike tens of thousands of other American soldiers who lost their lives in service to their country, I had the good fortunate to be able to say goodbye to Vietnam.

CHAPTER 7
Sergeant Cluff

Preston Cluff has few regrets about his twenty-seven years of active military service. One, however, sticks out in his mind.

"I never met Bob Hope," he says.

Cluff met a lot of other people in his military duties and I imagine they all felt the same way about him as I did: one heckuva nice guy.

The experience of writing this book has been an interesting one for me. My collaborator Tim Gregg has been the ultimate "color guy." Just as I do in the broadcast booth, I describe the action, the milestones of my life, and Tim provides the analysis. We've been to places writing this book I never expected to go.

Tim is a pretty tenacious researcher. He knows his way around the Internet. He's also a good interviewer, which has been another interesting experience. Usually I'm the guy asking the questions.

Our lives have numerous parallels. We both grew up in the Midwest. While I considered attending the University of Oklahoma, Tim actually went. We both majored in Broadcast Journalism and gained considerable practical experience during our undergraduate years working part-time at commercial radio stations. We also both joined and left fraternities. During the summer before his senior year, Tim lined up a student internship with none other than Chris Lincoln at KTUL-TV in Tulsa.

As we outlined this book, Tim expressed particular interest in my Vietnam experience. By the time he graduated from high school, the war had ended. Tim told me he felt a little out of his element when it came to helping me tell my war story. And so, he sought to find an "expert"—someone who could help us tell the tale.

Which is how I came to be reunited with Preston Cluff.

I had not spoken to Master Sergeant Cluff for more than 40 years. When I did—after Tim tracked him down in Alaska—Preston reminded me he was only a staff sergeant during the time we worked together in Saigon. I had him initially pegged at a higher rank. "Never wanted to go to sergeant-major school," he told me on the phone from his home in Eagle River, a suburb of Anchorage and bedroom community to Joint Base Elemendorf-Richardson. "Had too much fun doing what I was doing. I didn't want to be tied down to a desk or tethered to a commanding officer!"

Cluff grew up in North Conway, New Hampshire. Like me, he developed an early love of sports. Unlike me, he played high school football, basketball, and baseball. And, as he readily admits today, he also ran with the wrong crowd. While I was recreating baseball broadcasts with friends in front of the television set at home, Preston and his "friends" were stealing cars. Poor grades doomed his athletic endeavors his final two years of high school and he wound up on juvenile probation for accessory to auto theft.

"The Army turned out to be the best thing that ever happened to me," says Cluff. "Otherwise, I probably would have gone nowhere or worse."

After graduation, Preston knocked around for a time before deciding to get serious about a career he thought he could sink his teeth into: sports broadcasting.

Just about the time I headed off to Mizzou for my freshman year, the U.S. Army knocked on Cluff's door. Given his circumstances at the time, he was grateful. He was drafted in October 1965, and by June of the following year, he had arrived in country with the 196th Light Infantry Brigade.

Before joining the Army, Cluff put in a year at the Cambridge School of Business and Broadcasting located in Boston. The "business" side of the operation was a secretarial school, while the broadcasting curriculum dealt more with keeping a radio station on the air rather than grooming on-the-air talent. Still, Cambridge got Preston's foot in the door and proved invaluable in influencing his Army career.

For most of his first tour of duty in Vietnam, Cluff was a radio operator at battalion command which kept him away from the heaviest combat action. "I still dug foxholes and I saw my share of KIAs," he said, referring to the Army acronym for "killed in action."

When the time came for him to re-enlist, Preston went for as much gusto as Army life would allow. He put in for his extension requesting a hitch with AFVN. To his amazement, his request was approved and he moved to Saigon in May of 1967. He believes a good word from his battalion commander altered the course of his Army career.

By Cluff's arrival, AFVN was established in a secure facility located a block and a half from the U.S. Embassy in downtown Saigon. Previously, the military broadcast center had been housed, along with bachelor officers' quarters, in the old Brinks Hotel. That site came under attack on Christmas Eve 1964 when two Viet Cong, disguised as South Vietnamese military officers, detonated a car bomb in the hotel's underground garage, killing two soldiers and injuring more than 60 other people. The attack may have targeted entertainer Bob Hope, long famous for his USO-sponsored holiday tours of overseas military operations. Hope and his entourage were staying in a hotel nearby and were not affected by the blast.

"I never met Hope, but I met a lot of big names from the world of sports," Cluff remembers today. The Dan Patrick of his time, Cluff met and interviewed the likes of Bowie Kuhn, Tony Conigliaro, Willie Stargell, Dick Weber, Nancy Chaffee, and Johnny Musso during their USO-sponsored tours designed to bolster troop morale.

Cluff was a top-shelf sportscaster. If I had to compare his on-air style with anyone of note, Mel Allen comes to mind. While he lacked a signature catch phrase, when it came to Cluff's work—whether reporting scores or interviewing celebrities—his enthusiasm was infectious. He always seemed to be on the brink of proclaiming, "How about that!" in wonder at his own lot in life.

Away from work, Cluff and I didn't spend a lot of time together, and for good reason it turns out. It wasn't until we reconnected that I learned Cluff had a secret life in Saigon. While we both officially lived in the same hotel and frequently commuted to work together, Cluff's real home was a rented apartment some distance from his Army life.

"Yeah, it was probably illegal," Cluff says," but a lot of American soldiers did the same thing, and I think the military sort of looked the other way.

"Growing up, my family didn't have a lot of money. Dad wasn't around and Mom had to work two jobs to make ends meet. When I re-enlisted and got to Saigon, for the first time in my life, I had money in my pocket."

Cluff shared his apartment with a young Vietnamese woman and the two had a child, a boy who died as an infant of spinal meningitis. "That was tough," he says. "Since most of my personal life was off the military's radar screen and we weren't yet married, my son didn't qualify to receive Army medical benefits.

"For the second time in my life, I decided I needed to get straight with the program."

Cluff left Saigon for a spot with Armed Forces Radio and Television Services in Washington, DC. He served another twenty-one years in the United States Armed Forces. During that time, his first wife Phu died of a brain tumor. Preston and his second bride Jae chose to stay in Alaska following his retirement from the military there in 1992.

The Army remains in Cluff's blood. After retirement he landed a civilian position at the Buckner Physical Fitness Center on the Fort Richardson encampment. "Caught another break there," he laughs. As director of operations, Cluff was the man in charge for nearly fifteen years. "Couldn't get away from sports," he says. "Truth is, never wanted to get away."

Even though Preston Cluff and I went our separate ways such a long time ago, we came to share something in common, besides a love of sports and warm regard for our time spent in the military.

"Bill, you're not the only play-by-play guy to get his start with AFVN in Saigon," Cluff told me proudly. "While stationed at Fort Richardson working for the Alaskan Forces Network, I was the voice of the Anchorage Northern Knights, a Continental Basketball Association team. Doing those games was a blast. Pretty good brand of basketball, too.

"Really, who could believe how much fun I had in the Army!"

As both soldier and civilian, Cluff spent more than forty years in service to his country. He traveled a lot of miles, met a lot of interesting people—including his two wives and Bowie Kuhn—stayed mostly out of trouble, and served with both honor and distinction.

Now that we're back in touch, I'm looking forward to seeing Preston again. He and Jae have a second home in the San Antonio area, a place where they can escape the Alaskan winters. The Sergeant also told me AFVN veterans hold a reunion every year.   He thinks the next one will be in Tennessee sometime in the fall of 2012.   If the Astros don't make it into post-season play, I think I'll try to spend some time with my old Army buddies.

CHAPTER 8
9/11

The afternoon of Sunday, September 9, 2001, was a good one for fans of the Houston Astros.

Weather-wise, light rain fell intermittently throughout the day, but with the roof closed at Enron Field, the playing conditions were perfect. A better-than-average crowd of just over 35,000 saw the Astros play one of their best games of the year. Home runs off the bats of Jeff Bagwell, Moises Alou, Brad Ausmus, and Richard Hidalgo complemented a seven-hit complete-game pitching performance from Roy Oswalt as Houston shut out Milwaukee 8-0.

The win gave the Astros a five-and-a-half game lead in the National League Central Division, their biggest of the year.

Houston had Monday off before continuing its home stand with a three-game series against San Francisco. The Giants flew into town late on the evening of the 9th after posting a 9-4 Sunday afternoon victory over the Rockies in Denver. Slugger Barry Bonds hit three home runs in the game, including a three-run eleventh-inning blast, which both led his team to victory and boosted his home run total for the year to 63. Bonds was well ahead of the pace Mark McGwire had set when breaking Roger Maris' long-standing single-season home run record in 1998.

Days off in September are a precious thing for ballplayers. The season is long and both physically and mentally grueling. Like the Astros, the Giants were battling for a spot in the playoffs, standing just a game and a half out of the NL West lead. There was also the hoopla of Bonds' home run chase, although that was tempered somewhat—at least on the road—by his reputation as one of the game's least likeable players.

There were worse places for Bonds and his teammates to spend an off day than the Bayou City.

Houston has a reputation as a locale friendly to professional athletes. The temperate winter climate, reasonable cost of living, and absence of state income tax also make it a great place to live. It's a great place for the young and the rich from out of town to have a good time. At least that's what I've been told.

As for the life of a Houston-based big league broadcaster when the ballpark doesn't beckon? Well, in my case I guess you could say I'm a bit of a homebody. A day off during the season enables me to get some much needed rest and a tasty home-cooked meal. During the off-season, I try to spend as much time with Dianne as I can and play the occasional round of golf. That's the kind of stuff that makes me happy and how I was spending my time the day everything changed.

**

"Bill, wake up. An airplane has hit the World Trade Center."

There was urgency in Dianne's voice as she came into our bedroom. She turned on the television there and I slowly came to my senses. As I fumbled for my glasses, I heard an earnest tone coming from the news anchor on TV. With my sight restored, I saw the horrible black cloud billowing from one of the Twin Towers.

The pictures were shocking. Before long our phone began to ring as family and friends reached out in an attempt to process the unimaginable scene we were all watching on television. Then, the second plane appeared from out of that crystal blue sky and the horror was multiplied by a factor of two. Other planes crash-landed in Washington, D.C., and the Pennsylvania countryside. Our leaders told us the nation was under attack.

I have flown millions of miles in my broadcast career, most of the time on large passenger planes like those hijacked and turned into weapons of mass destruction on 9/11. Experts tell us airlines are the safest way to travel. We learn to accept the ordinary as routine.

Then came the horrifying events of September 11, which served as yet another painful reminder that nothing—even the most routine aspects of our daily lives—is ever a completely for-sure thing. Almost ten years to the day after the World Trade Center was destroyed, an entire Kontinental Hockey League team perished in a plane crash near the Russian city of Yaroslavl.

Months *before* 9/11, nearly a dozen members of the Oklahoma State University men's basketball program died when the private plane in which they were returning home went down in the flatlands of eastern Colorado. Fast forward again, and just two months after the crash in Yaroslavl, Oklahoma State's women's basketball coach and his top assistant lost their lives when the small plane in which they were making a recruiting trip fell out of the sky in central Arkansas.

Marshall and Wichita State Universities lost entire football teams when chartered flights failed to make it to their final destinations less than six weeks apart in the autumn of 1970.

No one is immune from the rough knocks which serve as counterbalance to the joys of life. Sometimes those blows can force us to our knees. The bad comes along with the good. Still, nothing prepared the world for what happened on 9/11

Once Dianne and I had connected with our loved ones, offering and receiving much-needed moral support, our attention returned to the ghastly images on TV. We sat side by side on the sofa in our family room watching in silence. I remember how tightly Dianne held my hand, squeezing her grip even more with every new revelation. Finally, I uttered the inanely obvious.

"No game tonight."

Baseball commissioner Bud Selig not only postponed all games that day, but also all games for the remainder of the week.

All commercial flights in the U.S. were cancelled for three days following the attacks and travelers from coast to coast, including fifteen Major League Baseball teams were stranded on the road. I was thankful to be at home with my wife. Many, many others weren't as fortunate.

After the World Trade Center towers collapsed, New York Yankees pitcher Roger Clemens rented a car and drove halfway across the country to be with his family in Houston. Several Giants and Astros took the same course of action from Houston, succumbing to an instinctive need to be close to loved ones in a time of crisis. For the next six days it seemed as if life could never return to the way it was before.

Then, slowly, something else nearly unimaginable happened.   Normalcy was given a fighting chance to be restored.

It was time to try and play ball again.

***

Wars can begin—and end—either with a whimper or a bang. When the first hijacked plane exploded into the World Trade Center, America found itself instantly thrust into both an altered reality and a state of war. On the other end of the continuum of conflict, the United States took nearly a decade before becoming fully involved in the political maelstrom of Southeast Asia during the 1960s.

Vietnam was also a different kind of war than had been seen to that time. The enemy frequently blended in with the general population. Women and children, previously the innocent bystanders of war's atrocities, became active and lethal participants. For the U.S., waging war in Vietnam became a tentative proposition. In addition, many were uncertain as to what it was we were fighting for.

Upon my departure from Saigon, I flew back to California for discharge and was processed out of the military at Oakland Army Base. Had it been baseball season, I might have stuck around to see what the Kansas City Athletics had become in their new incarnation as the Oakland A's. Under owner Charlie Finley, the team was set to dominate the game.

Thirty years later another airplane took me back to the Bay Area, this time on the leading edge of war. Vietnam didn't come to an official end until 1975 and the War Against Terror didn't manifest itself fully until the invasion of Iraq in 2003. But, as the Astros' team charter landed *safely* at San Francisco International Airport on the eve of the resumption of play in the aftermath of 9/11—and I wouldn't take safe landings for granted again for a long time—none of us on that plane were completely certain what the future held.

Only three times has Major League Baseball play been suspended by anything other than labor upheaval or an act of Mother Nature. The 1918 season was cut short after U.S. entry into World War I. On June 6, 1944, in recognition of the events taking place that day at Utah, Gold, Juno, Sword, and Omaha Beaches on the coast of France, big league baseball again went dark in deference to military action.

And then there was the aftermath of 9/11.

I spoke with several players on the flight to San Francisco. None were eager to play and a few voiced concern that an insufficient amount of time had passed since the attacks. At Ground Zero, the enormous pile of rubble still smoldered and the remains of victims were still being recovered.

Everything about that trip, at least until game time, was subdued. Manager Larry Dierker told me he had no plans to rally his squad. "This is a veteran ball club and I've found they don't respond to team meetings." He was quiet for a time before adding, "In my heart, I know I'm ready to get back to work, to let the people who did this to our country know they're not going to diminish our way of life."

In Washington, President Bush addressed a joint session of Congress and spoke of a nation "awakened to danger and called to defend freedom." Of our enemies, he promised justice would be done. He went on to ask Americans for a return to normalcy:

> "Great harm has been done to us. We have suffered great loss. And in our grief and anger, we have found our mission and our moment.
>
> "Freedom and fear are at war. The advance of human freedom, the great achievement of our time and the great hope of every time, now depends on us.
>
> "Our nation, this generation, will lift the dark threat of violence from our people and our future. We will rally the world to this cause by our efforts, by our courage. We will not tire, we will not falter, and we will not fail.
>
> "It is my hope that in the months and years ahead life will return almost to normal. We'll go back to our lives and routines, and that is good.
>
> "Even grief recedes with time and grace."

Both the Astros and Giants were idle when baseball officially resumed play on Monday, September 17. That day, nearly everyone in America was a Mets fan—the Yankees also had the day off—and New York prevailed at Pittsburgh 4-1. In St. Louis, Hall of Fame broadcaster Jack Buck, his body frail and ravaged by both Parkinson's disease and lung cancer, made an unexpected return to Busch Stadium. In one of his final public appearances he spoke of life and liberty:

> *"War is just not our nature...we*
> *Won't start, but we will end the fight.*
> *If we are involved we shall be*
> *Resolved to protect what we know is*
> *Right.*
>
> *"We've been challenged by a*
> *Cowardly foe, who strikes and then*
> *Hides from our view.*
> *With one voice we say there's no*
> *Choice today, there is only one*
> *Thing to do."*

In San Francisco, Astros outfielder Lance Berkman struggled to find right words.

"It will be tough for me to get my mind on baseball," Berkman told reporter Joseph Duarte of the *Houston Chronicle*. "At the same time, it's a reality we have to deal with.

"There isn't a whole lot we can do from a distance but pray for the people involved," Berkman continued, "I think it will help if we can get back on the field and try and get back in a normal routine and bring back some of the things (from) before the tragedy.

"We'll never forget it. But at the same time, we have to eventually move forward."

Almost 41,000 fans joined Berkman in an attempt to move forward as the Giants and Astros resumed their seasons at Pac Bell Park. Rather than wearing jerseys and caps, San Francisco faithful sported apparel featuring stars and stripes and the color scheme red, white, and blue.

During the pregame ceremonies that night, ballpark lights were dimmed and the crowd lit thousands of candles to honor the victims of the attacks. A choir sang "Amazing Grace," and firefighters and police officers joined the two teams on the field. In the broadcast booth, despite the steel and glass partitions, we were one with our fellow Americans.

I had seen and heard Buck's remarks in St. Louis the day before. Leading into our broadcast I referenced the Cardinals' Hall-of-Fame announcer, quoting briefly from his poem. Otherwise, pregame camera shots captured everything else that needed to be said. Both teams sported American flags newly-stitched onto the sleeves of their uniform jerseys. Fans held each other and cried. One homemade sign in the stands read "Deliver Us From Evil."

San Francisco held a 2-1 lead heading to the top of the ninth inning as pain gave way to purpose over the course of that baseball night. When Giants reliever Rob Nenn came out of the San Francisco bullpen, he was welcomed, not by the strains of his usual anthem, the Deep Purple song "Smoke on the Water"—which spoke of "fire in the sky"—but by an *a cappella* cacophony rising from the throats and hearts of the home fans in attendance. Just an inning and a half before, the seventh-inning stretch was permanently transformed as "God Bless America" replaced the ballpark standard, "Take Me Out to the Ball Game".

Looking for his 40th save of the season, Nenn faced Houston pinch-hitter Orlando Merced to lead off the ninth. Merced lined a single to center which brought up Jeff Bagwell. Down in the count one-and-two, Bags slapped another line drive past first base and into the right field corner. His triple tied the game 2-2.

Nenn struck out Berkman for the inning's first out, but then Moises Alou lifted a fly ball to center, deep enough to score Bagwell from third. As the top of the ninth came to a close, Houston owned a 3-2 advantage.

The lead held as Astros closer Billy Wagner struck out pinch hitters Shawon Dunston and Damon Minor in a one-two-three bottom of the ninth. Baseball was back and the Astros were back in the win column, as my friend Milo Hamilton likes to say.

I remember leaving the ballpark after the game feeling a great sense of relief. I did my best to make the broadcast business as usual and was glad the team had pulled out the win. Still, it took a while for the outcome of games to matter in the way they had before.

Houston swept the three-game set with the Giants. Barry Bonds was held without a homer until the fifth inning of the finale. The Astros returned home to face the Cubs sporting a four-and-a-half game division lead.

In the first game in Houston after 9/11, Astros fans were met with extra security at the entrances to Enron Field. Those precautions applied for broadcasters, too. During pre-game ceremonies, Eagle Scouts carried a massive American flag onto the field, bagpipers from St. Thomas High School played "Amazing Grace," and the Kingwood High School chorus performed the National Anthem. As the song ended, chants of "U-S-A, U-S-A" echoed around the ballpark, rekindling the patriotic fervor of our country's "Miracle on Ice" victory over the Soviet Union.

That night's game came to a less than memorable conclusion, at least for the home fans. Chicago won 12-4 as Sammy Sosa hit his 55th home run of the year.

The next afternoon Merced and Bagwell sparked a six-run fifth-inning rally; Merced with a bases-loaded triple and Bagwell with a two-run double. Houston took the game 8-4. The Astros won the rubber game of the set on Sunday besting Sosa's three-home-run outing with a three-run rally in the seventh. Wagner recorded his 37th save, and the Astros were a win away from going thirty games above the five-hundred mark.

Yet, they couldn't shake off the Cardinals.

St. Louis won twelve of fourteen games in response to Jack Buck's Busch Stadium return and after taking two of three at Houston and winning four more in a row, the Cardinals had completely erased the Astros' division lead.

Houston played abysmally over the course of the last two weeks of the extended season. Still, the Astros clinched a spot in the playoffs with a win in the opener of the regular-season-ending series at St. Louis. In fact, both teams were assured a spot in the playoffs. Houston won the finale 9-2, and although the two teams ended the year with identical 93-69 records, the Astros were named division champions on the strength of their head-to-head advantage over the Redbirds.

On October 4, I made the call of Barry Bonds' record-tying 70th home run at Enron Field. Later revelations have diminished the achievement in my mind, but seeing the mark equaled was a memorable moment. Bonds went on to break the single-season record with three more blasts against the Dodgers at Pac Bell Park. The Giants, however, missed the playoffs.

In the postseason, both the Astros and Cardinals lost first-round series. Behind the pitching dominance of former Astros Randy Johnson and Curt Schilling, Arizona won the National League pennant. In the American League, the New York Yankees appeared to be a team of destiny as they beat the A's and the Mariners to qualify for World Series play.

The Series went the distance. In the bottom of the ninth inning of the decisive seventh game, New York owned the lead and sent its version of a sure thing to the mound to seal the triumph. But the game, the Series, and the most difficult of seasons did not come to a storybook end. Closer Mariano Rivera gave up the tying run and then a soft line drive off the bat of yet another former Astro, Luis Gonzalez, capped the Diamondback's dramatic rally and gave Arizona the championship at home.

On behalf of its namesake city, the New York Yankees had fought the good fight. In the end, though, what mattered more than winning was enduring, persevering, and giving the best you had to give. The Yankees and the Diamondbacks did exactly that. I think we all did.

In a small, but not insignificant way, baseball helped put America back on its feet.

CHAPTER 9
"That's A Winner"

Growing up in Sedalia, my friends and I spent a lot of summer nights and weekend afternoons listening to St. Louis Cardinals baseball games on the radio. In my case, I didn't tune in because the Redbirds were my favorite team. I loved listening to the broadcasters, one in particular.

In 1954, St. Louis had three future Hall-of-Famers announcing their games. Two were rookies in the team's broadcast booth that year. Harry Carabina, more popularly known as Harry Caray, was the crew's veteran. In '52 and '53, Caray called games alongside former Cardinal player Gus Mancuso. A native of Galveston, Texas, Mancuso caught for five different big league teams and was a two-time all-star. Broadcasting was a bit of a moonlighting venture for Mancuso, who also served as a scout for the Cardinals.

Beer baron Augustus Busch—"Gussie" to the baseball world—bought the Redbirds before the 1953 season and after a year-long shakedown cruise with the club, wholesale changes were made throughout the organization. One of those changes made Mancuso a full-time scout again.

Enter Jack Buck and Milo Hamilton to the Cardinals' broadcast booth.

Hamilton had broken in as a big league announcer with the St. Louis Browns in 1953. One of the many changes Gussie Busch orchestrated after buying the Cardinals was purchase of Sportsman's Park from Browns' owner Bill Veeck. For years the two teams shared the facility and even though the Cardinals were the more successful tenant, the Browns actually owned the ballpark. When Busch bought it, he changed the name to Busch Stadium, less to honor himself than to market his eponymous beer company, although when it came to Gussie, one had to question his stated rationale.

Busch also was instrumental in "encouraging" Veeck to sell the Browns. The American League found buyers in Baltimore and St. Louis became a one-team baseball town. That left Hamilton without a job, but not for long. A talent then, as he has been with the Astros since 1985, Milo joined the Cardinals' broadcast crew in advance of the '54 season. Buck came aboard that same year after a season doing games for St. Louis' Triple-A minor league affiliate in Rochester, New York.

As a baseball play-by-play announcer, Jack Buck was always a man of precise language. Learning the craft seated between Harry Caray and Milo Hamilton, small wonder he employed an economy of words in his descriptions and accounts of a game.

By the time I attended my first game in St. Louis, Milo had moved on, leaving Caray and Buck in the booth alongside former Cardinal player Joe Garagiola. Like many fans of the time, I brought a radio to the ballpark to listen while I watched. I was astounded at the discrepancy between what I heard and what I saw with my own eyes, at least when Caray was calling the action.

A ground ball off the bat of Ken Boyer was a "hot smash," according to Caray. In reality, it was a routine two-hopper which resulted in an easy out. Buck, on the other hand, was a model of consistency and accuracy, which set the tone for my own broadcast style in years—and decades—to come.

Until his death in 2002, Jack Buck was my idea of the consummate broadcast professional. The more I listened to him—even after becoming a peer—the more I relished his subtly sardonic style and the more I thought of him as the "Thinking-Man's Announcer".

In his book *Moon Shots*, former Cardinal Wally Moon, a St. Louis rookie the same year Buck and Hamilton broke in with the club, remembered getting to know Jack during the team's travels by train to away games. Moon—the'54 National League Rookie of the Year—wrote, "Buck had a keen intellect, and his sharp mind and wit often had some players scratching their heads while others burst out in laughter."

Jack Buck grew up a Red Sox fan in Holyoke, Massachusetts. He and his family eventually moved to Cleveland where, as a teenager, Buck worked as a deck hand on the iron-ore boats which traversed the Great Lakes region. He served in World War II and was injured in action. After the war he attended Ohio State and, upon graduation, caught on as the voice of the Columbus Red Birds, the Cardinals' American Association affiliate. Two years later, at the age of 29, Buck was in the big leagues.

The '54 Cardinals were a mediocre team with more future hall-of-famers in the announcer's booth than they had on the field. While Stan Musial and Red Schoendienst were St. Louis icons who carried no airs or pretense, Harry Caray—a *bon vivant* if there ever was one—developed his own sizable and wildly enthusiastic following. Buck proved an able and affable sidekick. Caray and Hamilton, on the other hand, never quite meshed, at least personality-wise.

After one season, Hamilton left St. Louis and after several stops in his stellar career found a permanent and beloved broadcast home in Houston. Following Milo's departure and returning to the Mancuso mold, the Cardinals opted to put another catcher into the booth, hiring Garagiola. Like Caray a St. Louis native, Garagiola spent nine years as a mostly serviceable but unspectacular big league backstop, but behind the microphone, he was a phenom, the national pastime's own Will Rogers.   And like Caray, Buck, and Hamilton, Joe also would one day receive the Baseball Hall of Fame's Ford Frick Award for broadcasting excellence.

Caray, Buck, and Garagiola remained the Cardinals' announcing team through the end of the decade. In 1960, the club tried to squeeze in a *fourth* hall-of-famer, Buddy Blatner, also a native to St. Louis. Wisely, Buck stepped out of the mix, but having developed a loyal following of his own, he was welcomed back to the Cardinals in 1961. Buck remained in the booth on a mostly full-time basis until his official retirement at the end of the 2001 season.

While Blatner was an accomplished baseball announcer, his claim to immortality was as a table tennis champion. He won a world doubles title and was inducted into the U.S. Table Tennis Hall of Fame in 1979.

During my stints with both the Reds and Astros, I became acquainted firsts and then friends with Jack Buck. Over the years he superseded Caray as *the* iconic broadcast figure in Cardinals' history, yet, he was always down-to-earth, approachable, and immensely likable. He was a fixture on the St. Louis banquet circuit and rarely turned down an invitation to speak at a charity event. In time, he became nationally known and beloved for his network assignments, too. His sixteen-year stint calling NFL Monday Night games with former Kansas City Chiefs coach Hank Stram was legendary and a lot of fun for listeners. Their styles and personalities were dramatically different, but Buck choreographed the broadcasts to perfection.

In St. Louis, Cardinal fans still like to say, after a Redbird triumph, "That's a winner," one of the catchphrases Buck employed with aplomb. Nationally, he's probably best known for his calls of two memorable walk-off home runs.

In the 1985 National League Championship Series, the Dodgers and Cardinals were tied at two games apiece and the Game Five score knotted at 2-2 in the bottom of the ninth inning when shortstop Ozzie Smith came to bat. Smith had nearly equaled his career total for home runs that season with six, but the switch-hitter was not considered a power threat as a left-handed batter. Then, in dramatic fashion, Smith "corked"—Buck's word—a looping line drive barely over the right-field wall to give St. Louis the win. Buck encouraged Cardinal fans to "Go crazy, folks! Go crazy!" And, they did.

Three years later, Buck outdid himself as a baseball dramatist, this time on a national stage.

The 1988 World Series was an all-California affair: the Dodgers versus the A's. Oakland led Game One in Los Angeles 4-3 when Dodger manager Tommy Lasorda sent Kirk Gibson to pinch-hit off Athletics closer Dennis Eckersley. Gibson had injured *both* legs in that year's NLCS and, as the World Series opened at Dodger Stadium, the former Michigan State football standout had a stomach virus to boot. He was the last player anyone expected to be *in* the game, let alone decide it.

On Dodger radio, Don Drysdale likened the moment to "Casey at the Bat." On national television, Vin Scully, who had called the Dodgers' regular season games, told viewers, "...all year long, he answered the demands, until he was physically unable to start tonight—with two bad legs: The bad left hamstring, and the swollen right knee. And, with two out, you talk about a roll of the dice... this is it."

Gibson worked the count full with a Dodger runner on second base. On the national radio broadcast, Buck made his epic call:

> "We have a big 3–2 pitch coming here from Eckersley. Gibson swings, and a fly ball to deep right field! This is gonna be a home run! Unbelievable! A home run for Gibson! And the Dodgers have won the game, five to four! I don't believe what I just saw! I don't believe

what I just SAW!

"One of the most remarkable finishes to any World Series Game...a one-handed home run by Kirk Gibson! And the Dodgers have won it...five to four; and I'm stunned. I have seen a lot of dramatic finishes in a lot of sports, but this one might top almost every other one."

Gibson's only at-bat of the Series helped propel Los Angeles to a four-games-to-one triumph over the heavily-favored A's.

Another baseball moment defines Jack Buck, the person and the professional, about as well as any. When Mark McGwire hit his record-tying 61st home run for the Cardinals in 1998, Buck told his radio audience, "Pardon me while I stand up and applaud." And he did. But what he did not reveal was that he also wept, so moved was he by the moment and the men involved, McGwire as well as the previous record holder Roger Maris, whom Buck had befriended during the ex-Yankee's two-year stay with the Cardinals at the end of his career.

Alyson Footer is the director of social media with the Houston Astros and a native of Ohio. Jack Buck was one of her favorite broadcasters, too. She says being interviewed by Buck, during his final season with the Cards and her first year as a reporter for MLB.com, remains one of her biggest thrills in baseball.

I had that same experience and that same thrill. Though Buck's been gone for a decade, it seems like only yesterday he and I were sitting together in the visitor's dugout at Busch Stadium II. He posed questions to me—good ones—and I did my best not to sound inane, feeling very much like the young boy who developed such an admiration for the man's immense talent and likable nature a half century before.

Jack Buck created one of the most memorable sign-offs of all time. Sportswriter David Jones of the Harrisburg *Patriot-News* calls it baseball's greatest broadcast styling and one of the best of all time, right there between boxing announcer Michael Buffer's "Let's get ready to *ruuummbbbllleee*," and Howard Cosell's, "He could go all...the...way." Buck made it simple. He made it easy. He always made it inviting.

"Thanks for your time this time." Jack told his audience at the end of a game. 'Til next time, so long."

CHAPTER 10
The Trim-Comb

The Army changed me in some interesting and unexpected ways.

Since I was never in a real life-or-death situation, I can't say it toughened or hardened me. I did learn to prioritize, compartmentalize, and focus on the task at hand.

Most of all, the Army taught me humility. Basic training puts everyone on a level playing field. Status, popularity, looks, and wealth mean nothing there, and the elimination of social stratification remains a constant in Army life.

I asked Dianne recently how she thought the Army had changed me. She reflected for a moment and then smiled. "You certainly looked more your age when you got back home."

Dianne lived with her parents while I was in Southeast Asia. Upon my return, we rented a small apartment and ate lots of home-cooked meals courtesy of our mothers. My discharge from the service had been moved up, in part, because I decided to attend graduate school. My decision to go back to college was prompted, somewhat, by the fact it helped expedite my military discharge. Win-win.

I attended Central Missouri State University in Warrensburg, thirty miles east of Sedalia, but stayed there only one quarter. Still, the experience was beneficial in that the drive to and from school—in my new orange Monte

Carlo—gave me time to think. I was ready to get back into the broadcasting business and wanted to do so in a big way. My sights were set on a major-market sports job.

By law, WOAI-TV in San Antonio was obligated to give me my old job back—if I wanted it—but Dianne and I decided not to return to Texas. She hadn't been happy living there and I was now considerably advanced in experience, thanks to the U.S. Army.

WOIA-TV was owned by Avco Broadcasting Corporation, a company whose roots were in the aviation business. Avco was a conglomerate with interests in broadcasting, aviation, and manufacturing. Corporate headquarters were in Cincinnati.

Gene McPherson, my point of contact with the company as a returning veteran, was a vice president with Avco Broadcasting. He took an interest in me and played a meaningful role in the development of my career. After informing him of my decision not to return to San Antonio, he promised to be on the lookout for other opportunities within the company's family of stations.

In March, just as the commute to Warrensburg was beginning to get a little old, McPherson alerted me to openings at Avco stations in Dayton and Cincinnati. Dianne and I had perfected the art of resume writing and I was confident, once I got my foot in the door, I could land a job.

The Dayton station wasn't interested in me, but the news director at the television and radio affiliate in Cincinnati liked what he read about me on my resume and saw of me on the air-check tape I brought back from Saigon. An interview was scheduled.

At CMSU, most of my male counterparts wore their hair in the style of the day, shoulder length and longer. In the Army, I wore my hair, once it grew out from basic training, pretty much in the same style as I had in college and do today: neatly groomed and parted on the right. In graduate school, I toyed with the notion of letting my hair grow long. Dianne was all for the idea. My sister Jebby was against it. Or, maybe it was the other way around.

When time came for my interview in Cincinnati, Dianne encouraged me to get a haircut so I would look more "presentable." I hedged at the suggestion.

"I think it looks good," I said one evening, admiring my longer locks in the cracked mirror of our tiny one-bedroom Sedalia apartment which was within shouting distance of the wrong side of the tracks. "I think I'll leave it like it is." I'd noticed the host of ABC's *Wide World of Sports*, Jim McKay, sporting longer sideburns and hair nearly touching his collar.

"William Brown, this job opportunity is important to both of us and I'm not going to have you go off looking like *that*." Dianne only called me "William" on special occasions. "Besides, what is it they say in the Army? 'Look good, feel good'?"

The Virgo in me sometimes can be a little stubborn and I've never been the most patient person on the planet. Also, upon my exit from the military, I'd become more cost conscious.

While my frugality didn't apply to the purchase of the new Monte Carlo—I developed an affinity for that car which would be replicated with another vehicle years later—I did pinch pennies when it came to "less important" things. After so much time in pressed khakis and polished shoes, I enjoyed the more relaxed countenance of civilian life.

"Saaaaaayyy," I continued, a great idea newly minted in my mind, "have you seen the ads on television for the…" I couldn't quite pull up the product name. Then it hit me. "The 'Trim-Comb' I think it's called?" Dianne shook her head fearing the worst.

"And what would you do with one of *those*?" she asked, knowing full well my intention.

"I'd save a ton of money on haircuts, for starters! I'm going to get one."

I returned to the bathroom mirror and tried to imagine how good I would look if I cut my own hair. Dianne sighed and walked away, muttering something under her breath.

"When I get the job," I called out, "I'll take us out to dinner to celebrate. With all the money I'll be saving on haircuts, I'll be able to take you out a lot more!"

Did the Army teach me how to problem solve or what?

***

A fascinating animation from a company called Flowing Data can be found on the Internet. It shows the growth of Wal-Mart, from its 1962 inception in Rogers, Arkansas, to its nationwide expansion to more than 4,000 stores by the end of 2010.

Wal-Mart had come to Sedalia just before my return from Vietnam. It was a pretty big deal at the time. No one yet understood the impact the future retail colossus would have on smaller businesses in the cities it invaded and conquered. For a young couple fresh out of the military, Wal-Mart was a haven of low-price shopping with a wide selection of almost everything one could think to buy.

Including the Trim-Comb.

Dianne insisted on going with me the next day when I told her I was headed out to shop. She knew me well. I'd hoped to steal away and purchase the Trim-Comb on my own, but had to modify my plan. In Dianne's mind, the Trim-Comb debate wasn't over and I would face more resistance.

Not wanting my intent to seem too obvious, we meandered to and fro through the Wal-Mart aisles before we happened upon personal grooming products.

"Look, the Trim-Comb!" I exclaimed, somewhat surprised to actually find the product in Sedalia—so advanced did I imagine its cutting technology to be. Was it really available beyond the most fashionable salons of New York City and Beverly Hills?

"Bill, no!" Dianne said as I pulled a Trim-Comb box off the shelf.

"But, look at this guy." I pointed to the ruggedly handsome man on the front panel of the product's packaging. "Not a hair out of place."

Dianne finally gave in and let me bring the Trim-Comb home. When we got back to our apartment, I couldn't wait to try my new toy. I headed immediately toward the bathroom with the Trim-Comb still in its box and the box still in a paper sack. "If you need any help," Dianne called out, "you won't get any from me."

Perhaps if I had read the instructions, or been a little more patient, or watched where I was "combing," the Trim-Comb would have lived up to my expectations. Sadly, what I did manage to do was unintentionally slice off a fairly sizable clump of hair, and not in a place where it wouldn't be readily noticed. The missing swath was right there in plain sight, just above my forehead.

As I stared into the mirror and examined my handiwork—or lack thereof—I thought seriously about giving up on my television career. If I was going to walk around looking like *this*, I had to choose a line of work which kept me far from the public eye. I thought briefly about becoming a geologist. Certainly I seemed to have rocks in my head.

I trudged out of the bathroom to face my accuser. Dianne was busy in the kitchen. When I said the three words a woman most loves to hear—"You were right"—she turned to face me and her eyes nearly popped out of her head. She was speechless, but only for a moment. Then, her face slowly broke into a smile and that smile quickly turned into a chuckle, and if she hadn't covered her mouth with both hands,

I believe that chuckle would have escalated into a full-blown outburst of hysterical laughter.

At least she had the decency not to say, "I told you so."

Shaking her head, she grabbed me by the hand and led me back into the bathroom. There, she did amazing things with a pair of scissors, a brush, styling gel, and prodigious amounts of hairspray. I actually felt human again.

Three days later I left for Cincinnati where I nailed the interview and got the job.

***

We didn't need a very big U-haul to move our possessions to Ohio. The Interstate Highway System, championed by President Eisenhower in the '50s to ensure rapid deployment of the military in case of future domestic attack, was not yet completed, and so the 530-mile drive which might take nine hours today, pretty much a straight shot along I-70 to I-74, required more than fourteen hours in March of 1972. We got up early and arrived late the same day.

I had flown in for my interview and had taken a taxi to and from the airport. Otherwise, neither Dianne nor I had been to Ohio

Cincinnati sits in the far southwest corner of the state. Hoosiers and Kentuckians are welcome there, given the city's proximity to both Indiana and the Bluegrass State. Ohio's third-largest city—but biggest metropolitan area—goes by several nicknames. Syndicated sports-talk host Jim Rome, in the "jungle-hip" parlance he is known for, has labeled it "The Nati." More commonly, Cincinnati is called "The Queen City," thanks to a reference from Henry Wadsworth Longfellow; and "The City of Seven Hills," which is also attributable to Rome—the Italian capital—due to the geographic similarities the two cities share.

Dianne and I settled in the northwest part of the Cincinnati area, a suburb called Cheviot, hilly enough, but not one of the original seven promontories. Dianne found a job working as an accountant and I served as both a weekday booth announcer and weekend sports anchor at the market's top radio and television stations.

WLWT-TV and WLW Radio have been Cincinnati institutions for decades. Both stations were founded by Powel Crosley, who for many years also owned the Cincinnati Reds.

Crosley's story is integral to that of Cincinnati's. He lived his entire life there and was a successful inventor, industrialist, and entrepreneur. He built cars, manufactured radios and then large household appliances, and eventually became a media titan. He bought the Cincinnati Reds in 1934 during the depths of the Great Depression. While the club's previous owner had lost his fortune in the deflated stock market, Crosley's investments had gone back into his own companies. He purchased the team for well below market value, and soon installed lights for big league baseball's first-ever night games.

"The man with fifty jobs in fifty years"—as he liked to say of himself—Crosley became one of America's richest men. He was a visionary who gets credit for the development of the push-button radio, disc brakes, soap operas, and the world's most powerful radio station.

They don't call WLW radio "The Big One" for nothing.

Crosley founded WLW in 1922. The call letters stood for "World's Largest Wireless," and the radio pioneer succeeded in making his venture live up to the name.

WLW is a clear-channel station today owned by Clear Channel Communications. It is the only station in America designated to operate at its assigned frequency at night, thus making 700 on the AM dial a "clear channel" and easily picked up throughout much of North America.

The station first went on the air generating fifty watts of power, less than the light bulb by which you're probably reading this book. The station's original signal could not be heard beyond just a few miles and was additionally impacted by Cincinnati's hilly terrain. By 1928, Crosley had amped up his transmitter to 50,000 watts, the maximum power at which an AM station can broadcast today.

Crosley wanted and got even *more* power. He spent a half-million Depression-era dollars to develop a transmitter which could generate 500,000 watts. On May 2, 1934 President Franklin Roosevelt flipped a ceremonial switch and WLW indeed became the world's largest wireless, both by night and by day.

Throughout the rest of the country, a number of smaller stations also had been licensed to operate at the 700 kilohertz frequency during daytime hours. Amplitude modulation waves travel farther at night and thus a clear-channel station like WLW beams its signals great distances with no interference from the sun.

Operating at 500,000 watts, WLW was wreaking havoc during the day. Crosley didn't care and was allowed to continue to dominate the airwaves for several more years, attracting great numbers of national advertisers. The brute force of The Big One also enabled him to make his Reds' nighttime broadcasts available to the majority of Americans. Think of Ted Turner's Superstation in Atlanta—fifty years earlier.

An act of Congress was required—literally—to power WLW back down to 50,000 watts in 1939. In 1962, a year after Crosley's death, his company petitioned the Federal Communications Commission for a waiver to allow WLW to broadcast at three quarters of a *million* watts. The request was turned down "in the public interest."

***

There are few booth announcers in today's broadcasting world, but at one time they were among the most recognizable figures—at least voices—in radio and television. What exactly is a booth announcer? Two of the most well-known in recent *television* history were Gary Owens on *Rowan and Martin's Laugh-In*, and Don Pardo, whose distinctive baritone proclaims "It's *Saturday Night Live!*"

In the days when radio was live, the booth announcer served as the ringmaster for programming. He introduced shows, read commercials, and voiced the half-hourly station identifications. By the time I stepped into the booth at WLWT-TV, my responsibilities were more of an afterthought than a focal point. On most days, my biggest responsibility involved the utterance of a single line:

"WLWT-TV, Cincinnati, a member of the Avco Broadcasting Corporation."

For my first couple of days at the station, I may have spent a little too much time in the announcer's booth, such was my zeal for doing a good job. Throughout the day, I kept a close eye on my watch and would try to settle into the booth about five minutes before the bottom and top of each hour. I'd clear my voice frequently, practice my locution, and wait for a signal from the control booth.

"You know, you can record those ahead of time," someone pointed out one day. "In fact, we're doing away with the booth next month."

Good thing I had other responsibilities to keep me employed.

***

I don't recall now why the WLWT-TV sports department was located across the street from the news set, maybe because the sports guys were serving two masters—radio and television—and were more commonly associated with radio operations. I regularly worked in the building housing WLW radio, both in my sports and announcer duties, but on weekends, I was also a member of the "Action Five," "Eyewitness Five," "Local Five,' or just plain "Channel Five" news team. How the marketing department labeled us in those days, I fail to recall.

Our opening for the newscasts featured a long shot of the anchor desk and the meteorologist and sports anchor were required to be on set for the shot. For me, a lot of planning went into that five seconds of air time. You didn't just walk down the hall and plop into a chair.

If it was a boisterous day outdoors—wet, windy, or snowing—the sports anchor made the dash across the street from one building to the other with trepidation. Fortunately, I worked weekends, so downtown traffic was usually not an additional concern. I was advised not to worry about make-up for the opening shot as I would never be seen in close-up. Once the news anchor began his top story—and it was always "his" story because as anyone who's seen the movie *Anchorman* knows, there were no women news anchors in those days—I was free to go about my business until my sports segment later in the half-hour block.

While WLWT-TV had a pretty strict "no-ladies-allowed" news anchor policy in my early days at the station, it did not abide by a "no-mayors" edict. Jerry Springer became the city's top anchorman at Channel Five in the 1980's, ten years after his one term as Cincinnati mayor, and a few years before his syndicated television talk show became a national sensation.

Betsy Ross was another well-known Channel Five news anchor. She helped break barriers in sports broadcasting, too, both behind the ESPN *Sports Center* desk and as a women's college basketball play-by-play announcer, a job she still does today.

My obstacle-course training at military boot camp came in handy in my weekend sports anchor job. Not only was I running back and forth across Ninth Street, and occasionally up and down stairs when an elevator was slow to arrive, there was also the matter of getting scores up on "The Wall."

On-screen graphics were in their infancy in the early '70s, and broadcasting was still a decade away from the computer-based teleprompter. So, presenting the news, weather, and sports was low-tech compared to today. On weekends, I spent more than a little time managing the on-set menu board where we posted scores of the day. We called that "The Wall."

One of the first things I did on my weekend shifts was to slot that day's matchups on The Wall, placing team name-cards into the appropriate slots on the black menu board. Then, before the early and late newscasts, I would insert white numerals to designate the score. During the sportscast, an in-studio camera panned the board to showcase results.

My prowess in managing The Wall one day prompted Channel Five program director Bill Spiegel to call me into his office.

"Bill, Tony Sands' son has been in a car wreck," Spiegel told me. Sands was the station's chief meteorologist. "It's not too serious, but Tony has asked to take the next couple days off. As you know, his regular backup, Bill Myers, is on vacation, so, I need someone to fill in for Tony the rest of the week. You're my guy."

Spiegel hadn't really made the request in the form of a question, but I was eager to see if I could talk my way out of the assignment. Some people hate snakes; some people hate heights. I have always been terrified of reporting the weather: all those town names and locations to remember and temperatures to get right. And don't get me started about high- and low-pressure systems. As far as I'm concerned, there isn't anything more high-pressure than doing the weather on television.

I knew my limitations. I understood full well I simply wasn't a "Bobbi the Weather Girl."

Bobbi Keith was decades ahead of her time. By day during the Vietnam War, she was a secretary for the U.S. Agency for International Development in Saigon. At night, she morphed into "a mini-skirted heat wave who raised troops' temperatures," according to an official dispatch from the Army's 1st Cavalry Division issued during Bobbi's "Weather-Girl" tenure on AFVN from 1967-69.

Whether clad in her trademark miniskirt or wearing a weather-map bikini, Bobbi's nightly weather reports were a hit for viewers in Saigon. The blonde-haired and blue-eyed Keith was a heartthrob devoted to the men fighting in the field. At times, she was a one-woman USO tour, frequently volunteering to go into the field to boost troop morale.

Bobbi always concluded her weather reports with the line, "Wishing everyone a pleasant evening, weather-wise and 'other-wise'" with a flirtatious wink at the not-so-subtle innuendo. She would then break into her signature go-go dance at the close of the show.

By my arrival in Vietnam, Bobbi had met and married a network news reporter and had retired her Weather Girl routine. Still, she was always a ray of sunshine whenever she visited the AFVN studios. One evening, while we were on red-alert lockdown and destined to spend the night in our offices, Bobbi magically appeared, warming our hearts with her big smile and quenching our thirst with a case of cold beer.

Fortunately, I did not have to channel Bobbi the Weather Girl. Bill Myers returned early from his vacation—"I got bored," he said—and I was off the weather hook. To this day, I continue to have nightmares about being asked to do the weather. I suspect weather guys—and girls—would jump at the chance to do something as elementary as calling a baseball game.

But, I'll bet they'd love a rain delay even more.

CHAPTER 11
The Merry Mortician

The Cincinnati Red Stockings were baseball's first professional team and well worth the money. During the club's first pro season, 1869, the team began what turned out to be a 130-game winning streak. The club joined the National League in 1890 and, for the occasion, shortened its nickname to "Reds."

Elsewhere, Cincinnati hosted its first men's professional tennis tournament at the Avondale Athletic Club, present day site of Xavier University, in 1899. Hometown boy Nat Emerson won the event and would be a regular in the tournament field until he moved to the state of Washington in 1911. According to Wikipedia, Emerson "owned an apple orchard" in Yakima. If you know anything about apples and Washington state, you know Emerson landed on a veritable gold mine. "Golden delicious" you could say, although if you were referring to Emerson's early crops, you would be mistaken. The golden delicious apple, which today is one of the top varieties grown in Washington, wasn't introduced to America's palates until 1914, and then in Clay County, West Virginia, about 250 miles south and east of Cincinnati.

Tennis remains a vibrant part of the Queen City's sporting scene. In fact, the present-day Western & Southern Open is the latest incarnation of the oldest professional tennis tournament still held in its original city. Western & Southern, a diversified financial services company, has been associated with the tournament for many years.

In mid-summer 1973—and with a year under my broadcasting belt—I was given the second-most substantive television assignment of my career to that point. I had begun hosting the Reds' pregame show that spring, but being tabbed to do play-by-play of the Western & Southern tournament final—as best as the term "play-by-play" can apply to a tennis match—was good exposure. Local enthusiasts were eager for the possibility of an all "bad-boy" final between defending champion Jimmy Connors and Romanian Ilie Nastase.

No television station worth its FCC license could pass up a pairing like that, despite the likelihood of on-court profanities. WLWT-TV aired the final live from the Queen City Racquet Club. I had taken up the sport after covering the tournament the year before, so, I was considered the sports staff's resident tennis expert.

Nastase, as the top seed, breezed into the Sunday afternoon final. Connor stumbled in the semis, losing to Spain's Manuel Orantes. A little of the luster was lost from our broadcast, but in the end, Nastase proved capable of obliterating tennis decorum on his own. In fact, he almost single-handedly killed the tournament's longstanding run.

At his best, Nastase was a magician with his racket, much in the mold of Roger Federer a generation later. At his worst—temperamentally—Nastase could be just plain "nasty" in nature. He made the likes of Milton Bradley, Albert Belle, and—dare I say—Jeff Kent, look like choirboys.

Orantes won the opening set 7-5. From that point, the Romanian began his patented brand of psychological warfare, both on his opponent as well as the officiating crew. He questioned nearly every close call; argued with the chair umpire—sometimes obscenely—and did everything in his power to disrupt Orantes' concentration. Ultimately, Nastase prevailed, winning a tight three-set match.

With time to kill before the top of the hour, we stayed on the air for the trophy presentation. Everything was set on court but the winner was nowhere to be found.

Actually, he was fuming in the men's locker room, refusing to participate in the post-match ceremony. The delay grew uncomfortably long, and since we'd exhausted our commercial inventory for the telecast, I was forced to ad-lib to fill time. My broadcast partner, a local teaching pro, was knowledgeable about the sport and eventually, with little else to talk about, we began to speculate as to why Nastase was absent from the proceedings.

Tournament referee Jim Meakin—today a member of the Cincinnati Tennis Hall of Fame—approached Nastase after the final and told him he was levying $8,150 in fines for his unsportsmanlike behavior during the tournament. That was $150 *more* than the event's first-place prize money. When Nastase went ballistic in the locker room and refused to come back onto the court to receive his trophy, Meakin and tournament officials offered a compromise. Nastase would be penalized only $5,000 for his boorish behavior if he would go out and thank tournament sponsors. He did—long after we had signed off the telecast—accepting his trophy, thanking the sponsors, and vowing never to play in Cincinnati again.

Nastase became the world's number-one ranked tennis player a week later. He finished the '73 season with fourteen ATP tournament titles, including the French Open championship. Before year's end, Cincinnati officials announced they were pulling the event off the Association of Tennis Professionals calendar; but, at the last moment, another group of organizers rescued the tournament and moved it indoors to the Cincinnati Convention Center.

To my knowledge, Ilie Nastase never returned to town.

***

In the early 1970s, Cincinnati was a city with an abundance of sports heroes. I arrived in time to meet Bob Cousy, the basketball legend who was head coach of the NBA's Cincinnati Royals. Cousy joined the franchise as player-coach in 1969, but gave up his playing duties just seven games into the season. For a brief time he teamed with the incomparable Oscar Robertson in the Royals' backcourt. Robertson—a former college great in town—was gone by the time I got to Cincinnati.

Cousy's team went just 32-50 in its final season in the Gardens—the Cincinnati Gardens indoor arena. The Royals' best player was six-foot guard Tiny Archibald who averaged more than twenty-eight points per game. The next year, the team entered into one of the oddest arrangements in the annals of professional sports, splitting home games between two cities. The Cincinnati Royals became the Kansas City/Omaha Kings. Eventually, the franchise move to Sacramento and may have a Las Vegas residency in its future.

I also had the chance to cover the NFL's Cincinnati Bengals, who were under the guidance of another legendary figure: head coach, general manager, president, team owner, and founder Paul Brown.

My boss at Channel Five, Phil Samp, was the Bengals' radio play-by-play announcer. He held the post from the team's inception until 1990, a great run of twenty-three seasons. Samp was a fine mentor, but while a love of baseball flowed through my veins, Phil was a football man to the core. And, as Bengal fans will remember, what a voice he had!

The number-two sports guy at the station was the number-one announcer on the Reds' telecasts. Tom Hedrick was a house on fire. Known as "The Parrott" for both his non-stop chatter as well as his hooked nose, Hedrick spent two years in Cincinnati before taking a play-by-play job with the Kansas City Chiefs. He's also worked for the University of Kansas sports network, CBS Radio, and is still going strong today as a member of the Mass Media faculty at Baker University, his *alma mater* in Baldwin City, Kansas. Tom's book, *The Art of Sportscasting*, is a great resource for young broadcasters looking to break into the business.

I got my first break as a big league baseball announcer sitting next to Tom. But that story really begins with perhaps the greatest ballplayer/broadcaster who ever lived.

***

> *"You have to be the local man; you're paid a handsome salary to be the booster for your team. But, you also have to be a fair person."*

Waite Hoyt thus summed up his broadcasting philosophy in an interview with the *Cincinnati Enquirer* in 1976, four years after he said a final goodbye to his seminal broadcasting career. Thirty years earlier, he had defined his play-by-play job with the Reds in similar, although earthier terms.

In Curt Smith's fine book on baseball broadcasters, *Voices of the Game*, Hoyt recalled a conversation he had with Reds' team president Warren Giles when asked why his broadcasting style wasn't as "enthusiastic' as that of Cubs' announcer Bert Wilson:

> *"Why shouldn't Bert Wilson cheer? (The Cubs) won the pennant last year, didn't they? They've got a great park to play in and they got some stars...Your top hitter's a lousy .267...and your top pitcher's won eight games. What is there to cheer about? If I cheered like Bert Wilson with the bums we've got, people would think I was blind or the village idiot...or maybe both."*

Hoyt was 18, and tagged with the nickname "Schoolboy," when he made his debut in the majors with the New York Giants in 1918. He is better known for the Hall-of-Fame numbers he posted as the ace of the New York Yankees pitching staff in the 1920's. Eight times he won 15 games, - leading the American League in victories in '27 and saves in '28. A member of three World Series championship teams, Hoyt was elected to the Baseball Hall of Fame in 1969.

Toward the end of his playing career, Hoyt was labeled by an enterprising sportswriter as "The Merry Mortician" for his off-season job working in a funeral parlor. At the same time, Hoyt also began dabbling as a vaudevillian entertainer. He appeared on stage with the likes of Jack Benny, Jimmy Durante, and George Burns. He was anything but the village idiot.

His intellect and command of the English language led to his second career. "Radio had long seemed the logical choice," he explained. Hoyt became a popular host of radio programs in New York City. He signed on with the William Morris Agency and told them he wanted to be a baseball announcer. At the time, former players weren't welcomed as regulars in the broadcast booth, lacking, or so it was thought, a sufficient vernacular skill.

The Burger Brewing Company held the rights to one of three Reds broadcasts in the years leading up to World War II. Cincinnati won back-to-back National League pennants in 1939 and 1940 and Reds fans basked in the achievement. The Burger Beer people hoped to differentiate their broadcasts by exploring the possibility of bringing an ex-player onto the air. Waite Hoyt was asked to apply for the job.

During his interview, Hoyt chose not to mimic the call of an imaginary baseball game. Instead, he told a story about a little boy. Story-telling would become his greatest hallmark as a broadcaster and Hoyt became famous for the stories he told about his ex-Yankee teammate Babe Ruth.

Hoyt got the Reds' job and began announcing games in 1942. Just three years later, Burger consolidated the three

Cincinnati baseball networks and Hoyt's was the preeminent baseball voice in town.

Hoyt was one of two former ballplayers who paved the way for others to enter broadcasting. While Hoyt was informative and eloquent, in St. Louis, Dizzy Dean murdered both syntax and sentence structure. The two men couldn't have been more different personally and professionally. Both became as well-known for their announcing prowess— perhaps even more so—than their standout pitching careers.

As a broadcaster, Hoyt was also known for calling a game in the past tense, a style which was uniquely his own. "As I speak, what happened a moment ago is gone," he reasoned. For many years and because of budgetary considerations Hoyt did not travel to Reds away games, instead recreating them in a Cincinnati broadcast studio. And, oh how Reds' fans hoped for a rain delay.

On the day Ruth died, Monday, August 16, 1948, Hoyt remained on the air for two hours after the Reds 5-2 win in Pittsburgh. He spoke of Ruth the entire time. In the years which followed, Hoyt continued to hold court on Ruth, ensuring the Bambino's accomplishments on the field and importance to the game would never be forgotten.

He told a lot of other great stories, too, so many in fact, two record albums were released in the 1960's, entitled *The Best of Waite Hoyt in the Rain* and *The Best of Waite Hoyt in the Rain, Volume 2.* Four sides of vinyl, though, still didn't do Hoyt justice.

Hoyt officially retired as the Reds' full-time radio play-by-play man in 1965. He was 66 years old by the end of the season—his twenty-fourth with the club, but, Hoyt never completely left the booth. He remained a regular on Reds telecasts for several more years. Near the end of his final season—1972—Hoyt was hospitalized. His health problems weren't serious, but his absence left a vacancy in the Channel Five booth.

Ball games on local television in the '70's and '80's weren't as common an occurrence as they are today. In the '70s, Channel Five broadcast about three dozen Reds games each season; so Hoyt's absence wasn't of immediate concern. I thought I might have a chance to fill in, but it wasn't until the Wednesday before the next scheduled game that a decision was made.

I got another call to see Bill Spiegel in his office.

"When's the last time you did any baseball play-by-play?" Spiegel asked. *Officially*, I hadn't broadcast any games since college, but I had taken to sneaking into an empty Riverfront Stadium broadcast booth to revisit my old habit of announcing games into a tape recorder.

"This week," I said.

Spiegel gave me a double take.

"Well, throughout the season I've been practicing in an empty booth at the ballpark, taping myself to..."

"Oh, yeah," Spiegel interrupted. "Hedrick's told me about that. Some of the newspaper guys think you're a bit of a *prima donna*. I guess it does take a little fortitude to risk making a spectacle of yourself."

I hadn't thought of my efforts in those terms and, as fate would have it, I'm glad I never did.

"Anyway," Spiegel continued, "you're a pretty smart guy. You'll be taking Hoyt's place on Sunday's broadcast. Think you're up to the job?"

I was speechless, truly speechless. My heart nearly pounded out of my chest. This was the moment for which I had long dreamed.

"You'll fly to Houston with the club tomorrow. It's an off-day for the team, so you'll be leaving in the afternoon. You and Tom can sit together Friday and Saturday to prepare and Sunday you go on the air."

I just sat there, dumbfounded.

"So, what *do* you think?" Spiegel finally asked again.

All I could think to tell him was, "Thank you, Bill. You know how much this means to me."

Spiegel looked across his desk. He probably remembered when he was just getting started in the business.

"Try to find a little more to say on Sunday, okay?"

We stood, shook hands, and as I turned to leave, Spiegel added, "And, Bill, Happy Birthday."

I had just turned 25 years old.

***

The Reds won a lot in 1972, so much so in fact, that my baseball broadcasting debut was bumped up two days. Upon arriving with the team at Houston's William P. Hobby Airport, Hedrick discovered the station had decided to broadcast that night's game. A Reds' win would clinch the National League Western Division title. The team would have a second-year pitcher, Ross Grimsley, starting on the mound, and a rookie announcer making his baseball debut on the telecast. Ironically, my future broadcast partner in Houston, Larry Dierker, was the Astros' starting pitcher. Really.

If you don't believe me, look it up!

My performance that first night wasn't much better than my showing in Bill Spiegel's office. Sitting in front of a live microphone was a far cry from pretend-announcing. By the time we left the team hotel and headed to the ballpark, I had sweated through my undershirt. Since this was television, I would be seen as well as heard, but fortunately I had a sports coat I would wear on camera. Otherwise, those blotches of perspiration under my arms would have been mighty unsightly.

As it turned out, I didn't really soar that night, but "The Parrott" sure did.

When Hoyt was brought aboard the telecasts, station management instructed Hedrick to tone down his act as much as possible and give Waite time to weave his tales. Bringing Hoyt aboard was a boost to the ratings, although the fact the Big Red Machine was having an outstanding year that season also helped. With Hoyt absent in Houston, Hedrick was unleashed. Here was his chance to make up for lost time and unspoken words.

Imagine what a poor imitation of Waite Hoyt I must have been! I still sometimes chuckle about that: my trying to fill Waite Hoyt's chair *and* his shoes. Truth be told, I'm not sure I could do that today, 40 years later. I think Jim Deshaies—in his own fashion—comes remarkably close.

The Reds held a 4-3 lead over the Astros going into the ninth inning. During the commercial break, Hedrick took off his headset and rose from his chair.

"Little late to be going to the bathroom, Tom," I said with a nervous laugh. Where *was* he going?

"Headed down to the field, Bill," Hedrick said collecting his things. "Once the game is over we'll want to get post-game reaction from the Reds' locker room. I even brought my own poncho to stay dry after the champagne starts flowing."

His words were followed by a classic Bill Brown pregnant pause. Finally I asked somewhat timidly, "So, who's going to do the ninth inning?"

"You are," Hedrick smiled. "You'll be fine. I've heard you're pretty good with a tape recorder. Welcome to the big leagues!"

He walked out and I heard a voice in my headset: "Thirty seconds to air."

The Reds had brought on closer Clay Carroll in the bottom of the eighth, relieving Pedro Borbon who faced two batters and failed to retire a hitter. Long before Tony LaRussa popularized a bullpen-by-committee approach, Cincinnati manager Sparky Anderson was known as "Captain Hook" for his creative ways with a pitching staff. In Carroll, though—at least in the '72 season—Anderson had a pretty sure thing.

119

However, the Reds manager, unlike LaRussa, was not the master of the double switch. Carroll hit for himself in the top of the ninth—and singled. Joe Morgan also singled moving Carroll up a base, but Bobby Tolan struck out against Astros reliever Mike Cosgrove to kill the rally and a chance at an insurance run or two.

All that "base-running" must have worn Carroll out.

After doing a passable job describing the top of the ninth, I prayed for Carroll to breeze through the bottom of the inning and put the game away. While I had tried to calm my nerves by imagining I was simply talking into my tape recorder, a lot more than that was on the line. Cincinnati was looking to clinch a title.

In my original notes for the manuscript of this book, I wrote, "Clay Carroll nailed down the final three outs and the Reds won by a 4-3 score." Technically, that's true.

Carroll also walked the bases loaded, which had a sparse but noisy Astrodome crowd savoring a comeback. With the bases loaded and two out, the Astros most dangerous hitter, Cesar Cedeño, stepped up to the plate.

I'll be honest. I have very little recollection of any of this because I was terrified I was going to botch the job. A Cedeño base hit could conceivably have given Houston the win and spoiled Hedrick's post-game champagne shower. Worse yet, what if the game went into extra innings? Would Hedrick come back and relieve me?

A review of the box score at BaseballRegister.com reveals Cedeño hit into a fielder's choice, shortstop Darrell Chaney to second baseman Joe Morgan, for the game-ending and division-clinching final out. Grimsley got the win that night and Carroll notched his 33rd save. Dierker took the loss, pitching only two-thirds of an inning. When I asked him recently if he remembers why he was pulled so early, he said he had no recollection of any injury, although he did not make another appearance that season. Forty years after the fact, his memory isn't any better than mine.

I was back on the Reds' broadcast sidelines the next year, but in 1976 I finally landed a permanent play-by-play job with the club. When Hedrick left for the NFL, Charlie Jones came in to take his place. I saw very little of Charlie the two years he did games for Cincinnati. We only aired three or four home games a season, so Charlie was able to commute from his home in La Jolla, California, usually meeting the team on the road.

Charlie never really caught on with Reds fans, in part because he was always seen as an outsider. Jones was a fabulous football announcer, but in many respects Cincinnati has a small-town mentality. Reds fans wanted one of their own calling games.

Upon my selection to join Ken Coleman in the Reds' TV booth, I received a number of congratulatory letters and phone calls. The response was gratifying and encouraging.

Among the letters and cards I've held onto over the years—and which Dianne has preserved in the scrapbook she keeps of my career—one in particular has always stood out:

> *A quick but sincere note.*
>
> *My confidence was justified in your appointment to the TV post. If you'll pardon my immodesty, you'll recall a couple of years ago, I told you, and others, you were the man for the job—and it has come to pass. I am very happy about it and I know you'll become one of the best in the trade.*
>
> *I'm sure you'll find a home in the hearts of the public. I know you know Coleman well. But you are fortunate as he is a real man, and a comfortable guy, which means a lot.*

Bill Brown

Have fun—and have a big 1976.

Sincerely, Waite Hoyt.

CHAPTER 12
Big Red Machine

In my book—here, literally—Pete Rose gets credit for coining the phrase, "Big Red Machine."

On August 4, 1969, the Philadelphia Phillies pounded out twenty-one hits and scored seventeen runs off a quintet of Cincinnati pitchers. By the end of the third, Philadelphia held a commanding 9-4 lead. In the end though, the Reds countered with twenty-five hits and *nineteen* runs. Alex Johnson had four hits and four RBI, Tony Perez four hits and three RBI, Lee May two hits and four RBI, and Johnny Bench had five hits in the Cincinnati victory.

Rose went three for four for the Reds that day with four RBI. He reached base in six of his seven at-bats. Tim Crothers of *Sports Illustrated* reported Rose saying after the game, "We scored so many runs and it was still a close game, but the 'Big Red Machine' did it again and we're in first place."

Rose often talked about his first car: an overhauled and repainted 1934 Ford Coupe. As a Cincinnati-area teenager, he claimed to have called his ride the "Little Red Machine." Of course, Rose eventually earned a well-known moniker of his own. When Yankee pitcher Whitey Ford saw Rose sprint to first after drawing a walk in a 1963 spring training game, the New York Hall-of-Famer said derisively of the seemingly pretentious rookie, "There goes 'Charlie Hustle'." Rose liked the intended putdown, and made sure the name stuck, pretentiousness be damned.

The 1969 Reds finished third in the National League Western Division standings. By the next year, The Big Red Machine was finely tuned and ran off with the NL West title before sweeping Pittsburgh in the league's championship series. In all, Cincinnati won six division titles during the '70s and reached four World Series between 1970 and 1976.

The Reds lost the '70 Series to Baltimore in five games made memorable by Oriole third baseman Brooks Robinson's spectacular defensive play. In 1972, the Reds returned to the Fall Classic and were heavy favorites to best the Oakland A's. Reserve catcher Gene Tenace hit four home runs and drove in nine to spark the Athletics to the upset. Six of the seven Series games that year were decided by one run.

As much as I'd like to take credit for being Cincinnati's good-luck charm during the '72 season, the arrival of another new face in town actually elevated the Red machine to justifiably "big" status.

Young fans today know Joe Morgan from his network broadcast assignments. Joe is an outstanding analyst, yet he was a better second baseman, the only player at his position to win the Most Valuable Player award twice. He earned the honor in back-to-back seasons, 1975 and 1976, years in which the Big Red Machine rolled to consecutive World Series championships.

Cincinnati repeated as NL West champions in 1973. Rose was named the league's Most Valuable Player and three other Reds—Morgan, Tony Perez, and Johnny Bench—finished among the top ten in MVP voting. Cincinnati again was considered the best team in baseball, but, again the team fell short in post season play, losing to the Mets in the National League Championship Series. I did not get a return trip to the television broadcast booth, even as a fill-in, for reasons I'll explain later in this chapter.

Following the '73 season, there was an opening on the Reds' radio network. Cincinnati lost Al Michaels after only three years on the job. Not yet thirty years old, Michaels left for the West Coast where he covered baseball with the Giants in San Francisco and basketball with UCLA in Los Angeles. Michaels called legendary coach John Wooden's final season at the Bruins' helm, in which the Wizard from Westwood captured his tenth national championship.

From there, Michaels landed network assignment after network assignment. He achieved fame at the 1980 Winter Olympics and worked ABC's *Monday Night Football* for 20 years. In 2006, Michaels left ABC for NBC's Sunday Night Football broadcast, teaming with the incomparable John Madden.

The Walt Disney Company, which owns both ABC and ESPN, extracted a substantial price to let Michaels out of his contract. As part of a rather unusual deal, NBC granted ESPN increased usage of Olympic highlights and broadcast rights to Friday coverage of Ryder Cup matches in return for Michaels' services. Also in the deal, Disney reclaimed the rights to an obscure cartoon character which NBC's parent company had owned for more than seventy-five years.

Chances are you may have never heard of "Oswald the Lucky Rabbit." He put Walt Disney—the man—and his fledging entertainment studio on the map, but he didn't belong to Disney for long. Universal, which distributed Disney's animated productions—cartoons, if you will— snatched Oswald away from his maker in 1927. Not to be outdone, Disney retooled the look of the character, most notably rounding the floppy ears, and launched a new creation—Mickey Mouse—in 1928.

Not every broadcaster can lay claim to being "traded" for a cartoon character. Along with his many other awards and accolades, Al Michaels owns that distinction. The most unusual thing about any of the contracts I've signed through the years has been the telling lack of zeroes to the left of the decimal point, at least in comparison to the Michaels, Maddens, and Vin Scullys of the world!

***

The Reds won 98 games in 1974, just one fewer than the previous year, but finished second in the NL West behind the Los Angeles Dodgers. That season saw the debut of *Redscene,* a half-hour pre-game show which aired on Channel Five in advance of the station's prime-time telecasts. Hosting the show gave me a chance to spend more time at the ballpark and get more exposure, both with the players as well as viewers at home.

The Reds' clubhouse in those days was a haven for several of the players' young sons. I once did a story on Ken Griffey—not yet known as "Senior"—at his suburban-Cincinnati home. We shot footage of his two young boys tossing a ball around in the family's backyard.

Craig Griffey spent seven years playing minor league baseball. Older brother George Kenneth Griffey, Jr. amassed 630 big league home runs. Junior hit 210 of those following in his father's footsteps as a member of the Cincinnati Reds.

The two Griffeys actually played *together* in Seattle for two seasons. On September 14, 1990, the 40-year-old Senior and 20-year-old Junior hit back-to-back home runs off California pitcher Kirk McCaskill, the only time a father and son have hit homers in the same big league game.

Pete Rose, Jr. also grew up in the Cincinnati locker room and, he, too, ultimately played for the Reds. His entire Major League Baseball career amounted to eleven games as a September call-up at the end of the 1997 season. Wearing his father's famous Number 14, "PJ" made just one start in Cincinnati. While he finished with 4,254 fewer big league hits than his dad, Pete, Jr. totaled 1,877 hits of his own in twenty-one years of *minor league* ball. He's now managing the Bristol White Sox, Chicago's rookie league team and is said to have a promising future on the bench.

You know you've been around the game a long time when the number of father-son tandems whose games you've called adds up to more fingers than you have on both hands. Actually, a little research reveals that number is close to thirty in my case and includes the Bannisters, Bells, Bonds, Boones, Borbons, Canos, Drabeks, Fielders, Gordons, Grieves, Gwynns, Hairstons, Kendalls, Matthews, Mays, Niekros, Penas, Perez, Roenickes, Swishers, and Youngs.

***

The 1975 Cincinnati Reds were the best baseball team I've ever seen. Manager Sparky Anderson's club totaled 108 wins and swept the National League Championship Series. Joe Morgan won the first of his two MVPs, but the award that year just as easily could have gone to Johnny Bench or Pete Rose, who finished fourth and fifth for the honor. Tony Perez also received MVP consideration for his fine season.

Pitching-wise, *six* Reds starters won ten games or more. Fire-balling right-hander Rawley Eastwick tied for the league lead in saves with twenty-seven. In all respects, the Big Red Machine was finely tuned and firing on all cylinders with a capable helmsman behind the wheel.

When Sparky Anderson took over as Reds manager in 1970, the Cincinnati media was less than enthralled with the move. Just 36 years old—but looking twenty years older— and with no big league managerial experience, the *Cincinnati Enquirer* announced his hiring with the banner headline, "Sparky Who?"

By the time he had finished his nine-year run with the Reds everyone knew George Lee Anderson.

What I liked most about Sparky was the way he treated every reporter exactly the same while often giving the wildly divergent perspectives in answer to the same question. On a team full of superstars, Anderson also knew special players had to be treated differently from the rank and file. How he related to his players is what triggered the Big Red Machine's success.

"There ain't no genius who ever managed in this game," Anderson once observed. "Just because you're a manager don't make you no smarter than the next guy." That's the kind of material I frequently got from Sparky when we talked on *Redscene*.

In addition to hosting the team's pregame show, I also finally got another chance to fill in on a few late-season telecasts. Veteran announcer Ken Coleman had taken Charlie Jones' place as the Red's number one TV play-by-play man. Joining Coleman in the booth was former big leaguer Woody Woodward. I filled in for Woodward when he began splitting time between Cincinnati and Tallahassee, Florida, where he had taken the reigns as head baseball coach at his *alma mater*, Florida State University. And, just as the team had done following my fill-in announcing stint in '72, the Reds again reached the World Series in '75.

As weekend sports anchor for Channel Five, I covered all seven games of that classic matchup between Cincinnati and the Boston Red Sox. Unfortunately, I missed the one moment for which that Series is best known.

Game Six at Fenway Park was, simply, one of the greatest baseball games ever played. Boston—down three games to two—opened the scoring with three runs in the first. Cincinnati tied the game with three in the fifth and then scored two twice in the seventh and once in the eighth to take its own three-run lead. Then, In the bottom of the eighth, former Red Bernie Carbo hit a pinch-hit homer off Eastwick with two men aboard to tie the game.

At that point, those of us with television credentials made our way from the auxiliary level of the Fenway Park press box into the bowels of the old stadium to establish a foothold for the post-game press conferences. As Game Six went into extra innings, my group kept tabs on the action by crowding around a small black-and-white television in the back of the interview room.

And that's where I was when Boston catcher Carlton Fisk led off the bottom of the twelfth with a walk-off home run up the left-field line. As Fisk's fly ball sailed into legend, the Fenway crowd exploded into pandemonium. In the bowels of the venerable old stadium, the vibrations from the thunderous ovation loosened a dust shower from the basement's ceiling beams, peppering members of the media with a fine gray mist.

Game Seven the next evening was equally dramatic. The Red Sox again jumped out to an early three-run lead. Cincinnati again battled back to tie. As the contest moved deeper into the night, everyone watching wondered if another extra-inning thriller was in the offing.

The Reds took the lead with a run in the ninth. Joe Morgan's pop-fly single to center scored Ken Griffey. With Cincinnati just three outs away from its first World Series title since 1940, everyone expected the Reds' manager to bring in Eastwick to finish the game. Instead, Sparky Anderson played a hunch.

***

Will McEnaney was signed by the Reds as an eighth-round pick out of North High School in Springfield, Ohio. He missed a season of prep ball for his self-proclaimed "mischievous prankster" ways. But, he could be forgiven: He was a lefthander.

Why left-handers often seem to land on the peculiar side of the fence I can't say. I'm right-handed and being a down-to-earth pragmatist, the ways of the southpaw are often inexplicable to me. Take Jim Deshaies, another lefty. Please.

Eastwick and McEnaney—the Reds famed "Kiddie Korps"—played three years in the minors together. Eastwick, a right-hander, had matinee-idol good looks and the confidence that usually comes along with that blessing. McEnaney, naturally, was a bit of an oddball. Just for grins, he once crawled through the middle of a tarpaulin roller to steal a bag of baseballs from a ballpark security guard.

Both pitchers were top prospects, but McEnaney got the call to the parent club first, in 1974. The next season, Eastwick joined the Reds and quickly became Anderson's go-to guy in the bullpen. In addition to leading the National League in saves, he also finished third for NL Rookie of the Year. McEnaney became a set-up man.

Until Game Six of the '75 Series, Eastwick had been pretty close to a sure thing. He won Games Two and Three in relief and saved Game Five. He seemed destined to have a hand in all four Reds' wins, but Carbo's home run changed that.

When Anderson made his bottom-of-the-ninth-inning call to the bullpen in Game Seven, he chose not to bring in his right-hander. Instead, he went with McEnaney instead.

After twelve years running his own bathtub renovation company in Royal Palm Beach, Florida, Will McEnaney, like a lot of entrepreneurs, fell victim to the Great Recession. Beginning in 2009, "It just went down the tubes," he told reporter Joe Capozzi in an interview for *The Palm Beach Post*. The following year, after McEnaney landed employment as a sales representative for a sporting goods retailer, he picked up a second job to augment his income: serving as the full-time scoreboard operator at Roger Dean Stadium, home of the Class A Jupiter Hammerheads. Both the St. Louis Cardinals and Florida—now Miami—Marlins, also play Grapefruit League games there.

"I've never paid this much attention to a baseball game in my life," McEnaney said of his job keeping track of balls and strikes. "I mean, when you're in the bullpen, you don't pay attention to anything on the field." He pauses before adding sheepishly, "At least I didn't for most of my career."

Coming out of the Reds bullpen to nail down a World Series championship was one of the most nerve-racking moments of his life.

"I was twenty-three years old. I'd never been put in that position. I was scared to death."

He retired the Red Sox in order. Future Hall of Famer Carl Yastrzemski flied out to end the game. The aftermath of that moment was captured on that week's cover of *Sports Illustrated* which showed McEnaney jumping into the arms of catcher Johnny Bench.

A year later and after closing out yet another Cincinnati World Series championship, McEnaney was traded to the Montreal Expos. At about the same time, his mother died and his first wife divorced him. Without his accustomed support-system in place, McEnaney turned to drugs and alcohol and nearly killed himself when he crashed his car into a house while driving drunk. He played three more years of big league ball, but became a washout by the end of the decade. He bounced around the minors for a while and then disappeared, at least from baseball circles.

Now, he's back, albeit a little more "behind the scenes" than perhaps he'd like. Even in a somewhat diminished capacity, it's good to see him back. We had a nice chat in Jupiter during spring training prior to the 2012 season and McEnaney, as befits a lefty, has no regrets about the way his baseball life turned out. These days, Will seems at peace with himself.

***

By the 1976 season, I finally ascended full-time into the Reds' broadcast booth. Despite my lack of playing credentials, I became Ken Coleman's partner on game telecasts. Although Coleman had been in Cincinnati for only a year, he already had a reputation as one of the best in the business.

Ken Coleman broke into broadcasting when I was five years old. Beginning in 1952, he was the radio voice of Paul Brown's Cleveland Browns. Two years later, he began a ten-year stint televising Cleveland Indians' games. In 1965, he moved to Boston to replace Curt Gowdy on the Red Sox radio network.

The Red Sox failed to renew Coleman's contract following the 1974 season which led to his arrival in Cincinnati. Reds fans got a broadcaster who was as smooth as silk and who cared about both the team and the community. I couldn't have honed my craft with a better partner than Ken Coleman. He provided a wealth of good advice and was a constant source of encouragement, which, at the time, was much needed and appreciated on my end.

In my mind, the opposite of encouragement is criticism and the dictionary defines "criticism" in this way: "The act of passing judgment as to the merits of anything."

Everyone is entitled to an opinion. Criticism, though, cuts a little more deeply. I've never been much of a fan of what some people call "constructive criticism."

Bill Wuerch wasn't much of a fan of mine. And that was a problem for me back in the mid '70's, since Wuerch was the station manager at Channel Five.

We've all had bosses like Wuerch: difficult, demanding, and hard to read. He was also hard to please, at least when it came to my play-by-play work. Upon return from my fill-in assignment at the end of the '72 season, Wuerch called me into his office.

"Bill, I didn't care much for what I heard in Houston last weekend."

That got my heart to pumping.

"I realize it was your first time as part of the game broadcast, but I was really disappointed in your energy level. You sounded like you didn't want to be there. There was no life!

"I wanted to walk up behind you and stick a pin in your butt!"

I could feel the blood rushing to my head. His criticism seemed harsh and his opinion mattered a great deal. In a real sense, my future was at stake.

He continued for a time and then concluded our meeting. "I just don't think you're cut out for play-by-play. You're a fine reporter and you do okay anchoring the weekend sportscasts, although I'd like to see you have a little more energy there, too.

"Bill," he said to me, "I wouldn't hold your breath the next time an opening comes up for the Reds' job. I'm okay if you're chosen to do something on the pregame show, but I won't support you for a spot in the booth."

Thus, my absence from fill-in assignments for nearly three seasons.

When I shared the conversation with Dianne, I was steamed. I had been on top of the world upon my return from Houston. Wuerch not only had knocked me off that perch, but also had pounded my performance—and thus me—into the dirt. I was outraged and directed much of my frustration at Dianne.

"We found this job, we can find another," I told Dianne. "If they don't think I'm good enough, then what's the point of me staying in Cincinnati. If I have no chance for the Reds' job..."

I broke off. My emotions had the better of me.

Dianne sat quietly for a time. Equal doses of sorrow, pity, and unconditional love emanated from her gaze. Throughout our decades together, Dianne has always been the voice of calm and collected reason in our household. As I've said before, I'm not a very patient person and Dianne, early on, learned to give me space in my moments of ire. She has the uncanny knack of being able to soothe and calm me and then illustrate the pragmatic side of any situation.

I could have never made it in this business without her. She's helped thicken my skin, a must for people in my line of work.

"Maybe that was just Mr. Wuerch's way of challenging you to do better," she finally said. "It was just your first time. He couldn't very well have said you were the best he'd ever heard. He wouldn't be able to afford you if he said something like that."

Although Dianne chuckled, her attempt at humor was lost on me and I glared in her direction. Keep in mind, I was just twenty-five years old at the time. I'd been in the Army, but I was still pretty naïve about certain things.

Our discussion continued and I slowly regained my composure. Dianne was willing to do anything and go anywhere with me, but she eventually persuaded me to look at the situation rationally.

"He said he likes some of your work. You can build on that," she said. "Remember what you said when you got back from Houston? You told me you had achieved your childhood dream. Well, I don't think that's exactly true."

I looked at her with a puzzled expression.

"Your dream wasn't to do one or two games. You want to do this on a full-time basis and you and I both know someday you're going to get to there.

"Regardless of the title on his door, Mr. Wuerch is just one man. Yes, he's an influential man, but you can't let his words define you. Have you asked anyone else what they thought of the job you did last weekend?"

Tom Hedrick and I had talked on the flight home. He'd offered what I thought was good council. As I reflected on his remarks, I realized he had made the same general observations as Weurch.

"The 'ups' in life really aren't what defines us," Dianne continued. "The roller coaster is always going to come down, but most of the time, the 'downs' aren't nearly as bad as they initially seem. When we pick ourselves off the floor, life looks pretty much the same as it did before.

"You are a resilient man, Bill. See if you can take what Mr. Wuerch said a little less personally. Ask others what they think. Look deep into your heart. And then, just be you."

She gave me a chance to respond, but I fell silent in reflection. She stood up from her chair, bent over, and kissed me on the top of my head, leaving me alone with my thoughts.

We didn't send out any resumes. I realized there was some truth to what Wuerch said. I decided to work hard and put the setback behind me. I broadened my own personal network. I enjoyed the pre-game assignments and landed some nice additional opportunities: tennis, college basketball, hockey, and Bengals pre-season games.

Early in 1975, a memo circulated through the station. Bill Wuerch was leaving Channel Five to take another position within the Avco Broadcasting group. His replacement was a young southerner by the name of Jim Hart. His management style was a far cry from that of Wuerch. Hart was a humble Christian man from the Smokey Mountain region of eastern Tennessee. Everyone took an immediate liking to him and his vision for the station.

Thanks to Dianne's advice, I built up my "fan base," not only at Channel Five and WLW Radio, but also within the Reds organization. Soon, Jim Hart became a trusted adviser. He enthusiastically supported me for the Reds' job when Woodward's departure created an opening in the booth.

***

The Big Red Machine had been an awfully good thing for the people of Cincinnati, but following the 1978 season, the unthinkable happened. Twice. In the span of one week.

A ninety-win season is usually good enough for a manager to keep his job. The '78 Reds won ninety games under Sparky Anderson, but finished behind Los Angeles in the NL West standings for the second year in a row. In the mind of general manager Dick Wagner, second place wasn't good enough. He told Anderson he intended to shake up the team's coaching staff, to which Anderson's reply was, "Over my dead body."

"Captain Hook" got the hook on November 27, 1978, when Wagner fired Anderson.

One week later, on December 5, Pete Rose signed a free-agent contract with the Philadelphia Phillies making him, for a time, the highest-paid player in team sports. Rose's departure so soon after Anderson's termination was not coincidental.

Anderson wasn't unemployed for long. He took over as field boss of the Detroit Tigers in 1979 and five years later he became the first manager to win the World Series in both leagues.

Meanwhile, John McNamara had the unenviable task of replacing Anderson in Cincinnati. While the team missed Rose greatly, the club did add to its pitching staff by acquiring veteran Tom Seaver.

Seaver went 16-6 for the '79 Reds. With much of the Big Red Machine still intact, the team rebounded to post another 90-win season, good enough for the NL West title by a game and a half over Houston. Unfortunately, another powerhouse had emerged in the National League's Eastern division, a team with its own inspirational identity. The "We-Are-Family" Pirates swept the Big Red Machine in the NLCS.

The steady Reds won eighty-nine games in 1980 and then posted the NL's best record in '81. That year, though, saw the first mid-season players' strike, the fifth work stoppage since the union's first labor action in 1972. The strike began on June 12 and forced the cancellation of more than seven hundred regular-season games. By the time play resumed on August 10, the fans had had enough. Ballpark attendance figures and television ratings dipped sharply. The baseball commissioner's office decided to split the season in two—a common practice at many levels of the minor leagues—creating the first divisional round of post-season play.

When the strike began, the Reds were a half game behind the Dodgers in the NL West standings. Thus, Los Angeles was declared the first-half champion. The second half of the season consisted of just over 50 games and with their spot in post-season play assured, the Dodgers coasted to a .500 mark. Meanwhile, the Reds won nearly sixty percent of their games in the second half, but at the finish line, Cincinnati stood a game and a half behind the second-half champion Astros.

Cumulatively, Cincinnati would have won the '81 West title by four games, but given the unique set-up by which baseball sought to salvage the season—and bolster revenues with an additional round of post-season play—the Reds were the ultimate bridesmaids, twice removed.

The next year, Cincinnati lost 101 games. Attendance at Riverfront Stadium frequently dipped below 10,000 paying customers and TV ratings were sometimes almost non-existent. Reds manager John McNamara did not survive the season. At the end of the year, I also was fired from my job.

When Ken Coleman returned to Boston in 1979, I took over the Reds' number-one television job. I felt confident and capable and enjoyed both the work and the responsibility. Veteran broadcaster Ray Lane became my partner and we enjoyed working together. Before coming to Cincinnati, Lane worked many years with the legendary Ernie Harwell in Detroit. A native Michigander, Lane settled back in the Detroit area upon his retirement and he lives there today. In 2009, Governor Jennifer Granholm declared October 3, 2009 as *Ray Lane Day* throughout the state of Michigan.

Lane had been out of baseball prior to landing the Reds' job. After my firing, he and I talked at length about my future. He told me to stay the course and never lose confidence in my abilities. I told him at minimum, I hoped never to suffer through another 100-loss season. We laughed.

Ironically, my spot in the Reds' booth was taken by another native of Detroit, Ken Wilson. Soon, Pete Rose returned to Cincinnati to manage the Reds, but that that ended badly when he was accused of gambling on baseball games, even some played by his own team. Ultimately, he was banned from the sport he loved so dearly.

Like Sparky Anderson, Ken Coleman got back to the World Series, too. He left Cincinnati after the '79 season and returned to his native Boston. Back behind the Red Sox microphone, he called the team's 1986 pennant run and described for his New England radio audience the nightmare that was Mookie Wilson's ground ball rolling between the legs of Bill Buckner.

I watched that game at home. By 1986, home was Los Angeles. I had been out of baseball for four long years.

Good fortune, it seemed, was no longer on my side.

CHAPTER 13
Triskaidekaphobia

I considered omitting Chapter 13 from this book.

Many hotels, particularly in the U.S., do not have a 13th floor. Formula 1 drivers are prohibited from racing with the Number 13. There were 13 people present at the Last Supper and we know how that turned out. All the fuss about the end of days in the year 2012 is a result of the Mayan calendar reaching the conclusion of its 13th b'ak'tuns on December 21, 2012. A b'ak'tun is roughly 394 years.

The fear of the Number 13 is called triskaidekaphobia. People who fear Friday the 13th are said to suffer from paraskevidekatriaphobia, which, I assure you, will be the longest word in this book. At least one Friday the 13th occurs in every calendar year. In 2012, there are three, perhaps a bad omen.

Spooky people born on Friday the 13th include outlaw Butch Cassidy, Cuban dictator Fidel Castro, film director Alfred Hitchcock, actor Steve Buscemi, and the Olson twins: Mary Kate and Ashley.

Not everyone is a triskaidekaphobe. Italians consider the number lucky. In the Jewish faith, a boy celebrates *Bar Mitzvah* when he turns 13 and becomes responsible for his own actions. When Wilt Chamberlain made the varsity basketball team at Philadelphia's Overbrook High School, he brought his uniform home to his mother and asked her to take off the Number 5 and sew on his favorite number instead: 13.

Among today's generation of all-time NBA greats, two-time MVP Steve Nash wears Number 13 with the Phoenix Suns. Miami Dolphin quarterback Dan Marino is arguably the NFL's most famous Number 13. Sweden's Matt Sundin played 21 seasons in the National Hockey League, scoring 564 regular-season goals while wearing Number 13 for three different teams.

Not a single member of the Baseball Hall of Fame wore Number 13 in his career. In fact, the number has been retired by only one major league team. That team is Cincinnati and the player so honored was a vital cog in the workings of the Big Red Machine: shortstop Dave Concepción.

I had the good fortune of watching Davey—as he was known during the early years of his career—blossom into a transcendent player.

On the Web site BaseballReference.com, Concepción is reported to have worn Number 50 at some point early in his career. According to Cincinnati's official Web site and MLB.com reporter Mark Sheldon, Concepción was handed Number 57 when he first reported to the Reds' big league camp in the spring of 1970. But the jersey didn't fit, literally or figuratively.

"I was too skinny, and it (didn't work) with my long name," Concepción said.

Tall and thin as a rail when signed as an amateur free agent at the age of 19, Concepción first asked to wear Number 11. That number was already taken by fellow rookie Hal McRae, who had appeared in seventeen games with the team the year before.

Finally, Concepción settled on Number 13 in honor of his mother Ernestine who had been born in his native Venezuela in 1913. Numbers didn't really matter, though. Concepción was just happy to be part of the team.

As he matured into a big leaguer, Concepción and Woody Woodward split time at shortstop for two seasons. Before his trade to the Reds, Woodward had worn Number 14 throughout his career in the majors. Pete Rose also wore that number. Upon his arrival in Cincinnati, Woodward chose Number 6 instead.

Concepción hit .260 his rookie year. His average dipped to .205 and .209 the next two seasons. With plenty of offense elsewhere in the Big Red Machine lineup, manager Sparky Anderson didn't care about Concepción's bat. He became a Cincinnati starter because of his fielding ability, particularly his range on the left side of the infield. Bolstered by Anderson's assurance he was an everyday player for the foreseeable future, Concepción got off to a torrid offensive start at the outset of the 1973 season. His batting average hovered around .300 until he broke his leg in a game against Montreal and was lost for the year on the eve of making his first appearance as an All-Star.

Then the fan outcry began. Concepción was encouraged to choose a new uniform number.

"People started writing letters," he recalled. "'We don't want you to be unlucky'," he remembered some of them saying. "I said, 'Don't worry about it. I broke my leg because I slid on top of the base.'

"After (that), my whole career changed." He kept the number.

In 1974, Concepción hit a then-career-high fourteen homers and won his first Gold Glove Award for defensive excellence. The next year, he was a Gold Glover, an All-Star-Game starter, and a vital piece to the Reds' championship season. By the end of the '76 campaign, which culminated with another World Series title, Concepción was simply the best player at his position in the National League.

For the next half dozen years, Concepción was a fixture as the NL's starting shortstop in the All-Star game. He was named MVP of the 1982 All-Star Game in Montreal. He had his best overall season in 1979 with career highs in runs scored (91), home runs (16), and RBI (84). Over the course of his first decade in the big leagues, Concepción transformed himself from a light-hitting defensive whiz to a complete ballplayer. When the Big Red Machine began to be dismantled, he became a fixture in the middle of the Reds' lineup. Concepción batted third for most of manager John McNamara's tenure with the club.

Concepción remained the Reds' everyday shortstop until midway through the 1986 season. In a game against Montreal, he suffered a broken hand and was placed on the disabled list. One month later, with the Reds' fortunes in the National League West fading, the team brought up a promising young prospect.

Barry Larkin was a 22-year-old Cincinnati native the Reds had been grooming as Concepción's heir apparent. Larkin made his major league debut on August 13, 1986. Two days later, he got his first start. He remained the team's regular shortstop for the rest of his nineteen-year career.

Remarkably, Concepción continued to make significant contributions despite losing his starting job.

In 1987—at the age of 39—Concepción had one of his best seasons. In a utility role, he played every infield position, committing just five errors on the year. While Larkin made the All-Star team and batted .296 with an OPS mark of .776, Concepción hit .319 for the season with an OPS of .761.

In 2012, Barry Larkin was voted into the Baseball Hall of Fame. No question he is richly deserving of the honor. Larkin gives Concepción credit for helping him find his way as a Major league ballplayer.

Larkin vividly recalls the first time he met Concepción, his boyhood hero. Cincinnati was at Detroit for an exhibition game with the Tigers before the start of the 1984 season. Larkin was a sophomore at the University of Michigan, on his way to becoming a two-time All-American and a first-round draft pick. Dave Parker, newly acquired by the Reds, introduced the two.

"Parker parades me into the locker room," Larkin told John Fay of the *Cincinnati Enquirer*. "Dave Concepción is sitting there, a guy I idolized as a kid. Parker walks up to him and says, 'Hey, Davey, this guy is going to take your job.'

"Davey looks at my hands. He saw all the calluses from my training in the weight room. He said, 'You're not going to take my job. Your hands are too hard'."

When Larkin joined the Reds just two-and-a-half years later, Concepción invited him to stay at his home.

"Davey was at the end of his career. He knew I was coming, but he welcomed me into his house. He took me out on the field and taught me how to do the bounce throw to first base. He talked to me about the different phases of the game.

"He even taught me meringue and salsa with the understanding I was the guy who was trying to take his job."

Larkin was an All-Star eleven times. Concepción made nine All-Star teams. Concepción won five Gold Glove awards; Larkin captured three.

Offensively, Larkin was the premier player at his position. He won nine Silver Slugger awards, presented annually to the top offensive player at each position. Concepción won the Silver Slugger award twice. For his career, Larkin batted .295 with 2,340 hits and 960 RBI. Concepción's career numbers: .267—2,326—950.

Larkin won the National League Most Valuable Player award in 1995. He was a top-ten finisher for the honor only one other time in his career. Concepción also was a top-ten selection twice, including a fourth-place finish for the award in 1981.

Five years after Concepción's retirement, he became eligible for induction into the Hall of Fame. He received less than seven percent of the vote in 1994 and over the course of his fifteen years of initial eligibility, he never earned more than a paltry 16.9 percent of ballot mentions from the Baseball Writers Association of America.

Part of what made Concepción a remarkable player—and teammate—was that he managed to keep his ego in check despite craving a bigger share of the Reds' spotlight. On a team with so many extraordinary players, Concepción undeservedly blended into the background. Frequently he would approach me after I wrapped up a pre- or post-game interview. "Hey, Bill, when are you going to talk to me again?" he would laugh. Over time, I realized his good nature belied the fact he did not feel he was receiving his due. I suspect he feels that way to this day.

His English wasn't the best early in his career. The sports press adored and felt more comfortable with Cuban infielder Tony Perez, already a well-respected veteran by the time Concepción became a part of the team. Most significantly, there were not a lot of column inches or extra interview minutes left with the likes of Bench, Rose, Morgan, Griffey, and George Foster occupying the media's attention.

No doubt about one thing: Dave Concepción was part of the greatest infield in baseball history.

But does that fact, along with the sum of his own body of work make Concepción worthy of induction into Cooperstown? I say yes.

Luis Aparicio is the only Venezuelan player currently in the Baseball Hall of Fame. He was a full-time starter at shortstop in each of his eighteen years in the big leagues. He was the 1956 AL Rookie of the Year with the White Sox and a thirteeen-time All-Star. Aparicio won nine Gold Gloves.

Growing up in the picturesque setting of Ocumare de la Costa, Venezuela, Concepción idolized Aparicio. It was Aparicio's Number 11 Concepción hoped to wear as a Reds rookie when the Number 57 uniform proved too big for his slender frame.

Offensively, Concepción's career achievements are statistically comparable to Aparicio's. The greatest disparity exists in at-bats—Aparicio had about 1,500 more—runs scored and stolen bases. Aparicio was a top-of-the-order sparkplug. Five inches taller, Concepción molded himself into a more complete offensive player. Arguably, he could be considered the precursor to the modern era of slugging shortstops, players like Larkin, Robin Yount, Cal Ripken, Jr., and ultimately Alex Rodriguez, another member of baseball's Number 13 club.

Long-time *Cincinnati Enquirer* sportswriter Bob Hertzel, a good friend and fellow Mizzou journalism grad, calls Dave Concepción a Hall-of-Fame-caliber player.

"I voted for Davey when he was on the ballot," Hertzel says today from his retirement home in Morgantown, West Virginia. "He, Aparicio, and (Ozzie) Smith were similar offensive players."

The author of acclaimed books on Pete Rose and the Big Red Machine, Hertzel says Concepción's prowess in the field, like Smith's, should not be overlooked.

"In 1974, Sparky Anderson said of Concepción's defensive play, 'Maybe somewhere there has been a man who played shortstop as well as he does, but I assure you there has never been a man who can cover the amount of ground he covers'."

For Concepción to attain baseball immortality, it will have to be through the Hall of Fame's Veterans Committee. In 2011, that group righted a long-standing wrong by enshrining Chicago Cub Ron Santo.

If it were up to me, Davey Concepción would certainly get into the Hall of Fame, too.

***

Growing up in the Appalachian Mountain region of southwestern Virginia, Billy Wagner was a boisterous lad. He was also a natural-born right-hander, but he didn't stay that way. After breaking his right arm as a youngster and impatient for his bones to heal, Wagner decided to give his other wing a go. In reasonably short order, he became a proficient left-hander. Thus, Wagner will always be cursed—or blessed, depending on your outlook—with the mindset and outlook of a southpaw. So, is it any surprise he chose to make the Number 13 his uniform of choice?

"Billy the Kid" is the Houston Astros' career save leader. His total of 422 saves for five different teams is fifth-best on baseball's all-time list. His career rate of 11.9 strikeouts per nine innings exceeds that of every pitcher who has thrown a minimum of 1,000 innings. When Nolan Ryan set the single-season strikeout record in 1973, he fanned roughly twenty-eight percent of the batters he faced. Over the course of his sixteen-year career, Wagner struck out one-third of the hitters who stepped to the plate against him.

For a power pitcher, Wagner was a bit on the smallish side. Throughout his career, clubs listed his height at 5'10". I always thought that figure a bit "lofty."

Billy's father, known throughout Smyth County, Virginia, as "Hotsey," was a fine baseball player in his own right. Some thought he was destined to be a big leaguer himself. Instead, the day after his high school graduation in 1970, he married his sixteen-year-old girlfriend Yvonne. Thirteen months later, William Edward Wagner was born in Marion, Virginia.

Wagner's parents faced an uphill battle to raise their son, not only because of their age, but also because their families couldn't stand each other. In a classic "Hatfield-and-McCoy" scenario poor Billy was caught in the middle.

Billy's parents divorced when he was five and for the next several years he and his sister bounced among various family members. Lacking in almost every basic necessity, Billy became a bitter and resentful child.

"It wasn't that (my parents) didn't love me," Wagner told Wayne Coffey of the *New York Daily News,* "They just didn't know what to do. When you are 10 years old and they ship you off to the next person, your first thought is nobody cares."

Wagner called himself a "red-chip kid" growing up. As one of the poorest children in school, Wagner received a red token which entitled him to free meals. "I was as embarrassed as any person could be," he said of being forced to take handouts.

In the ninth grade, Wagner moved in with an aunt and uncle, Sally and Jack Lamie. They lived in the tiny unincorporated town of Tannersville, about fifteen miles north of Marion. To this day, Wagner considers Tannersville as his childhood home, the place where his life began to take on some semblance of normalcy. The Lamie's provided Billy with stability and consistency. Their son Jeff, Billy's cousin, provided Wagner an athletic role model.

Sports became both sanctuary and catharsis for Billy.

At Tazewell High School, Wagner excelled in all sports. By his senior year, he had made a name for himself on the pitching mound. He hoped to play somewhere in college. But at 5'3" and 130 pounds he was deemed too small to be a legitimate prospect, a reoccurring theme throughout his career. Astros' owner Drayton McLane, upon meeting Wagner for the first time, told him bluntly, "I thought you'd be bigger."

With no scholarship offers, Billy followed Jeff to Ferrum College, a small Division III school about two hours east of Marion. Ferrum did not offer athletic scholarships, so Wagner pieced together a variety of financial-aid options—along with a $24-a-week job at the school library—to fund his education. He hoped to play on the Ferrum football team with Jeff, but instead he was encouraged to concentrate on baseball. During his sophomore year, and after a five-inch growth spurt, Wagner averaged 19.11 strikeouts per nine innings for the Panther baseball team, an NCAA record. Pro scouts began to take notice.

In the meantime, Billy had taken notice of Sarah Quesenberry, a member of the Ferrum women's basketball team. They began dating and soon realized they saw eye-to-eye on most things, and not just because Sarah was a couple of inches taller than Billy. When Wagner met Sarah's father Steve, the two men quickly bonded.

"He knocked me all over the driveway when we played basketball," Wagner remembers fondly, "He was a big man and loved to try to put me in my place. He treated me just like one of his own. We had a great time."

After his sophomore season at Ferrum, and followed by an outstanding summer in the Cape Cod League, Wagner became one of the top baseball prospects in the country. Houston selected him as the twelfth overall pick in the 1993 amateur draft. The Astros gave him a $500,000 signing bonus. But leaving Ferrum wasn't easy. Sarah had one more year of school before earning her degree, and moving on also meant Billy wouldn't be able to hang out with Steve.

Wagner had a promising first year professionally, pitching at the Class A level in Auburn, New York. That November he proposed to Sarah and the two were married in the fall of 1994. Heading into the 1995 season, Wagner seemed on track for a spot in the Astros' starting rotation. On May 16, Houston placed Billy on their forty-man roster. A promotion to the big league club seemed imminent. Billy called Sarah to give her the good news.

At two o'clock the next morning, Wagner was awakened by another phone call from his wife. Her father Steve and stepmother Tina had been shot to death outside an apartment complex in Hillsville, Virginia, murdered by Tina's sister's estranged husband. Sarah had talked to her dad shortly after getting the news that Billy might soon be a big leaguer. Steve was immensely pleased.

Despite his own chaotic and tumultuous past, Wagner stood firm for his new family. He was a rock of stability upon which his wife and those closest to her could mourn the terrible loss. To help console his family, the Astros gave Billy a bereavement leave.

Four months later, on September 13, 1995, Wagner made his major league debut at Shea Stadium in New York. He threw six pitches to retire the only Met batter he faced. It was his only appearance in a Houston uniform that season. He was allowed to rejoin Sarah and the two of them spent the off season coping with their enormous loss.

Over the course of his Houston career, Wagner saved 225 games and posted a 2.53 earned run average in 464 appearances. His last year with the team, 2003, he led the National League in appearances with 67 and finished second in saves with 44. Inconsistency spelled the end of Wagner's days as an Astro.

Billy played two years in Philadelphia, and then signed a $43-million free-agent contract with the Mets. His three seasons in New York were considered a disappointment by many fans there.

After splitting the 2009 campaign between New York and Boston, Wagner inked a one-year deal with Atlanta where he regained the mojo which had made him a dominant force for much of his career. Playing in manager Bobby Cox's final season, Wagner announced in May that 2010 would be his last year, too. And, at the age of 38, Billy found himself in one final pennant chase.

On the last day of the 2010 regular season in a must-win game against Philadelphia, Wagner came on in the bottom of the eighth inning with Atlanta holding an 8-4 lead. In what would be his last major league appearance as a closer, Billy gave up a single, a double, and a walk in the eighth and the Phillies cut the Braves' advantage to a single run.

Cox sent Wagner back to the mound in the ninth, and, not surprisingly for those who followed the ups and downs of Billy's career, he struck out the side. By night's end the Braves were headed into post-season play.

Wagner deserved to see his career end in storybook fashion with a trip to the World Series. Instead, the Braves bowed meekly to the San Francisco Giants in the divisional series. Wagner appeared in just one game, pitching only one inconsequential inning.

Otherwise, Billy Wagner went out in style. He appeared in 71 games during his farewell season, recording 37 saves. He struck out 104 batters in 69.1 innings and posted a microscopic ERA of 1.43.

"I'm totally content with not playing baseball," Wagner said recently. "I love watching it. I love talking about it. If I miss anything, it would be some of the guys I played with and competing on the field. Other than that, you can keep it."

Wagner long ago left behind the hardscrabble existence of his youth. He'll never forget, though, the experiences he had as a boy. Six years ago, Billy and long-time friend Erik Robinson started the Second Chance Learning Center. The mission of the organization is to help the economically-disadvantaged children of Virginia's Appalachian Mountain region stay in school.

Billy and Sarah and their four children still live in the Old Dominion State. Home now is a 120-acre farm in the foothills of the Blue Ridge Mountains, outside Charlottesville. He's intent on putting his past forever behind him. When he announced his retirement, Wagner explained he wanted to spend more time with his family.

And if anyone knows the importance of a commitment like that, it's Billy the Kid.

CHAPTER 14
Flights of the Concord

For every Billy Wagner or Davey Concepción, hundreds of other baseball sagas have less happy endings. The end of my seven-year run as a Reds broadcaster is one of those grim tales.

"Brown Axed," the headline read in the *Cincinnati Enquirer*. Readers' might have wondered if Paul Brown had been dismissed as president of the Cincinnati Bengals football team. While he had left the sideline as the team's coach at the end of the 1975 campaign, Brown remained as team president and part owner. In fact, he and the Bengals were going strong having reached the Super Bowl at the end of the 1981 season. When the "Brown Axed" story broke, the Bengals, as well as the rest of the National Football League, were in the midst of a nearly two-months-long mid-season players' strike.

The hatchet which had fallen was squarely upon my own head.

Just as a bad team can't fire all its players, a television station in a ratings decline can't find a new audience. Affecting change, or at least the illusion of change, is achieved much more easily by eliminating the man at the top. I finally had sympathy for and a new perspective on every manager or coach who'd ever been dismissed.

I'd received the bad news the day before the story broke in the newspaper. Program director Bill Spiegel came up to my desk.

"Can I see you for a minute?" Honestly, I thought I might be getting another plum assignment.

When we reached his office he closed the door and the two of us sat down on opposite sides of his desk. Spiegel was usually a pretty gregarious guy, but for a brief time the two of us just looked at each other. Finally he gave me the bad news.

"We're going in a different direction with the Reds' games," he said. "Our numbers are down and our advertisers are screaming at us. The ball club isn't happy and..."

I cut Spiegel off.

"What do you mean the ball club isn't happy? I wouldn't imagine they're very happy since attendance went into the toilet this year. But, what does that have to do with me?" I had somehow managed to channel Waite Hoyt.

Spiegel paused. "Bill, all I can say is that this goes way above me." He fell silent again for a moment. "Think about it. There are others involved in a decision of this nature."

Surprisingly, I took some solace in his remark, although I wasn't sure quite sure what he really meant.

"If they can fire Sparky Anderson, they can get rid of anyone."

So had "they" yanked the plug on my career? And just who would "they" actually be?

If anyone deserves credit for building the Big Red Machine it's Bob Howsam. As the club's president and general manager from 1967 to 1977, Howsam assumed almost total control of the franchise. The Reds' stringent dress code and facial-hair policies were a reflection of his conservative nature. But, when it came to sports management, Howsam was without peer.

Prior to his arrival in Cincinnati, Howsam and his father Lee helped launch both the American Football League and baseball's Continental League. In fact, both ventures were christened in the same year, 1959. The Howsams were the original owners of the Denver Broncos, and while the Continental League never got off the ground, the threat of competition forced Major League Baseball into expansion mode in the early '60s.

Howsam spent two years as general manager of the St. Louis Cardinals before moving to Cincinnati.

Stepping down as GM of the Reds following the 1977 season, Howsam turned over operations of the club to Dick Wagner. After missing the playoffs two years in a row, Wagner fired Anderson. Then, in 1980 former Western & Southern chairman William Williams and his brother James bought the Reds. At the time, the Williams family also owned controlling interest in the Bengals.

I couldn't imagine my dismissal was orchestrated at the levels of a Dick Wagner or even the Williams Brothers, but Spiegel seemed to be making that implication. Irrespective of my small part in the proceedings, the Reds continued to make an adequate number of other bad moves to keep the team floundering both in the standings and at the ticket window. Less than a year after my termination, Wagner and the Williams Brothers also had departed the scene. Marge Schott bought the team in 1984 for $13 million.

"So, when's my last day?" I asked Spiegel as he seemed ready to conclude our meeting.

"Well, Bill, that depends on you. Actually, we'd like to keep you on here at Channel Five. You can continue with your other responsibilities as long as you'd like."

"Really," I said, and not in the form of a question.

"Absolutely. Of course, there will be a slight reduction in your compensation."

"How much?"

"About half."

A common tactic for employers wishing to avoid paying unemployment benefits is to create an untenable work environment for their unwanted employees. I'm not sure whether or not Spiegel had that in mind, but basically, he was dropping my pay scale to the level it had been before I got the Reds' job. It didn't take long for me to realize my days in Cincinnati were numbered.

I had given no thought whatsoever to changing jobs. But when I did, I quickly discovered the job market was tight. By the end of 1982, the American economy had been in the doldrums for nearly two years. The nationwide unemployment rate was nearing eleven percent. I knew I had a marketable skill set and was still young enough that eventually I could land another decent job, but I couldn't wait forever.

Family life wasn't about just Dianne and me anymore.

***

How did people ever get along without text messaging? It sure would have come in handy for me on February 8, 1974.

I was on the courts at the Queen City Racquet Club and life was generally good. Dianne and I were expecting our first child and she was well into her ninth month. Her due date was still about three weeks away so she gave me the green light to hit a few tennis balls before I went to work.

We take instantaneous communication for granted these days. I do have a Facebook account, as does this book, but I don't twitter or "tweet." If you knew my cell phone number, you could give me a call anytime and anywhere, even in the broadcast booth. I can't promise I'd be able to pick up, but you could always leave a message.

I'm usually pretty good about returning calls, particularly if you were so inspired to try to find me after purchasing this book. In fact, if you "Like" this book on

Facebook and post a favorable comment to the page, I can almost assure you I'll send out a thank-you reply. If that isn't "relationship marketing," I don't know what is.

"LOL."

While Facebook, the Internet, and personal computers are products of the imaginations of people whose technical capabilities far exceed my own, a cell phone definitely would have come in handy when Dianne's water broke unexpectedly while I was doing my thing at the Queen City Racquet Club.

We not only had a Plan A in place, but also Plans B and C—sort of standard operational procedure when you have an accountant and a fussbudget in the same family. No stone goes unturned and every eventuality is anticipated, except for the premature-birth scenario.

"Excuse me, Mr. Brown," one of the young teaching pros came up to my court. "Your wife just called. She said she's having the baby.

"She also said you would know what that means."

Immediately I cut short my match, collected my things, and dashed out to the parking lot. Then I realized the pro had said nothing about whether or not Dianne was on her way to the hospital. I reached for my cell phone but I had left it about twenty years into the future. I ran back into the clubhouse and called Dianne at home. She answered.

"Honey, are you okay?" I asked. "Are you having the baby now? Did you find a ride to the hospital? What can I do for you? Why are you having the baby NOW???"

"Bill, Bill. Settle down. It's okay. I've called the doctor and I've got a ride and why don't you just plan on meeting me at the hospital."

And then Dianne added, "Would that work for you?"

"Sure. Absolutely. You bet." Of course it would work for me. Since we lived on the west side of town and I was on the far north side of town, I was pretty useless as far as offering much in the way of immediate assistance.

"Listen, I'm so sorry I'm not there for you right now," I told Dianne, still in somewhat of a panic. "You know, I had a feeling that tennis was a bad idea this morning. Do you have your bag packed? Do you have the checklist we made? Don't leave home without the checklist!"

"Bill?" The line was silent as Dianne awaited my reply.

"Yes?"

"Just settle down, okay? Do you know how to get to the hospital?"

"Of course."

"Well, why don't you meet me there, okay? Just go to the admissions desk and I'm sure they'll be able to tell you where I am." I was glad one of us was in our right mind.

"And, Bill, one other thing."

"Yes, anything, just name it!"

"Don't forget to breathe."

I was a pretty proud father-to-be. I'd bragged that Dianne and I were having an "off-season" baby. We hadn't particularly planned it that way, but the fact our child was due before the start of the baseball season was a relief. Not that I was making many trips with the team, but I was still in stand-by mode hoping another fill-in opportunity might come my way.

I'd heard stories of how distracting the birth of a baby can be for a ballplayer.

We sometimes forget that baseball players—athletes in general—are also people, more or less, just like you and me. The games they play professionally constitutes their jobs. We pay to see them in their workplace.

Today, ballplayers are richly compensated for their efforts; but, as we all know, money doesn't buy happiness. As John Lennon once said, "Life is what happens while you're busy making other plans."

Johnny Bench had a horrible year in 1976. From the time he broke into the league as a 20-year-old catching phenom in '68, Bench had been a prodigiously productive player. But, in '76, he suffered through a miserable season, thanks in part to an early shoulder injury. His RBI count was exactly half what it had been when he won his first MVP award in 1970. His home run total dropped from the previous year by a factor of two and his batting average dipped to a career low of .234.

Bench also had other things on his mind. The year before, he had met and married a beauty queen from South Carolina in the most sudden of whirlwind romances. Vickie Chesser had finished runner-up in the 1970 Miss USA pageant and Bench had first spotted her in a toothpaste commercial on television. One of the perks of being someone like Johnny Bench is that a pretty girl on TV isn't beyond your reach.

Four days after they met on a first date in New York City, Bench proposed. Six weeks later, on February 21, 1975, they were married in Cincinnati's Christ Episcopal Church. By the end of the year, they were discussing their marital problems on the *Phil Donahue Show*.

By the time they should have been celebrating their first anniversary, they were living apart. Since Phil Donahue was no Dr. Phil, airing out their dirty laundry on national television turned out to be a bad idea. Their life had become a soap opera and all of Cincinnati was enthralled. Divorce proceedings got messy and dragged on throughout much of the '76 season. Bench's play suffered from the psychological toll.

I can't say for sure, but my guess is the divorce was finalized right around the end of the regular season. Even with Bench at less than his best the Reds still ran away with the NL West. He had just two hits in the last week of the season; only fourteen hits in September. Then, as postseason play began, Johnny Bench suddenly got hot. He batted .333 in the National League Championship Series, and hit a sizzling

.533 to claim MVP honors in the Reds' World Series sweep of the Yankees.

The cloud had lifted. Baseball's once most-eligible bachelor was again a single man specializing in the run-producing extra-base hit.

To save my own marriage, I knew I needed to get to the hospital before Dianne gave birth. Fortunately, we both arrived in the nick of time. Truth be told, since Dianne *was* about three weeks early in her delivery and also a *reasonable* person, our marriage was never in *real* in jeopardy.

Welcoming Allison Kara Brown into the Brown lineup proved to be a banner day.

***

As I write these very words Allison is celebrating her birthday in Willmar, Minnesota. She lives there with her husband Alan and children Luke, Emma, and C.C. Our Allison is a pretty special lady, married to a good and decent man, and their kids are adorable because they take after their grandmother and not me.

I get to see my grandchildren at least three times a year and now that Luke has turned ten, he and his dad sometimes meet me for ball games when the Astros are in the northern reaches of the country. One of the perks of the team moving to the American League in 2013 is that Allison's home is only about one hundred miles from downtown Minneapolis. Trips to Twins games will be extra special for me.

I was an absentee dad for much of Allison's life. Baseball season is a little tough being gone so much. When she still lived at home, Allison might have told you that off-seasons were hard, too, because I was constantly trying to make up for lost time. As an only child, she grew up with a pretty intuitive sense about what was going on with me. I call that our special father-daughter bond.

One of the stories she loves to tell people took place in Cincinnati. Dianne and I were attending the open house at Allison's elementary school. As is the custom at those sorts of affairs, teachers and parents spend equal time gushing over the children. Driving home after the event, Dianne asked me if I had learned anything about our daughter that night. "Yeah," I said. "I didn't know she was in the second grade. I thought for sure she was a third-grader."

You can't always tell the players without a scorecard.

***

The loss of my job was a shock to our family unit, but Dianne and Allison did their best to keep my spirits up. I remained at Channel Five while looking for other work. Despite the down economy, opportunities began to present themselves. A job doing Triple A baseball came open in Columbus, Ohio. I would have been willing to take a step down the proverbial career ladder and move to radio, but I wasn't crazy about the idea of also being the morning-drive sports anchor. A 4:30 a.m. wake-up call on the heels of a night baseball game wasn't my idea of a good time.

I interviewed for a television job with the Minnesota Twins. In addition to calling about 40 baseball games a year, I would also have hosted between-period reports on Minnesota North Stars hockey telecasts. For years I'd convinced myself the hockey end of the deal wasn't really all that appealing to me, but to be honest, I suspect I was never offered the job. Dick Bremer got the position in the Twin Cities and he's been there ever since.

For months I pursued a position with the Home Sports Entertainment network out of Pittsburgh. I told Dianne I really wanted the job. Sometimes you have to be careful what you ask for.

After the Entertainment and Sports Programming Network went live on September 7, 1979, executives at Warner Cable imagined the same concept also could be a money-making proposition on a regional basis. Thus, Home Sports Entertainment was born about the time I was looking for a new job. I learned Pittsburgh would be one of HSE's first markets and for months I made phone calls to a single-point of contact within the company. That individual was former New York Giants football coach Allie Sherman.

In his first two years as head coach of the Giants, Sherman guided his team to back-to-back NFL championship game appearances. Both times New York lost to Vince Lombardi's Green Bay Packers, but Sherman won the league's Coach of the Year award in both 1961 and 1962. The Giants reached a third-straight NFL title contest in 1963, but bowed to the Chicago Bears. Their fortunes fell precipitously from there, and by 1968 chants of "Goodbye, Allie" famously echoed throughout Yankee Stadium.

Sherman was fired as coach of the Giants before the 1969 season. He would never coach again.

When Warner Cable put together its HSE concept, the company knew it needed a few big names to provide credibility. That's where Sherman fit in. And, he was extremely good at one part of his job. Every time I talked to him to check on the progress of the Pittsburgh operation, Sherman was friendly, affable, and optimistic. He could have sold a cow pie to a cattleman. He certainly sold me on the HSE proposition but it took him forever to finally offer me a job.

Allie Sherman was a great front man, but his management skills, at least in my estimation, were grossly lacking. I learned quickly in my new job what it must have been like to be a New York Giant in the '60s. The guy hated to lose.

I moved to Pittsburgh and left the girls in Cincinnati so Allison could finish out the school year. Let's see, she would have been...in the third grade? Fourth? Who remembers.

Much of HSE's programming was live sporting events. I was "sports director," which meant I was in charge of all operations originating in our home studio. I did some play-by-play assignments, but the Pirates were in capable hands with the venerable Bob Prince and his two ex-jock sidekicks: Steve Blass and Willie Stargell. I spent a lot of time in their broadcast booth and truly enjoyed getting to know all three men.

The network also carried the woeful—at the time—Pittsburgh Penguins. If Sherman negotiated the contract with the Pens, which I'm certain he did, he got taken to the cleaners. The network also paid too much for the rights to Pitt, Penn State, Duquesne, and Robert Morris college games, but I did get to do some mid-major basketball broadcasts. And, if I remember correctly, there was also some tennis that year. Fortunately, Ilie Nastase was long-retired from the game.

It probably would have been a good thing if Sherman had spent more time selling ads than making programming decisions and yelling at his people—which happened to me on a couple occasions. He hired competent men such as general manager Jim Gilligan and program director Bernie Seabrooks, but Sherman wasn't good at delegating responsibility.

About a year after HSE first went on the air in the Steel City, Warner shut the money-losing operation down. So, I was out of a job again, and this time I not only had a family to support, I also had a mortgage to pay.

Thank goodness for my trusty AMC Concord station wagon.

By this time, the car certainly was racking up the miles. After taking the Pittsburgh job, I commuted to and from Cincinnati until the girls moved. After HSE went out of business, I took another cable job—back in Cincinnati. With another school year to finish and a home to sell, I did the commuting thing again, this time in the opposite direction. The Concord served me ably.

Sports Time Cable Network was the brainchild of the people at Anheuser-Busch, Inc. The business model was basically the same as HSE without the maniacal ex-football coach calling the programming shots. Anheuser-Busch was a dominant nationwide presence as a sports advertiser and the company had proven capable in its ownership of the St. Louis Cardinals. Gussie Busch would have been proud as his old company hoped to find synergy on the programming side of the sports equation.

I was initially impressed with management. Sports Time moved its Cincinnati operations into a state-of-the-art studio which put Channel Five to shame. I had a good feeling about the job. Unfortunately, after about a year, that venture, too, went out of business. While another regional sports network had fallen by the wayside, the folks at ESPN continued growing along their merry way.

Actually, the HSE concept did not fail in all markets. In places like Dallas and Houston it proved to be a hit, ultimately morphing into Prime Sports and then Fox Sports Network. HSE/Prime/FSN has been the home of the Houston Astros since 1983, but that relationship soon will change. Beginning in 2013, when the Astros move to the American League, the team's telecasts will be originated by Comcast SportsNet Houston, a joint venture with the Houston Rockets.

As Sports Time shut its doors, many eligible employees took advantage of something called an "assignability" clause. This meant that if the network could find its people other opportunities commensurate in pay to their old jobs, Sports Time would not be liable for the balance of its contracts. I was "fortunate" to be assigned a new position in Southern California. Dianne and I had never considered ourselves

"West-Coast types," but a job was a job and there was a certain allure about living in Los Angeles.

My new opportunity was with the Financial News Network, but I wasn't putting my sporting past in the rearview mirror. FNN was embarking on a new approach to its programming and was looking to add sports to its evening mix. Even though I'd heard that song and dance twice before, I decided to roll the dice again.

I sold Dianne on the idea, calling the new opportunity an "adventure." And, as with any good explorer, it was up to me to pioneer our westward expansion while Allison finished yet another school year.

Poor kid.

***

Somewhere in Arizona—I don't recall exactly where— the Concord and I stopped for gas. An "alert" mechanic pointed out that the back end of the station wagon was considerably lower than the front. I had the car loaded to its limit since it would be a while before the girls joined me in L.A.

I couldn't disagree with his observation.

"Now that you mention it, that doesn't look good." I tried my best to sound like I had even a small clue as to the mechanical workings of a car. "I'm headed to Los Angeles, so I still have a ways to go. Think I'll be able to make it out there like this?"

The young man stooped to eye the ground clearance at the back end of my car. "Maybe," he offered, "and maybe not."

Just as I was about to become a little irritated with his manner, he continued.

"You could make it, I'm not saying that you won't. But, you really don't want your car to break down in the middle of

163

nowhere, and between here and there you'll find a lot of nowhere."

He suggested I invest in a set of "helper springs" for the back wheels. Certain I was being scammed but unwilling to run the risk of fending for myself on the side of the road, I agreed to let the mechanic bolster the rear suspension of my vehicle.

That turned out to be one of the best things I'd ever done, not as good as getting married or having a daughter, but a lot better than boot camp, Allie Sherman's programming decisions, and Brussels sprouts.

The adjustment not only smoothed out the rest of the ride, but also added several years and tens of thousands of miles to the road life of that trusty AMC wagon.

Part of the appeal of the Los Angeles opportunity was that I wouldn't be working for a start-up company. FNN had gone on the air in 1981 and was growing. I figured people would always have an interest in money matters.

The aim of our new team was to launch a four-hour block of weeknight sports programming. Fittingly, our part of the broadcast day would be called "SCORE."

While starting yet another new job, I was tasked with finding yet another home and I had no intentions of trying to buy in the L.A. market. A realtor uncovered what seemed to be a real steal on a rental property in Canoga Park. Unfortunately, just as the girls were ready to head west for their part of the move, the pipes in our new home broke and the house flooded. I shared news of this minor catastrophe with Dianne's mother, who recommended I not tell my wife until after she arrived in California.

That was the last time I attempted to hide the truth from my better half.

Dianne was not pleased to see our new home in its state of disrepair. Despite my efforts to put a positive spin on it— "We're getting new carpets"—other repairs which were also sorely needed were not being addressed. My "punishment" for lack of full disclosure arrived the next day when the moving van showed up. The driver was unable to find anyone locally to help unload the truck, so, in my usual hurry to get things done, that task fell, literally, onto my shoulders.

Eventually we got the house in order and Dianne and Allison took nicely to living in L.A. I mean, what's not to like, save for the occasional smog alert, epic traffic jams, earthquakes, mudslides, and the pretentiousness which goes along with the city's signature *Hollywood* lifestyle.

But I digress.

Admittedly, I grew comfortable at FNN/SCORE. For the first time in a while, I wasn't looking over my shoulder waiting for the other shoe to drop. My family and I spent a lot of time seeing the sights and entertaining the many friends and family eager to pay us an extended visit. No one came to see us— save for our parents—when we lived in Pittsburgh...and Pittsburgh, it turns out, is a really underrated town.

Still, I wondered if a career in sportscasting would ever provide the sort of comfort and security I longed to give my family. We could never have met our financial obligations if Dianne hadn't agreed to go back to work—making Allison a quasi-latchkey kid. Fortunately, Allison made friends easily— she's always had one of the most effusive personalities you'll ever encounter—and also had a good sense for avoiding bad situations. She was about as well-adjusted as any young girl who had bounced around from town to town and school to school could be.

There comes a time in every sportscaster's life—in fact, this "truism" exists throughout the broadcasting industry— when a person seriously ponders the possibility of giving up the dream and entering the "real" world. That moment for me came in California when a friend of a friend offered me a chance to explore an opportunity with a company called Paychex.

The money was good. I passed the management aptitude test with flying colors. And the work hours promised to be steady and reasonable. Over the course of the previous four-and-a-half years, I had been apart from my wife and daughter maybe twenty percent of the time, and that didn't count all the nights and weekends I worked in a studio somewhere. Both Dianne and I knew far more stability growing up and we worried that my lifestyle could have an adverse effect on our daughter.

In the end, it was a close call, but I decided to stick with what I knew best.

CHAPTER 15
Comeback

One of my favorite Bible verses comes from the Book of Romans: "Suffering produces perseverance; perseverance, character; and character, hope."

I call that the formula for a comeback.

Lance Berkman, known as "The Puma" during his playing days in Houston, was the 2011 National League Comeback Player of the Year with the Cardinals. If anyone understands what it takes to make a comeback, it's Berkman, who, in his first year in St. Louis, helped the Redbirds win a World Series championship.

In an off-season appearance at Houston's First Baptist Church this past winter, Berkman spoke pragmatically of his latest award. "Every kid dreams of someday winning 'Comeback Player of the Year'," Berkman joked. "What 'comeback' really means is that you weren't very good for a while. Personally, I would have preferred never to have had to make a comeback in the first place."

Me, too, Lance. And good luck in your recovery from your knee surgery. Keep in mind if you're not as fleet of foot as you were before, we'll be in need of a designated hitter in Houston come the 2013 season.

When you think about it, life really is about comebacks. We get knocked down and we get up again. And there are different kinds of comebacks. Consider the following variations on the word:

> A batted ball hit back to the pitcher: *a "comebacker"*
>
> A rally from a deficit in runs scored: *"The team pulled off quite a comeback!"*
>
> A pithy remark, quick reply, or retort: *"Dierker had quite a comeback to the reporter's question."*
>
> A return to a former position or status: *"Newt Gingrich failed in his effort to make a political comeback."*
>
> A forgettable 2007 movie starring Carl Weathers and directed by Tom Brady, (but not the Tom Brady you're thinking of): *"Why don't you act like a barbell and get benched."*
>
> What the other and more well-known Tom Brady was unable to pull off in the final minute of Super Bowl XLVI: *"My husband cannot throw the (expletive deleted) ball and catch the ball at the same time," a disgruntled Mrs. Brady said after the game.*

With a steady job in Los Angeles, I really hadn't been thinking about making a baseball comeback of my own. On the heels of my experiences in Cincinnati and Pittsburgh, I realized there were worse things than being "gainfully employed."

Occasionally while in Los Angeles, I was able to rekindle relationships from my sporting past. Such was the case when I arranged to do an interview on SCORE with former Reds GM Dick Wagner. After leaving Cincinnati himself, he took over as general manager of the Astros and seemed pleased to hear from me when I called in advance of his team's series at Dodger Stadium. He told me he would be in town with the club and would be happy to do an in-studio interview with me.

After the interview, Wagner casually inquired if I had considered getting back into the play-by-play business. I told him Dianne, Allison, and I were content where we were. I did not realize—until he called me again the next day—that

Wagner had an ulterior motive for his seemingly innocuous question.

As general manager of the Reds, Wagner had overseen the dismantling of the aging Big Red Machine. The team's subsequent failure had cost both of us our jobs. Three-and-a-half years later, he not only had put together another winning ball club in Houston—the team won the NL Western Division championship in 1986—but also seemed interested in renewing our working relationship.

Shortly after Houston's '86 playoff run ended, Wagner called me again. He said the club had a broadcast opening and encouraged me to apply for the job. After his initial inquiries, Dianne and I had talked at length about the possibility of me getting back into baseball. We had been living in Los Angeles for two years and while we valued the stability of my job, the city's size and cost of living were beginning to wear on us. In addition, we also had concerns about the societal influences Allison was experiencing.

The decision was unanimous among the Browns. The time was ripe for a comeback.

I put my resume and demo reel together and sent them to the Astros' director of broadcasting Art Elliott. Given Wagner's persistence, I felt good about the possibilities, but I also knew that if I got the job, I would be filling some awfully big shoes.

***

When Houston was awarded a National League expansion franchise on October 17, 1960, team owner Roy Hofheinz intended to do baseball in a big way—"Texas style," you might say. Three months before the beginning of the team's inaugural season in 1962, land was broken south of the city's already thriving Texas Medical Center and adjacent to the temporary stadium in which big league baseball would get its start in the Lone Star State. Hofheinz—known as "The Judge" and a former Houston mayor—promised the team's permanent facility would become "The Eighth Wonder of the World."

The Judge intended for every facet of his new baseball operations to be first class, including his radio broadcast team. He already had one announcer in his employ. Alabama native Loel Passe had served as the voice of the minor-league Houston Buffs—also owned by Hofheinz—since 1950, and was a favorite with local fans. Finding the right voice and personality to jive with Passe took a little more time. After a nationwide search, The Judge got his man.

Robert Eugene Elston was born on March 26, 1922, in Fort Dodge, Iowa. Around the time of his 20th birthday and after having landed a job at a local radio station, Elston called his first major league game, a Fort Dodge exhibition between the Cubs and White Sox as the two Chicago teams barnstormed their way toward the opening of the 1942 regular season. Twelve years later, in 1954, Gene Elston was a full-time member of the Cubs broadcasting crew. His reputation grew quickly.

In 1958, Elston and Hall-of-Fame pitcher Bob Feller teamed for the Mutual Broadcasting Network's *Game of the Day*. In late 1960, Elston was set to take the Reds' radio job, but when Cincinnati GM Gabe Paul was hired to run the new Houston franchise, he brought Elston with him to Texas.

Houston baseball fans got a full season's worth of previews as Elston and Passe spent 1961 announcing Buffs games together. By the time the Colt .45s were ready to begin play, the club was already recognized for having one of the best broadcasting tandems in the business. In 1965, the duo, along with everyone else—players and fans alike—moved "indoors" as Hofheinz's dream of the world's first air-conditioned domed stadium became a reality.

By the time of his dismissal after the 1986 season, Gene Elston had become as much of a baseball institution in Houston as the Astrodome or Hofheinz himself. While I was eager for the opportunity to resume my baseball journey, I was also a little intimidated about the prospect of replacing a living legend like Elston.

Several weeks after submitting my resume, Art Elliott called to schedule an interview. He said I was one of three candidates under consideration for Elston's job. Rather than asking me for a convenient time to come to Houston, he told me my interview would be the following Thursday, at nine o'clock sharp. I booked my flight and arranged for a day off from work—but not two days. Given my track record, tempering my optimism was not difficult.

After arriving in Houston on the "red-eye" flight, I checked into a hotel and caught a couple hours of sleep. A taxi shuttled me to the Astrodome where I met Elliott and was greeted warmly by Wagner. My meeting with team officials was easy and relaxed. I aced that part of the interview process.

Elliott and I then drove to the HSE headquarters where I anticipated talking with management and staff. Instead, I was asked to audition for the job.

Really?

Elliott told me he had decided to put his three finalists through an audition process even though each of us already had submitted demo tapes. He wanted to see how we would perform "under pressure." Each of his candidates would announce three innings from a videotape of one of the Astros' broadcasts from the year before.

"Bill, come in and make yourself comfortable," Elliott said, gesturing toward a conference room inside the HSE studios. A technician followed us inside.

"I think we have everything you'll need." The table was set up in much the same fashion as the broadcast booth had been in Cincinnati. There was a monitor, headset, scorebook, and media guides. Elliott was serious about the process.

"We've already filled out the scorebook to the point of the game where you'll begin the audition," he said.

"So, we're just going to turn the sound down and give it a go," I said to myself. Who knew the experiences of my youth would come in handy so many years later.

"You'll get thirty minutes to prepare and then we'll give you a live countdown," Elliott said. "Is there anything else you might need?"

"Who are the Astros playing here?" I asked referring to the monitor on the conference table. "The Dodgers," I was told.

I hadn't announced a baseball game in more than four years. Since I didn't submit my application until the baseball season was over, I didn't have a chance to brush up on my skills, although I wasn't expecting a live audition to be a prerequisite for employment. I'd *thought* a lot about baseball after scheduling the interview, but I hadn't really done anything to prepare other than get better acquainted with the Astros organization. I thought my resume, demo reel, and past association with Wagner would sufficiently state my case. Not so, it appeared.

I checked out the scorebook, thumbed through the media guides, and made a few notes. I didn't want to over-think what I was about to do. I asked the technician a couple questions and after about ten minutes told him I was ready to go.

The audition went well. My reserve of broadcast clichés came back quickly. Unlike many of my peers, particularly those of the generation which preceded me, I've never really had a signature catchphrase—a "Holy Toledo!"—in my oratorical bag of tricks and I wasn't about to try to throw one in as a part of my audition. I've always taken great satisfaction and comfort in being a steady performer on the air, a tour guide for the viewer, if you will.

I got my audition off to a good start and was able to generate momentum. I later learned one of the other candidates was so unnerved by the process he asked for a "do-over" about two minutes into his run. Kiss...of...*death*.

It was an odd feeling—and I can see how a re-do would have been a tempting proposition—not being able to survey the playing landscape. Much of baseball is about anticipation, not only in advance of a game, but preceding every pitch. A great deal of information is communicated by the positioning of defenders or how far a runner takes a lead off base. A good baseball announcer is always analyzing and anticipating. For my audition, I was at the mercy of what was being shown on the monitor in front of me.

At one point Los Angeles sent a pinch-hitter into the on-deck circle. There was a brief shot of the player, but I couldn't see the uniform number or the name on the back of his jersey. Fortunately, I had watched a number of Dodger games the previous season. One of the bonuses of living in L.A. was getting to hear Vin Scully on a regular basis. I tuned into his broadcasts often—either on radio or TV—just to admire his skill. As a result, I knew the Dodgers well enough to recognize Bill Russell and speculate how his at-bat might influence the game.

That little extra insight may have gotten me the job.

After the audition was finished, I told Elliott the experience had been enjoyable on the whole. I recounted my days as a kid practicing in front of the family television, and joked that I hoped it would give me an edge in the selection process.

"I was really impressed with your left-hander in that game," I said to Elliott. "He had the Dodger hitters tied up in knots. I asked your technician how to pronounce his last name and I sure hope he gave me the right information. How did the game end?"

"Kid threw a two-hit shutout," Elliott told me. "We won that game 4-0.

"We got Jimmy Deshaies from the Yankees. We think he'll be a good one."

I caught an early flight back to Los Angeles and arrived home by mid-afternoon. I called Dianne at work and told her things had gone well. With the rest of the day my own, I offered to pick up Allison at school. I was eager to see what my daughter thought about the possibility of another move.

Allison was on the front steps of her school in an intense discourse with a group of girls when I arrived to take her home. She didn't see me in the car, so rather than embarrass her with a honk of the horn, I decided to embarrass her by introducing myself to some of her friends.

She was still dominating the conversation as I approached from behind. When Allison began to notice the strange looks on the faces of her friends, she turned and saw me. My daughter shrieked with delight and rushed up to give me a hug.

We had enrolled her in a private school, so she was dressed in her standard uniform. Admittedly, Dianne and I had become concerned with her evolving fashion sense outside the classroom. Although we tried to tone down her wardrobe a bit, her after-school attire always seemed a little over the top to me. She was spending a lot of time watching something called "MTV" and I wasn't completely on-board with that. Frankly, the changes we thought we were seeing in our daughter were one of the big reasons Dianne and I were hopeful we could leave California.

Allison asked me how things had gone in Houston.

"Pretty good, sweetheart. I have a good feeling about this one."

She introduced me to her friends and when she told them where I'd been and what I'd been doing, none of them seemed too impressed, although they were polite in their indifference.

"So, when will you find out about the job?" Allison inquired. She was nodding her head excitedly.

"I don't know. Soon, I hope."

"Me, too!" she exclaimed. "I sure hope you get the job. I think it would be *great* to live in Texas!"

Behind her, four sets of eyes flew wide open and four jaws dropped to the ground.

"But we don't *want* you to leave, Allison," one of them moaned.

"Yeah, that would be, like, *totally* un-cool," another observed.

"*Totally*," her two remaining friends echoed. I could tell my baby was on the precipice of becoming a "Valley Girl."

Three weeks later, Art Elliott called and offered me the job. Dick Wagner phoned soon after and said he was pleased with the opportunity to be working with me again.

The Browns were heading back to Texas.

***

The Concord and I made the long drive east—nearly 1600 miles—to start my new job. I was ecstatic to be back in baseball and hoped I could drive as far as El Paso my first day on the road. In mapping my route, I was surprised to learn the distance from Los Angeles to El Paso was about the same as from El Paso to Houston. Texas was a pretty big place.

If you've never driven through far West Texas, the landscape there is almost other-worldly. The Concord seemed to balk at the notion of tackling the high desert and the car stalled on the second day of the trip about three-and-a-half hours east of El Paso. Miraculously, I was able to coax the vehicle into a service station near the town of Fort Stockton. Despite the fact it was still early on a Sunday morning and the station was closed, an attendant magically appeared. He quickly diagnosed the problem as a minor one and soon completed the repair.

While he tinkered with the engine, the two of us engaged in small talk. He told me he lived in a trailer behind the station and regularly tended to travelers in need. After he finished, he wrote up a bill and handed it to me.

"This amount doesn't seem right," I said. "It looks like you've only charged me for the parts. What about labor?"

"I'm a Christian man," he replied, "and I do my best to observe the Sabbath. I do okay with this job and I'm happy to help people. But, since the Lord prefers for me not to work on Sunday, I really can't take your money for my time."

And then, in the next breath, he asked, "Have you received Jesus Christ as your Lord and Savior?"

I told him I had.

The Concord got me safely to Houston and remained a part of our family for another six years or so. I'll admit it was a somewhat emotional day when we finally traded her in. While I felt a strong attachment to the car—sort of a "man's-best-friend" kind of relationship—the wagon eventually became a bit of an embarrassment to Dianne. In time, the roof liner began to sag. I used map pins to keep the fabric out of my eyes and never bothered to get it replaced. Finally, after giving Astros' shortstop Craig Reynolds a ride home—and telling Dianne about it—my wife put her foot down. Soon thereafter, I parted ways with my motorized *kemo sabe*.

We've managed to keep from putting quite so many years or miles on our cars since then and I don't get nearly as attached to them as I used to.

***

176

I hit the ground running in Houston and as the club prepared for spring training, the vice president of marketing Ted Haracz arranged a meeting with the broadcast crew. There were five of us: Larry Dierker, Milo Hamilton, Bill Worrell, Jerry Trupiano, and me.

Gene Elston's dismissal was still a source of considerable discussion around town and I expected to catch some of that flak. I had been told the move was made in an attempt to find a "better chemistry" among the announcers. A cohesive mix would be important given Haracz's plans for the upcoming season.

Haracz intended to co-mingle his radio and television crews. Milo as the new lead announcer, would do innings one through three and seven through nine on radio. I would call those same six frames on television. In the fourth, in an increasingly popular trend among ball clubs at the time, Milo and I would switch seats. Milo would step into the TV booth, while I would call the middle three innings on radio.

While I would be working with Milo, technically, I would never work *with* Milo. Had that arrangement been put into place before my arrival, Elston and Hamilton—two broadcasting titans and eventual members of the broadcasting wing of the Baseball Hall of Fame—might have been able to coexist.

And my move to Houston might never have happened.

Upon Hamilton's arrival in 1985, he and Elston had a difficult time meshing styles and personalities. Milo, as fans know, is a "rah-rah" guy. Elston was not. Since Elston was the lead announcer, he set the tone for the broadcasts. His demeanor was more casual and conversational than Milo's, who can make a routine single to right field sound like the second coming...of Babe Ruth.

Neither Elston nor Hamilton were willing to change his way, nor, frankly, should either have been asked to do so. Had their roles, or styles, been reversed—with a high-energy guy opening and closing the game—they might have had a chance to click. Instead, their pairing proved awkward and the situation became a tenuous one for both. Something had to give. Elston became the odd man out.

More changes to the team's broadcasts were in store, which was why Haracz wanted to meet. In a figurative game of musical chairs, yet another familiar voice would soon depart the club.

Dierker, Worrell, and Trupiano would be the broadcast analysts, or "color commentators" as they're known in the business. As a former player, Dierker was comfortable in that role, but Worrell and Trupiano were also talented play-by-play guys. Trupiano had served the club as an able utility man in the booth, working two innings of radio play-by-play on road games. He was better known to local listeners for his play-by-play assignments with the football Oilers, basketball Rockets, and hockey Aeros. He was a diligent and hard-working sportscaster.

Bill Worrell had been added to the Astros telecasts the previous season. He played baseball at the University of Houston and upon graduation landed a job at KPRC-TV, where in four short years he was elevated to sports director of the NBC affiliate. He helped launch HSE in Houston in early 1983, and then joined both the Astros and Rockets crews in 1986. He's been the television voice of the city's NBA team ever since.

Once Haracz explained the new plan, silence filled the room. Trupiano's play-by-play duties had been eliminated and he was obviously unhappy about the decision. To his credit, he did a good job of keeping his feelings in check. I feared replacing Elston *and* taking Trupiano's innings would make me the bad guy before anyone had the opportunity to get acquainted with me. Already my new job seemed to be off to a rocky start.

Upon the Astros arrival at their spring-training complex in Cocoa Beach, Florida, Trupiano met with Wagner to plead his case. Wagner listened, but told Jerry the team was committed to the new broadcasting assignments. Wagner emphasized that Trupiano was still important in the team's plans, but Jerry had taken the position hoping to build upon his resume as the city's most versatile sportscaster. Instead of getting more air time, he would be getting less. After he and Wagner talked, Jerry resigned.

Catching up with Trupiano before he left camp, I expressed my regret at how things had worked out. He was cordial and knew I wasn't to blame. Fortunately, he stayed plenty busy. He continued to call Oilers and Southwest Conference football games and then, before the 1989 season, he landed a job with the Expos. In 1993 he moved to Boston and was a member of the Red Sox broadcast crew through the 2006 season.

***

I loved being back in baseball and working with a team of great broadcast professionals. I was doing far more games—about 150 a year—than I ever had in Cincinnati. And, I enjoyed the radio side of the equation. Television guys have to be careful not to say too much during a broadcast since the viewer can see the action. That's not the case in radio.

Although I didn't mention it at the time, I thought rotating announcers was a terrible idea. With less than ninety seconds to pick up our things, walk down the hallway, and switch seats, neither Milo nor I had any idea what the other had already talked about to the previous audience. We regularly repeated ourselves and that had to grate on truly discerning listeners and viewers. Both broadcasts suffered from a lack of continuity our fans deserved, but that's the way we did things for ten years.

The team's fast start in '87 gave me an opportunity to get comfortable in my new job. Unfortunately, the good times did not last. The team eventually settled into mediocrity and the philosophical differences between Wagner and manager Hal Lanier became pronounced. As the season progressed, the whole team seemed to be on pins and needles. And to make matters worse, owner John McMullen really didn't seem to care.

Hofheinz had turned out to be a better visionary than club owner and in 1975 he lost the team to creditors. McMullen purchased the franchise four years later. A limited partner in the New York Yankees until he bought the Astros, McMullen was quickly rewarded with Houston's first division title in 1980. Soon, though, his interest in the team began to wane with his purchase of the NHL's Denver franchise in 1982. He promptly moved that club to his home state of New Jersey and soon the Devils seemed to occupy most of his attention. Although the Astros won another division crown in 1986, by then McMullen had become an absentee owner—in the worst sense of the word.

By the end of the '87 season, the team had fallen twenty games in the standings from the year before. Wagner resigned as GM, citing an untenable working relationship with his owner as the reason for his departure. Lanier lasted just one more year as the manager, and what followed were some lean times.

Upon our move to Houston, Dianne and I decided to plant our roots firmly in the Texas soil. We once again became home owners, but as the '87 campaign played out and the front-office drama began to unfold, I started to question whether or not the purchase of a house had been a good idea.

To make matters worse, shortly after Dianne and Allison moved to town they were involved in a car wreck. The girls had dropped me off at the Astrodome in advance of a road trip and on their way home were pancaked on the freeway between two eighteen-wheelers. Miraculously, they escaped serious injury, although Dianne suffered a detached retina in the accident. Our second car was totaled.

Thank goodness we still had the Concord to keep us going. And as 1987 came to an end, I wondered how many more miles I might have to drive before landing in a place of personal contentment and professional satisfaction.

CHAPTER 16
Brethren

I'm sure it must be annoying when broadcasters go to extreme lengths *not* to give up on their teams. After all, numbers don't lie and no sport is more entrenched in the sanctity of numbers than baseball.

Individual success in baseball is ritualistically determined by averages and probabilities. Team success—or failure—is based on a more fundamental arithmetic.

Over the course of an entire losing season, like the 1982 Reds' and 2011 Astros' 100-loss campaigns, keeping the excitement alive can be a difficult challenge for an announcer. But woe to the play-by-play man or woman who assumes the outcome of a single game has been determined before the final out is made.

Baseball miracles do happen. But by "miracle," I'm not referring to the Biblical kind. I'm pretty certain God doesn't favor one team or player over another. I believe in the power of prayer, but not so much when it comes to seeking divine intervention with runners on second and third.

Which brings me to Tim Tebow.

Yes, of course I realize Tebow is a quarterback and not a third baseman, but I'd like to make a quick observation about the phenomenon of "Tebow-mania."

I don't think God had anything more to do with Tim Tebow's comeback victories for the 2011 Denver Broncos than he did with the young quarterback's sub-standard play that same season. By all accounts, Tebow has brought the Good Word to millions of people. I'd seen athletes "tebow"— the act of genuflecting on one knee with head bowed to fist— or something like it, plenty of times before the former Heisman Trophy-winner came along. I suspect Tebow's on-field prayers are less about personal accomplishment or vanquishing foes than simply giving praise and thanksgiving to his Creator. He seems to be the real deal in that regard.

I applaud Tebow and wish him well in New York. But Tebow is not alone as an athlete of strong spiritual conviction. Others, like Kurt Warner, Curt Schilling, Craig Reynolds, Lance Berkman, Albert Pujols, and Zach Johnson also come to mind.

It's no secret in Houston that I'm a man of faith. I get requests on a regular basis to speak in front of church groups. During the off-season I accept as many of those invitations as possible.

The great Negro League player Buck O'Neill drew similarities between baseball and religion. Of baseball, he said, "It taught me and it teaches everyone else to live by the rules, to abide by the rules." In addition, baseball is a sacrificial game. With the sacrifice bunt and the hit-and-run, players give up their own chance at individual glory for the greater good of the team.

Of course, there has been no greater sacrifice for mankind than that which took place on the cross at Golgotha.

The Bible says "to whom much is given, much is expected," and not to sound blasphemous here, but when a team is staked to an eleven-run lead after just three innings of play, what normally follows is the expectation of easy victory.

Washington Post sports columnist Tom Boswell writes: "Baseball is a religion that worships the obvious and gives thanks that things are exactly as they seem. Instead of celebrating mysteries, baseball rejoices in the absence of mysteries." I must disagree with my esteemed colleague.

How else would you explain what happened on the night of July 18, 1994?

By the time Milo and I switched broadcasts during the opener of the mid-summer series between the Astros and the Cardinals, the outcome of the game seemed no longer in doubt. Houston starter Brian Williams was shelled for six runs in just an inning and two thirds of work. Reliever Tom Edens was ripped for five more runs in his one and one-third innings on the mound. As I settled into the radio booth to start off the fourth inning of play, the Astrodome scoreboard read: St. Louis 11, Houston 0.

With a game of this nature, broadcasters have to search for the more personal story lines to keep things interesting for the audience. A struggling reliever might find his good stuff or a reserve infielder could come up with a great defensive play. These are the sorts of things which can provide highlights during what we in the business like to call "garbage time."

When Dave Veres gave up a leadoff double to start the fourth, I feared St. Louis was about to expand on its lead. But Veres settled down and retired the Cardinals without giving up another run, an accomplishment which elicited a sustained-yet-somewhat-mocking cheer from the Houston crowd. In the bottom of the inning, the Astros finally touched St. Louis starter Allen Watson for two runs.

Young lefty Mike Hampton, not yet the $100-million starter he would later become, pitched the Astros fifth and sixth, retiring all six batters he faced. Meanwhile, Houston added two more runs in the fifth to cut the Cardinals lead to 11-4, prompting this on-air exchange between Larry Dierker and me:

> Bill Brown: *"If a huge comeback is possible for the Astros today, the relief pitching is setting a nice tone and the offense has gotten into the game."*
>
> Larry Dierker: *"The Cardinals have had a hard time*

stopping teams this year, and their bullpen is suspect."

Those remarks were about as far as we were willing to go to suggest Houston could pull off a comeback of—if you'll pardon the expression—Biblical proportions. The complexion of the game, though, did seem to be changing.

Watson walked leadoff batter Craig Biggio to start the home half of the sixth inning. When Kevin Bass followed with a double, St. Louis manager Joe Torre pulled Watson in favor of reliever Frank Cimorelli. And that's when the floodgates opened. Before the inning was over, the Astros sent seventeen batters to the plate!

In scoring eleven runs in the sixth, Houston managed only seven hits. Four St. Louis pitchers combined to walk five Astros in the inning and also hit a batter. Biggio, Bass, Ken Caminiti, Luis Gonzalez, and James Mouton all reached base. Journeyman outfielder Mike Felder, who answered to "Tiny," hit a two-run triple which was the biggest blow of the frame.

By the time the inning was over, Houston led 15-11 and would go on to win the game 15-12. That comeback remains one for the record books, as the largest in both Astros and National League history.

The next night, St. Louis held on to its double-digit lead, blanking Houston 10-0. As I said, God does not play favorites when it comes to sports.

All in all, 1994 could have been a good year for the Astros, but it turned out to be the most regrettable of seasons for baseball as a whole. Three weeks after its historic comeback, Houston stood just a half game behind Pittsburgh in the newly-created NL Central Division. Then, on August 12, the players went on strike and the rest of the season was cancelled. For the first and only time to date, the World Series wasn't played.

Jeff Bagwell was the National League MVP that year, the first and only time an Astro has won the award. There's a good chance he might not have garnered the honor had the season been allowed to run its course. Bagwell was lost for the year on August 10, suffering a broken hand when hit by an Andy Benes pitch in a game against the Padres. At the time of the strike, San Francisco's Matt Williams had forty-three home runs, well ahead of the pace to break the single-season home-run record. San Diego's Tony Gwynn was batting .394 when the season was called off, otherwise he might have had a shot to become baseball's first .400 hitter in more than fifty years.

Ken Griffey, Jr., who had forty home runs at the time of the strike, put it best: "We picked a bad season to have a good year."

Actually, Griffey may have "misremembered," or chosen to use the "royal 'we'" in making that comment. At the time of the strike, Seattle had a record of 49-63. Remarkably, the Mariners were just two games off their division lead. Had the Astros been in the AL West *that* year, they would have held a 13-1/2 game advantage at the time of the strike.

Instead, baseball "was without form, and void, and darkness was on the face of the deep" until the walkout was finally settled on April 2 the following year.

***

I grew up a Methodist and as a boy I attended First United Methodist Church in downtown Sedalia. My father taught a Sunday school class there on the legal aspects of the trial of Jesus Christ. Members of the congregation raved about it, but I was too young to be in the know. Dianne and her family were members of the nearby Calvary Episcopal Church, which is where she and I were married.

While there may be no atheists in foxholes, I sort of got out of the habit of going to church while in Vietnam. Not until after Allison was born did Dianne and I decide again to make church-going a regular part of our lives.

Thanks to a recommendation by one of my tennis buddies, Associated Press sportswriter John Chace, the Browns began attending White Oak Christian Church on Cincinnati's northwest side. Dianne and I enjoyed the church's vibrant spirit and sense of community. On March 19, 1978, Dianne and I were baptized together there. Five years later we baptized Allison at the same church. She reflects on that time:

> *"My dad's faith is very firm and I've often seen him moved by a sermon or worship song.*
>
> *"I knew my parents had been baptized as children, but I think it says a lot about both of them that they went through the process of baptism by immersion as adults. Even though I was just a child at the time, I still remember some of the family discussions we had about what baptism really meant. At first I think Dad was sort of against the idea. He thought it seemed to point toward 'works' rather than 'faith.'*
>
> *"One of their friends, Mike Stohler, finally convinced them to go through the immersion process. I was only four years old at the time and I can't honestly say I remember the event. But when it came time for my own baptism, I was extremely excited.*
>
> *"I was scheduled to be baptized on Easter Sunday, but Mom got sick that day. I begged and pleaded with her to let me go on with the baptism as planned, but Mom would have none of it. So, I was baptized the next Sunday and the best part about the experience was that I was baptized by my dad.*
>
> *"Ours was the first father-daughter baptism in the church's history. After it was over and we were leaving the baptistery, I remember seeing several of the choir members in tears. It was a very touching moment and an unforgettable experience for both Dad and me."*

White Oak was a non-denominational church and we hated leaving there when we moved to Pittsburgh, but we took great delight in returning a year later. The Browns believe the church experience supersedes denominational preference. We've run the gamut over the years. I've even attended mass with Jim Deshaies a few times when the ball club has been on the road.

Presently, Dianne and I attend Jersey Village Baptist Church. I've been approached about becoming a deacon, but as long as I spend my summers also attending services at the "church of baseball" (as the Annie Savoy character called it in the movie *Bull Durham*), I can't give that important ministerial duty the attention it deserves. Hopefully, I will be able to someday.

***

Dianne and I have church friends, baseball friends, friends who are neighbors, and long-distance friends with whom we've kept in touch through the years. As we moved from city to city, it seemed we were always "adopted" into families which helped to smooth the transitions. Friendship and fellowship have been critical to our lives.

Upon our arrival in Cincinnati, Gene and Peggy Hille befriended us. We had Thanksgiving dinner in their home every year. In Houston, Dan and Sue Walsh have done the same thing and we feel as if we're a part of their immediate family.

Interestingly, two members of my high school graduating class are now living in Houston. I get to see or talk to Barry Wallace and Jim Johnson on a fairly regular basis. Unlike me, they were two of the top athletes in our school. In 2011, our high school's former football coach, Earl Finley, came to Houston to compete in the Senior Olympics. Barry and Jim had kept in touch with Coach Finley through the years and the four of us met for dinner one night. We mostly reminisced about the "good old days." Well, the three of them reminisced. I listened, reflected, and laughed. It was a special occasion.

In my baseball travels I've also been able to reconnect with other old friends and classmates from Sedalia. In advance of one of our high school reunions, a committee of volunteers compiled a list of contact information which has enabled me to touch base with old acquaintances from coast to coast. In Washington, D.C., I'll call Bill Post and we'll get together for lunch before a Nationals' game. In Atlanta, Chuck France and his wife are usually up for a get-together when the Astros are in town to play the Braves.

Tony Monsees is a realtor still living in Sedalia, but I occasionally see him in St. Louis or when Dianne and I go back to Sedalia to visit her mother. My sister Jebby and her husband Steve live in Denver and enjoy watching the Rockies play, so, we're able to get together every time the Astros venture to the Mile-High City.

In San Francisco, Randy and Mary Short like to have lunch at various places in the Bay Area. We marvel at how far we've come in life, from Sedalia to the cozy atmosphere of a Sausalito cafe.

Speaking of San Francisco, over the years I've seen four fair balls hit into the water beyond the right field concourse at AT&T Park. More significantly, at least on a personal level, I've actually toured "McCovey Cove."

That part of San Francisco Bay just outside the Giants' home field is unofficially named for the team's Hall-of-Fame first baseman Willie McCovey, also a member of baseball's elite 500-home-run club. As Barry Bonds chased the single-season home-run record in 2001, he reached McCovey Cove eleven times. Bonds is the only player to deposit two home runs into the water in the same game.

Bill Brown

As Bonds neared Mark McGwire's record, seeing the Cove filled with small water craft, mostly kayakers, became a common sight. On the afternoon of September 29, 2011, Bonds dropped his 69th homer into the murky deep. Since baseballs are buoyant, it floated to the surface. The ensuing scene rivaled the Battle of Midway as a flotilla of seagoing vessels fought for position and possession of the historic ball.

A few years ago, I was a pretty avid kayaker myself. I owned a kayak and enjoyed exploring rivers and bayous throughout the Houston area. When the Giants moved into their new stadium in 2000, I vowed I would someday test the waters outside the ballpark. That day came early in the 2003 season.

Catching a late afternoon flight from Houston, we arrived in San Francisco shortly after sunset on a Sunday to open a three-game series with the Giants the next day. The Astros had won seven of their first nine and began play on April 14 with a half-game lead in the NL Central Division. The team would remain competitive for the rest of the season.

After a good winter of kayaking and feeling fit and confident, I decided to get my closer look at McCovey Cove. The team hotel was a short distance from the ballpark and a kayak rental establishment was just north of the Giants' home field. Since it was a Monday, the South Beach area was quiet and as I recall, I might have been the only kayaker out that particular day. Reversing my usual routine, I decided to have an early lunch and then follow that with my workout—on the waters of San Francisco Bay.

The attendant helped me select a kayak and eager to begin the adventure, I hopped into the craft. I received pre-launch instructions—the do's and don'ts of water safety—and may not have paid as much attention as I should have. Soon, I was pushed into the cold waters of the bay and my paddling journey began.

I headed south toward the ball field and soon found myself in McCovey Cove. I tried to imagine what it might take to scramble for a home run ball and wondered how often a boater flipped his kayak in pursuit of a memento. Given the chill of the bay waters, I was pleased I would be spending my time during the game that night in the press box rather than McCovey Cove.

Paddling further south for a time, I then doubled back and headed northward to get a close-up look at the San Francisco-Oakland Bay Bridge.

As I made my way back by the kayak shop, the proprietor saw me and gave a friendly wave. "How's it going?" he shouted out. "Lovin' it," I replied. He turned his attention to other things.

Approaching the bridge, I could hear the rumble of cars from the span's lower deck. The water became a bit more choppy, but I continued along and considered it an achievement as I made my way into the shadow of the immense roadway. I remember reading somewhere that at the peak of construction in the 1930s, the bridge project consumed six percent of America's total steel output.

Coming out from under the bridge, I veered onto a more northwesterly heading. One of my favorite places in San Francisco—the Embarcadero—came into view. In making the turn from the east side of the city, the waters became more difficult to maneuver. But as the sights, sounds, and smells of San Francisco filled my senses, I caught a rush of adrenalin, and wound up paddling all the way to Fisherman's Wharf. I glanced at my watch and realized I had already exhausted my one-hour rental time. I needed to turn back.

When I did, I ventured into a whole new world of pain. Unknowingly, I had paddled into a series of crosscurrents which were much stronger than I had realized. In fact, they were so strong on the return trip, I found myself making little headway. The faster I paddled the slower I went. Panic set in for a time and I soon was exhausted. I'd planned to take a short nap before the game, but as my struggles continued, I realized that luxury would have to be struck from my afternoon itinerary.

I finally made it back to the kayak-rental pier a few minutes after four. I'd been on the water for close to two-and-a-half hours and I was exhausted. At first the proprietor good-naturedly kidded with me about my tardiness since it meant more money in his pocket. His mood quickly changed when I innocently told him how far I had gone. Apparently, the bridge area and points beyond were strictly off limits due to safety and liability concerns. He had covered these restrictions in his dos and don'ts and, as he pointed out, I'd even signed a form acknowledging I would abide by the rules.

Paying my overage charges, I gave the attendant a sizable gratuity as an apology for my venture into troubled waters. By the time I got back to the hotel, Deshaies was waiting for me in the lobby. I had told Jim of my plans for the afternoon and once he saw me drag in he broke out in laughter. I told him I felt worse than I looked and encouraged him to head over to the ballpark without me.

"I'll be right behind you," I said unconvincingly.

Actually I made it to the stadium in plenty of time and called a 4-2 Giants win. In the second inning, Bonds homered into McCovey Cove off Houston pitcher Wade Miller. Bonds' last blast into the Bay came on August 8, 2007, his final season before legal issues stemming from incessant accusations of steroid use ended his career. That homer came off Tim Redding of the Washington Nationals. Redding, by the way, was a member of the Astros' starting rotation in 2003.

In all, Barry Bonds hit 35 home runs into McCovey Cove. One Houston player has reached the watery abyss at the time of this writing—Lance Berkman. He did it on May 15, 2008, off Giants pitcher Vinnie Chulk.

***

*"There is no friend like an old friend
who has shared our morning days,
no greeting like his welcome,
no homage like his praise."*

--Oliver Wendell Holmes, Sr.

One of my good friends in Cincinnati was Roy Mays, a minister and fierce fellow combatant on the tennis court. He made a positive impact on the lives of all his friends before he died of cancer years ago. Roy was one of those rare individuals who lived his life with zest and never stopped helping others. John Chace wrote for both the AP and the *Cincinnati Enquirer* before taking his journalistic talents to Miami where he basks in retirement joy these days. He not only helped Dianne and me find a great church, he remains a great friend to us both.

Closer to home, Tal Smith was the general manager of the Astros when I first met him in 1980. Under his watch, the Astros were on the way to their first division title and I had Tal on the Reds' pregame show that year. After I moved to Houston and he returned to the Astros franchise in 1994, Tal and I became good friends.

Tal is unquestionably one of the brightest men in baseball. He remembers names and details dating back to his youth in Framingham, Massachusetts. After graduating from Duke University and spending a brief period of time as a sportswriter, Tal got his break when he joined the staff of general manager Gabe Paul in Cincinnati. Paul not only brought Gene Elston to Texas when he assumed the helm of the new Houston franchise in 1960, he brought young "Talbot" with him, too. Tal had various responsibilities with the ball club in its earliest days, but perhaps his biggest contribution was his work with Judge Hofheinz in the development of the Harris County Domed Stadium.

After twelve seasons in Houston, Tal left to serve under Paul in the New York Yankees' front office. His arrival coincided with that of George Steinbrenner and he helped rebuild the Yankees into a powerhouse. Tal returned to Houston in 1975 when he was named general manager of the club. He proved instrumental in convincing John McMullen to sell his shares of Yankees stock and buy the Astros in 1979. A year later, in a move which shocked the baseball world, McMullen fired Smith following the Astros' 1980 West Division championship season. Tal stayed in Houston and started a consulting company, advising teams on salary arbitration cases. His firm's record through the years has been very good.

Tal returned to the Astros in 1994, shortly after Drayton McLane bought the team. His tenure as president of baseball operations continued until McLane sold the club to its current owner Jim Crane. Tal's third stint with the Astros ended in the winter of 2011.

One of Tal's neighbors in Houston is also a great friend. Gerry Hunsicker has worked in the Tampa Bay Rays' front office for several years and has been instrumental in elevating the team from the depths of its long-maligned past into its current status of annual contender. Hunsicker and Rays GM Andrew Friedman—a Houston native—have managed to stay competitive with both the Yankees and the Red Sox despite a payroll discrepancy of well over $100 million.

Gerry is one of the class acts in all of baseball. He served as the Astros GM from 1995 to 2004 and built the team which reached the World Series in 2005. Those years were heady times for the organization and all of us regretted that Gerry wasn't there to see the club finally reach the Fall Classic.

I've already talked briefly about the two former Astros pitching standouts who have been my partners in the broadcast booth: Larry Dierker and Jim Deshaies. You'll read more about them—and from them—in the pages to come.

I've formed solid friendships with several other former Astros players, too. I have a ton of respect for Craig Biggio, Jeff Bagwell, Terry Puhl, and Craig Reynolds. All four were outstanding players and all four continue to make important contributions today. Biggio and Bagwell remain with the Astros in advisory capacities.

Terry Puhl is the baseball coach at the University of Houston-Victoria. A native of Melville, Saskatchewan, Terry also coached the Canadian national team at the 2008 Beijing Olympic Games.

Craig Reynolds today serves as teaching pastor at Second Baptist Church's North Campus in Kingwood, Texas. I'm fairly certain he and Dierker are the only ones in my circle of local baseball friends who ever rode in the AMC Concord, sagging headliner or not.

Even though Major League Baseball has become a multi-billion-dollar business, it still fosters fraternities of caring and considerate human beings. That point was driven home in early 2012 when the Astros' organization scrambled to put together a retirement party for the team's longtime equipment manager Dennis Liborio.

Dennis retired after more than thirty years on the job. His friends at Damian's Cucina Italiana restaurant in Houston decided to throw him a dinner party to honor his years of service, not only to the ball club, but also to the local Italian community. Liborio is intensely passionate about his heritage. Thanks to Damian's a scholarship in Dennis's name has been set up with the Texas Italian-American Sports Foundation.

By the time the decision was made to honor Liborio, we had only two weeks to get invitations out and plan the party. Despite the short notice, the response was tremendous. Nolan and Ruth Ryan arranged for a private plane to fly them in from the Dallas area where Nolan is president of the Texas

Rangers. They also brought team executive Rob Matwick and coach Jackie Moore along. Both Matwick and Moore have ties with the Astros and thus, are friends with Liborio.

Other attendees included former Astros pitcher and team comedian Charley Kerfeld from Seattle and former GM Bill Wood from Comfort, Texas. Umpire Joe West also flew in from Florida to join the gathering.

One of the highlights of the evening was a story West told about an after-game encounter he had with Liborio in Chicago. Apparently Liborio was with Mike Hampton at a bar when West happened to walk in. Joe came up to Liborio and began a conversation, not recognizing Hampton. As was the fashion of the day, Hampton was adorned in an open-colored shirt and sported multiple gold chains. West asked Liborio, "Who's the guy with the Mr. T starter set?"

Hampton overheard the comment and fired back, "Hey, Fatso, why don't you mix in a salad every now and then?"

Liborio turned to Hampton and suggested, "You might want to tone it down a little, Mike. Mr. West here is going to be calling balls and strikes when you pitch at Wrigley Field tomorrow afternoon."

The retirement party was a big success and made for a memorable night for Dennis and his wife Geraldine. Baseball can be a thankless taskmaster at times, but the game creates strong bonds which form special circles of friends. Dianne and I know how fortunate we've been to call Houston home for the past two-and-a-half decades and there's no place we'd rather be.

Working at a job you enjoy is good. Having caring friends is great. Being able to give back to others, though, may be the best feeling of all.

As you read on you'll discover that's one of the reasons I decided to write this book.

CHAPTER 17
Forever Irene

The modern, scientifically-engineered rose, its color vibrant, its long stem striking in a bouquet or vase arrangement, is but a pretender to a certain breed of horticulturalist. The vast majority of roses today bear surprisingly little resemblance to their ancestors. While beautiful of bloom, many species are difficult to grow, finicky in nature, and not particularly suited for the real world.

If these flowers were human, Irene Hunsicker would have had little patience for their kind.

Irene loved roses. So when the *Houston Chronicle* held a contest in late 2008 to name a new strain of what's called an "antique rose," fittingly, Irene was selected to be its namesake. She was the overwhelming pick, based on the efforts of many caring friends who sent in letters of recommendation. As a result, Mike Shoup, the owner of the Antique Rose Emporium in Brenham, Texas, affixed the new sobriquet to his 1663 varietal, a hardy, fragrant, and persistent flower which remains a popular seller.

A rose by any other name would *not* smell as sweet as "Forever Irene."

Irene Hunsicker died of cancer two years later. In her final months, she took care to stop and smell the roses when she could. The rose garden outside the Main Building of the M.D. Anderson Cancer Center in Houston was one of her favorite places. Any time she had a check-up, test, or treatment scheduled, she always tried to take at least a few moments to savor the sweet smell and appealing vista of that special tract.

When owner Drayton McLane hired Gerry Hunsicker to be general manager of the Houston Astros, he didn't realize he was getting a package deal. Irene, in her own right, was a force with which to be reckoned. She knew no strangers, took no prisoners, and brought numerous ideas to the organization. When the going got tough, "Attila"—as she liked to call herself—got going.

She championed local causes. She organized the players' wives into a meaningful benevolent entity. She made friends, lots of friends. She raised an extraordinary daughter, Kelly.

Meanwhile, her husband was building a pretty good ball club.

Just two seasons after replacing Bob Watson as Astros GM, Hunsicker and the team began a string of four divisional championships in five years. Under Gerry's watch, Houston increased attendance each of its last four years in the Astrodome, then moved into a new downtown stadium called Enron Field. The good times continued. If not for the Atlanta Braves, the Astros easily could have been the dominant team in the National League.

Only Gerry, Kelly, and Irene's inner circle of family and friends knew of her physical struggles through the years. Plagued with allergies and asthma since childhood, Irene later also suffered immune system disorders, heart problems, and chronic joint pain. She probably should have gone on the disabled list numerous times, but Irene wasn't one to experience life from the sidelines.

Then, sadly—and almost inevitably—the unthinkable occurred. Irene took ill in the Astrodome shortly after the conclusion of the Astros' final regular season game. She was rushed to the hospital and a series of tests were performed. Within days she got the sobering news: Irene had cancer.

The nurse had become the patient.

***

Irene Henry grew up in the small community of Collegeville, Pennsylvania, not yet the thriving suburb of Philadelphia that it is today. There she met Gerry Hunsicker and their lives became permanently entwined as sweethearts in the eighth grade. After high school, Gerry played baseball at St. Joseph University in Philadelphia. Irene studied at the nearby Lankenau Hospital School of Nursing. At an early age, Irene knew she wanted to help people and she found healthcare to be an ideal pursuit.

Upon Gerry's graduation, the couple married and moved to Miami where he became an assistant baseball coach at Florida International University. Irene worked in a local hospital and the young couple thrived. Gerry earned his master's degree at FIU and in 1978 landed his first job in the big leagues working in the Astros' front office for general manager Tal Smith.

The move to Texas enabled Irene to advance her own education. She enrolled at the University of Texas Medical Branch School of Nursing in Galveston, and earned her graduate degree in nurse administration. At the same time, she held down a full-time job as an emergency room nurse, and volunteered in the infirmary on game days at the Astrodome.

Nursing is a rewarding but sometimes thankless job. Good nurses have to be tough customers because they face nothing but sickness and disease day and night. I'm a lousy patient, as Dianne will attest. I can't imagine putting up with a full ward of people like me, but Irene did. Irene expected her patients to get well. She almost willed them to good health.

Although the Hunsickers left Houston when Gerry became director of minor league operations for the New York Mets, by the time Irene was diagnosed with uterine cancer, she and her family were back in Houston, comfortably ensconced among friends and admirers and within an easy drive to the M.D. Anderson Cancer Center which would be at the forefront of Irene's care for the rest of her life.

Given her years as a nurse, Irene knew illness well. She always considered it to be a bitter rival; her mission to conquer it on her patients' behalf. She began her own personal battle in much the same way. When she started her initial rounds of chemotherapy, she kicked things off with a "mango tango" party. As her health improved, she became a dynamic advocate for others. She raised money for the hospital's research arm. And, given her powers of persuasion, oh how Irene could raise money.

Seeing an opportunity to use the Astros' name to fight cancer, Irene mobilized the Astros Wives Organization into a fund-raising machine. Along with Jennifer Everett, Christi Ensberg, and several others, Irene resurrected a past fan favorite: a wives' cookbook. It was called *From Home Plate to Your Plate* and upon its release in 2004, the book proved a big local hit. Sales of the book totaled more than $160,000. Proceeds benefitted M.D. Anderson's research initiatives.

Technically, Irene's cancer never went into complete remission. Her chronic immune system issues worked against her doctor's treatments. She did bounce back from her initial diagnosis, but the cancer was a formidable foe. She took much comfort from the Astros' success on the field.

In 2004, Houston reached the playoffs as the National League Wild Card qualifier. The team won its first-ever post-season series with a divisional round victory over the Braves. In the National League Championship Series, Houston reached a seventh-and-decisive game to quality for the World Series. But the win—at least in '04—never came.

The team seemed poised for more seasons of championship play. Houston fans eagerly awaited "next year" and the 2005 campaign did not disappoint as the Astros won their first National League pennant.

Sadly, Gerry and Irene Hunsicker were not a part of that ride.

Hunsicker's sudden departure at the end of the 2004 season left the Astros' organization in a temporary state of disarray. Gerry and owner Drayton McLane are both driven men and during their time together in Houston, they often seemed to be of contrary opinions. Although Hunsicker left Houston with a year remaining on his contract, there was a silver lining to the shakeup. Gerry and Irene had the chance to spend more time together and they made the most of the opportunity.

The two traveled extensively, as much as Irene's health would allow. By this time Gerry was an investor in a horse farm and Irene loved to be around the majestic animals. The Hunsickers kept their home base in Houston, enabling Irene to stay close to valued friends as well as her medical team. She also spent as much time in her garden as her health allowed.

Irene inherited her love of plants and flowers from her mother Jean. Throughout her married life, indoor plants— when the Hunsickers were young and just getting started— and later outdoor gardens of various size and complexity, kept Irene busy when Gerry was out of town. She came close to earning certification as a Master Gardener.

A year after leaving the Astros, Gerry was named a senior vice president for the Tampa Bay Devil Rays. Irene's health was sufficiently improved for him to return to the game, although Gerry told friends his wife was tired of having him underfoot.

As Christmas approached, the Hunsicker family had much for which to be thankful. Irene's iron will served to counterbalance her physical problems and she was having more good days than bad. People in the know gave Gerry much credit for the Astros' success in 2005. All in all, the year was filled with many figurative roses and the Hunsickers did their best to stop and smell every one of them.

About this time, Irene and her daughter Kelly began a blog which enabled family, friends, and an ever-growing legion of admirers to keep close tabs on her condition. Irene knew staying on top of her disease meant getting all her worries, concerns, and fears into the open. Her blog helped do that.

First Post
Posted by Irene Hunsicker on January 15, 2006 at 9:37 AM

Didn't get much sleep in the hospital last week. I am trying to use every modality from relaxation techniques that I used when I taught Lamaze. Laughing will increase my t-cells so I intend to laugh my way through this crappy disease. Some of you may not know I had a nickname in nursing school. My friends said they liked me in the dorms but didn't necessarily like working with me and dubbed me Attila the Hun. I am back in Attila the Hun mode and out to kill those cancer cells. Will give you an update after I have my toxic juice (chemo). I will be an inpatient at MD Anderson. Love, Attila.

B-cells produce natural antibodies which help the human body ward off potentially harmful invaders. T-cells are a form of white blood cells which are the body's first line of internal defense. Irene's newly-diagnosed Non-Hodgkin lymphoma involved the malfunction of both sets of cells, a rare occurrence with a poor prognosis.

One of Irene's closest friends was Jonnie Smith, wife of Tal Smith. Tal hired Gerry to work with the Astros on two separate occasions and the two families spent considerable time together. Jonnie says Irene was constantly on the lookout for new medicine and new medical techniques to fight her disease.

"At her sickest, I used to cook meals for Irene," Jonnie says. "She and Gerry lived just around the corner from Tal and me. She and I shared a lot: triumphs, heartaches, even a housekeeper.

"Long before her cancer, Irene was extremely well-read when it came to advancements in the treatment of disease. After she got sick, she once told me she had learned that a certain kind of dietary fibre had been proven to boost the immune system. She asked me to look up recipes high in that form of roughage. What I fixed might not always have tasted very good, but Irene was determined to do everything in her power to ward off her disease."

Jonnie said Irene also believed in the power of prayer. Throughout her twelve-year fight with cancer, doctors were continually amazed at her series of turnarounds. Prayer gave Irene both relief and hope.

"IN HIS GRIP"-----REMISSION
Posted by Irene Hunsicker on April 10, 2006 at 9:02 PM

Today is one of the best days of my life!!! My testing from last week came in today. Everything reveals that I am in remission from both of my cancers. My Doctor looked stunned...then we hugged each other. What a testimony to Easter Week that I have been given this miracle. Yes, I am totally attributing this to the power of God through caring friends, family, and prayer. I feel like the weight of the world has been lifted and we can go forward.

There is some reservation with all this good news. Staying in remission is difficult with this rare cancer. I have an 80 percent chance of having a reoccurrence within 9-12 months...SO PRAYER WARRIORS, IT LOOKS LIKE I NEED TO BE PERMANENTLY ON YOUR PRAYER LIST.

Have a wonderful Easter with your families...love, Irene

Nearly a year later, Irene blogged that she was determined to "giv(e) up chemo for Lent." The disease had returned and was again spreading. Yet, as the year progressed, the cancer again seemed to move toward remission. The Devil Rays gave Gerry time off whenever things got too bad, but in 2007 things were mostly good. Irene began working with a trainer, returned to a regular regimen of tennis, and celebrated her thirty-fifth wedding anniversary.

She even started calling herself the "Energizer Bunny."

Believe the Unbelievable
Posted by Irene Hunsicker on December 18, 2007 at 7:23 PM

'Tis the season to be Jolly...
Because Irene is a medical folly!!!

No...I have not been into Gerry's wine room. I am just high on life! And you would be too if they told you two years ago that your life span was 6 months to two years. Well, it's official. We just broke that dastardly milestone. So everything seems like a gift to me! I have had so much support from loving friends, family, and even acquaintances. It's been really an amazing ride.

Another amazing ride took place in 2008 as Gerry's Rays—the team shortened its name trying to cast aside a dismal past—went from "worst to first." Tampa Bay's thirty-one game improvement was one of the biggest swings ever and after knocking off the White Sox and the Red Sox in the American League playoffs, Irene and Gerry finally got their moment in the World Series spotlight. The fact the Rays lost to Philadelphia didn't diminish the experience for Irene one bit.

Happy Thanksgiving
Posted by Irene Hunsicker on November 29, 2008

No we didn't beat the Phillies but they used cruel and unusual weather to get us off our game. But worst to first was an amazing experience. Best we have had in baseball so far. The Rays have been amazingly good to us and signed Gerry to another three years with more focus for him on the farm system.

I was remiss in updating the blog after my colonoscopy for abnormal pet scan. Well, at least I had a good reason. Long story short. I got hives for 8 days from a medicine they gave me for the colonoscopy and was ready for a padded cell. Uncontrollable itching is really an awful experience. It went away and I got cluster migraines for 5 days which I never had before. To say I was cranky, dejected...is an understatement.

But good news was on the horizon.

Merry Christmas & Happy New Year!
Posted by Irene Hunsicker on December 22, 2008 at 1:00 PM

Happy Holidays!

Wow! Did I get the best gift ever. I feel absolutely great! What a special treat to feel good, have energy, stamina, and nothing hurts. I forgot what this feels like.

To top this off, I had a rose named after me. "Forever Irene." It's carefree, no thorns and spicy! It is available by phone or email to the Antique Rose Emporium. Part of the proceeds from each rose will be donated to Dr. Barbara Pro's Research at MD Anderson. I passionately love gardening, so to me this is like getting (an) mvp award at the world series...and a legacy. A naming contest in the Houston Chronicle spurred Diane Henson and Kelly to mobilize into action. Forty friends wrote in letters. I am (indebted) forever for the gift you have given me this holiday.

For the first time she signed her post "Forever Irene." She took a liking to that name.

Sadly, Irene did not live forever. None of us do.

Late in 2010, Irene made her final trip to Florida and went sailing with Gerry. While on the open water, a school of dolphins swam next to their boat and stayed with them for much of the afternoon. Irene was breathless with excitement and saw the pod as a good omen. When they got back to shore, she could barely walk. She asked Gerry if she could sit quietly on the dock while he went to get the car. I can imagine her using that time alone to savor the joy she must have felt that day. Even at the end, she still embraced the blessings in her life.

Like the rest of us who knew Irene, Judy Dierker—wife to Larry—thinks often of her dear departed friend.

"Our strongest connection was our faith," Judy says, "We would bow our heads and pray for each other to have strength, courage, and hope as we each dealt with the hurdles we faced in life. My friendship with Irene formed a tapestry bound together by the many things we shared.

"Her wit, wisdom, and indomitable spirit were gifts I still treasure. Forever Irene was a rose plucked too soon. I miss my friend."

CHAPTER 18
Dome, Sweet Dome

"It's hard not to be romantic about baseball.
This kind of thing, it's fun for the fans.
It sells tickets and hot dogs."

Brad Pitt as "Billy Beane"
from *Moneyball*, the movie

While author Michael Lewis is now best known for the two movies based on his books, *The Blind Side* and *Moneyball*, he is not a sportswriter by training. I'm tempted to suggest that sportswriters require no real training except house training, but the experience of writing this book has given me a new appreciation for the craft of the print journalist. Turns out, it's a lot easier to talk about something than to write about it. I'll keep my day job.

The above quote is not from the real Billy Beane, long-time general manager of the Oakland A's, nor is it attributable to Lewis. Columbia Pictures bought the film rights to the best-selling book in 2004. Stan Chervin wrote the initial treatment which lured Brad Pitt to the project. With Pitt on board, Steven Soderbergh was hired to direct the movie and Chervin was replaced by screenwriter Steve Zaillian, who had won an Academy Award for his work on *Schindler's List*. In 2009, Columbia shut down the project, unhappy with the direction Soderbergh and Zaillian wanted to take the story.

Although not a baseball fan, Brad Pitt is a product of the University of Missouri and so, knows a good thing when he sees it. He tenaciously kept the *Moneyball* project alive and ultimately the movie was given a second life. With only one previous major film credit—*Capote* in 2005—Bennett Miller was hired as the new director. Another Oscar winner, Aaron Sorkin, authored a third version of the script and that's the movie which was made. Chervin, Zaillian, and Sorkin received an Academy Award nomination for Best Adapted Screenplay, but theirs was anything but a tidy and organized collaboration. Feelings got hurt and heads rolled, all for the good of the collective cause.

Such was also the case in the real-life story on which the movie and the book were based.

As a financial writer, Lewis was intrigued by Beane's use of quantitative analysis in the gut-feel world of major league baseball. The subtitle for the book which followed is "The Art of Winning an Unfair Game." "Science" might have been a more accurate description of how Beane achieved his break-through success which has gone on to universally influence the sport. Through principles normally the domain of economics and statistical probability, Beane leveled the playing field between rich teams like the New York Yankees and Boston Red Sox and less-well-financially-endowed small-market clubs like his own Oakland A's.

The 2012 Houston Astros are taking this "Moneyball" approach.

Beane's story, as written by Lewis, is a fascinating one. In both the book and the movie, he gets the lion's share of the credit for the A's 103-win season in 2002 and the record-breaking twenty-game winning streak which propelled the club into the playoffs that year. Cast as a "villain" in the film is Oakland manager Art Howe.

The Howe portrayed by Oscar-winning actor Philip Seymour Hoffman, in no way resembles the Art Howe I know.

The real Howe played for the Pirates, Astros, and Cardinals, and managed the Astros for five years after my arrival in Houston. He was charged with helping to rebuild the club, much as he did later in Oakland.

Howe was already on board as A's manager when Beane was promoted to GM in 1998. A year later, Beane added stat-whiz Paul DePodesta to his staff, and Oakland's fortunes began to turn. In my mind, Howe deserves much credit for those A's teams' success.

Films "based on a true story" often play loose with the facts. While truth can be stranger than fiction, rarely is the unadulterated truth entertaining without a certain degree of "creative license." We've certainly encountered that in the writing of this book.

In talking with Art not too long ago on the Fox Sports Houston postgame set, he told me he was initially asked to play himself in the movie. Apparently Soderbergh planned to use real baseball people to portray minor characters, choosing a "docu-drama" approach to tell the story cinematically. Any time a director chooses to use "real people" instead of actors, problems often ensue. That's probably the reason the production was shut down. When Miller was brought on board to direct, he brought his *Capote* star with him. Hoffman won an Academy Award for his portrayal of author Truman Capote—and he played Howe about as far from his *Capote* character as possible.

In a way, Art should be glad for that small favor.

Howe fears *Moneyball* might hurt his chances for landing another job in baseball. The good news, as I have told him, is that the movie got people talking about him again. In the right situation—as Howe has said himself—I believe Art would make some club an excellent manager and I hope he gets the chance.

I know another baseball story which would make for a pretty entertaining couple of hours at the Cineplex. Although aging and well past the prime of life, the main character remains beloved by many and a symbol of great change in the game of baseball. Producers interested in the project will be encouraged that this well-known icon won't demand a single penny for story rights.

Someday, maybe we'll get to see a movie about the Houston Astrodome. Being romantic about the old girl isn't difficult. And she already has a supporting role to her credit.

***

I got my first glimpse of the Dome in 1970. My employer at the time, WOAI-TV in San Antonio, had acquired a block of tickets to an Astros' game and somehow two wound up in my possession. Dianne and I made the three-and-a-half-hour trip to Houston and I'll never forget my first glimpse of the stadium, sunlight bouncing off of its gleaming acrylic-paneled roof.

Famed Texas novelist Larry McMurtry once said the outside of the Dome looked like "the working end of a deodorant stick." Perhaps.

Today, the Astrodome sits lifeless and appears even more diminished in stature. Reliant Stadium dwarfs the once-famed building. With hard edges and a retractable roof, Reliant seems even to bully its neighbor. Tom Kensler of the *Denver Post* wrote that visitors unaware of its historical significance might mistake the Astrodome as a "glorified tool shed."

If only it still had such a noble purpose.

No one was calling the Harris County Domed Stadium "a tool shed" when it was unveiled to the media on February 8, 1965. More than 200 members of the local and regional press were escorted onto a darkened field. Construction was ongoing as the facility was still a few weeks from its maiden voyage.

Then they turned on the lights.

"Another world" –Lou Maysel, *Austin American*

"Moving into the dome is like going from a tent show into a grand opera house."—Clark Nealon, *Houston Post*

"It just overpowers you"—Johnny Lyons, *Victoria Advocate*

"Alice was right. There is a wonderland."—John Wilson, *Houston Chronicle*

"No team will ever be worthy of this stadium. It's that great."—Mickey Herskowitz, *Houston Post*.

Words failed me the first time I saw the Astrodome, in large part because of the explosion of color inside the stadium. The playing surface—first called "ChemGrass" then later "Astroturf"—was a vivid shade of green. Seating was color-coded by elevation, from the "Lipstick Red" of the field boxes to the golds and bronzes of the upper level seats. The club- and loge-levels and the seats outside the stadium's fifty-three luxury boxes—which became known as "sky boxes" because of their location high above the field—featured darker hues: black, purple, and blue.

Almost anywhere you sat, the seats were plush, wide, and extremely comfortable. I have no recollection of the outcome of the game we saw that day.

On the drive home, I could not stop talking about the experience of watching a baseball game indoors. If someone had told me I would make my debut as a major league broadcaster inside the Astrodome just two years later and then work there full time for another thirteen years, well, I would have had a hard time imagining that scenario. Equally improbable was the stadium one day becoming an antiquated relic.

Houston concluded its thirty-five year Astrodome run with three consecutive divisional championships. The teams' final regular season game there was one for the ages. Yet, even before the franchise moved into a new downtown ballpark, the Dome held a dark secret. The facility had grown decrepit, cramped, and hopelessly outdated.

Today, it's shrouded in darkness—literally—and its future remains unclear.

***

Plans for a domed stadium helped solidify Houston's bid for a National League expansion franchise in 1960. That same year, the Houston Oilers began play in the fledgling American Football League. In a matter of just a few months, the City of Houston became a big league player in two professional sports.

From its beginnings, the Harris County Domed Stadium was intended to be a multi-use arena, shared by baseball and football tenants alike. One of the venue's many innovative design features was its movable blocks of field-level seating. More than 10,000 seats shifted along tracks to accommodate the configuration of both baseball and football fields. Oilers' owner Bud Adams enthusiastically supported construction of the stadium and the plan was for his team to begin play there in 1965.

Adams reneged on his commitment, citing an unfavorable lease agreement with the Houston Sports Authority which oversaw management of the Dome. The Oilers played from '65 to '67 at Rice Stadium before the matter was finally settled. The University of Houston, meanwhile, quickly made the Astrodome its football home and soon the Cougars—playing as an independent—were one of the most prolific offensive teams in college football, destined for admission into the Southwest Conference.

The Astrodome also played host to a number of other notable events.

October 8-17 1965—Over the course of ten days, evangelist Billy Graham drew more than 700,000 people, including President Lyndon Johnson, to his "Crusade for Christ." Graham called the Astrodome "a tribute to the boundless imagination of man."

February 4-6, 1966—"Bloodless" bullfights took place in the Dome despite the objections of the Texas attorney general's office. More than 100,000 people attended the three-day extravaganza.

November 14, 1966—Boxer Muhammad Ali defended his heavyweight championship against Cleveland "Big Cat" Williams in front of a record crowd of more than 34,000. Photographer Neil Leifer rigged a remote-control camera in the Dome's gondola some eighty feet above the ring. Leifer calls his famous overhead shot of Ali moving to a neutral corner with Williams flat on his back "the best picture I ever made." Less than six months later, Ali was arrested in Houston for refusing induction into the U.S. Army.

January 20, 1968—Elvin Hayes scored 39 points to lead the University of Houston basketball team to a 71-69 win over top-ranked UCLA. Hayes out-dueled Bruins All-American Lew Alcindor in the contest which ended UCLA's forty-seven-game winning streak. The game was played in front of a then-record crowd of 52,693.

February 27-March 1, 1970—Elvis Presley attracted more than 200,000 fans to six shows at the Houston Livestock Show and Rodeo.

December 5, 1970—The movie *Brewster McCloud*, about a loner living in a bomb shelter inside the Dome, held its world premiere in Houston. The story's counter-culture themes left many Houstonians perplexed.

January 8, 1971—Daredevil Evel Knievel set a world record jumping his motorcycle over thirteen cars in front of an Astrodome crowd of more than 41,000 people.

September 20, 1973—Billie Jean King defeated Bobby Riggs in the tennis "Battle of the Sexes." The 55-year-old Riggs entered the much ballyhooed event as a five-to-two favorite. The consummate hustler, Riggs purportedly bet against himself and threw the match, losing in straight sets.

June 15, 1976—Heavy rains forced the only rainout in Astrodome history. Flash floods surrounding the stadium area prevent the umpiring crew from getting to the ballpark. After the game was called, Astros and Pirates players dragged picnic tables onto the field to share their pre-game dinner spread with the handful of fans who braved the elements to get to the park that night. Or so the story goes.

November 20, 1978—Rookie running back Earl Campbell ran wild, gaining 199 yards rushing as the Houston Oilers beat the Miami Dolphins. Howard Cosell called the Monday Night Football matchup the greatest game he had ever seen.

October 28, 1981—The Rolling Stones performed before nearly 60,000 people in the largest non-rodeo concert in Houston to that time.

July 25, 1986—Opening ceremonies took place in the Astrodome to launch the U.S. Olympic Festival. The event featured four hundred drill-team members and six hundred fiddlers between the ages of six and nine.

September 25, 1986—Mike Scott's no-hitter against the San Francisco Giants clinched the NL West title for Houston and sealed the NL Cy Young Award for Scott.

October 15, 1986—The New York Mets advanced to

the World Series with a 7-6 sixteen-inning NLCS win over the Astros. The contest was the longest playoff game ever until the Astros and Braves went eighteen innings at Minute Maid Park in 2005.

August 17-20, 1992—The Republican Party held its national convention inside the Dome, forcing the Astros on a record-breaking twenty-six game road trip. Houston did not play a home game from July 27 to August 24. Imagine the clothes a broadcaster would have to pack for an excursion of that duration. Before heading out of town for that trip, Dianne jokingly asked if I would be packing a steamer trunk.

Other interesting and notable events also played out inside the Dome, but the Mets and Astros could fill an entire chapter of great—and curious—Astrodome moments. On August 30, 1999, Edgardo Alfonzo went six for six with three homers and five RBI as New York throttled the Astros 17-1. No comeback for the Good Guys that night and no overtime pay for the guys in the booth.

On April 15, 1968, New York and Houston played twenty-three innings of scoreless baseball. Utility infielder Al Weis' fielding error on a Bob Aspromonte ground ball in the bottom of the 24th inning allowed Norm Miller to score in Houston's 1-0 victory, the longest major league game ever played to an outcome. Fortunately, I was still in college at the time.

And, on April 28, 1965, during the Astros' first homestand in the Dome, New York Met broadcaster Lindsey Nelson stationed himself along a catwalk inside the gondola to call Houston's 12-9 victory. The game lasted almost three-and-a-half hours. I never knew about this stunt while working in the Dome, otherwise, I might have been tempted to try it myself. I've broadcast a couple games from the Crawford Boxes at Minute Maid Park, but honestly, I prefer the comforts of our spot in the press box.

There's just no place like home.

Keep in mind I was a regular visitor to Houston during my days broadcasting Cincinnati games. I always enjoyed working in air-conditioned comfort, and, as I recall, the food in the media dining room, particularly the barbecue chicken, was outstanding.

Before the Dome opened, people wondered if curve balls would break as effectively indoors as outside. That was never an issue. Former Houston pitching great Joe Niekro confounded hitters inside the Astrodome for almost eleven seasons with his knuckleball. Nolan Ryan pitched nine years for the Astros. He threw the fifth of his seven career no-hitters inside the Dome against the Los Angeles Dodgers on September 26, 1981.

Texans are proud of their traditions and Astrodome traditions were plentiful. The original scoreboard stretched 474 feet behind the center field pavilion, contained 1,200 miles of wiring and 50,000 light bulbs, and cost $2 million to manufacture and install. Perhaps the most popular scoreboard feature was the animated cartoon character "Chester Charge," who appeared regularly on the 1,800-square-foot video screen. Any time an Astro hit a home run, the entire scoreboard erupted in a light and sound show which was always a hit with fans.

When improvements were made to the Astrodome in 1989, Bud Adams wanted considerations given to his football team. The original scoreboard gave way to 18,000 additional seats, but in the end, Bud moved his franchise to Tennessee at the end of the 1996 NFL season.

Another popular Astrodome tradition was public address announcer J. Fred Duckett. A native Houstonian and Rice University graduate, Duckett was the Colt .45s original public address announcer. He continued those duties when the team moved into the Dome and held his position until 1992. Duckett became celebrated for his home-field pronouncements each time Jose Cruz came to bat. Duckett extended the popular Puerto Rican's last name into a lengthy "Cr-u-u-u-u-u-u-z." In addition to his job with the Astros, Fred sold insurance, taught history, and was the track coach at Awty International School for several years. He died of leukemia in 2007 at the age of 74.

For the past eighteen years, including the final six seasons inside the Dome, Bob Ford has handled public-address duties for the Astros. He may have one of the best voices in all of sports and he's truly a nice guy. When Bob is under the weather he's been ably replaced by my close friend Mike Acosta, the ball club's authentication manager and a veritable jack of all trades.

Speaking of sick days, I've had a few. Like most of my television peers, I feel duty bound to work every game if possible because of the ample time off I have once the season ends. But, I'm no zealot. When Allison got married, I was where I was supposed to be which was giving her away.

As I've aged, I've tried to take better care of my voice. Admitting that my vocal chords aren't quite what they used to be is a little like a pitcher saying he's dropped a few miles per hour on his fastball. In 2010, I lost my voice in Milwaukee and missed a couple games. In his mid-80s, Milo Hamilton is one of the real iron men in the business. Although he's been doing only home games and select road series for a few years, he's always had an incredible track record. He never seems to tire and that distinctive voice is always strong and true.

At one time or another, a playground, children's library, barber shop, bowling alley, movie theater, beauty parlor, chapel, and a presidential suite featuring Louis IV furniture have popped up inside the Astrodome. The Astros' administrative offices were housed there, too, until the team moved downtown. For me, an off-season visit to the Dome— to check in and pick up mail—meant parking near the loading dock on the home-plate side of the stadium and then, once inside, walking halfway around the park to get to an elevator which would take me to the ninth floor. The walk always did me a lot of good, although I never did find the bomb shelter in which Brewster McCloud was said to have lived.

***

Mickey Mantle hit the first home run in the Astrodome. One can imagine Astros pitcher Turk Farrell intentionally grooving one to the Yankee standout just to ensure his own place in Dome lore. Of course, Mantle's blast took place in an otherwise meaningless exhibition game. Philadelphia's Richie Allen—later known as Dick—clubbed the first official home run in the first regular-season game played inside the Astrodome—April 12, 1965. Bob Aspromonte was the first Astro to homer indoors on April 24, 1965.

Ken Caminiti hit the Astrodome's final home run in the last big league game ever played there: October 9, 1999. His three-run shot excited the home partisans, but Atlanta won a 7-5 decision to capture its National League Divisional Series against the Astros. Caminiti was a frequent hero during his days in a Houston uniform—and was also a National League Most Valuable Player as a rival. His story is one of the franchise's—and baseball's—great recent tragedies.

Caminiti made his debut with the Astros the same year I did: 1987. In his first game, he tripled and homered. He was a solid third baseman while in Houston, but after moving to San Diego, his offensive numbers exploded. He earned NL MVP honors with the Padres in 1996. Years later, he admitted to steroid use during his prime years as a player.

Performance-enhancing drugs turned out to be the least of Caminiti's problems. Through the years, perhaps because his hard-nosed style of play led to frequent nagging injuries and a reliance on pain-killers—or because he was as intense off the field as on—Caminiti became addicted to hard drugs.

By the time he returned to Houston in 1999, he had already spent time in rehab. He openly discussed his demons and his teammates and friends constantly offered their support. Ken, though, never got his life turned around. He died of a drug overdose in the Bronx, New York, on October 10, 2004.

Craig Biggio was one of Caminiti's closest friends. After they became established as Astros teammates, the two pooled their resources and bought a ranch near the small South Texas town of Sabinal, about an hour west of San Antonio. They called their property "Cambo Ranch."

In time, as Caminiti's personal problems mounted, Ken gave up his stake in the property, but the two friends remained devoted to each other. Former *Houston Chronicle* columnist Richard Justice wrote eloquently about that relationship on the morning Biggio collected his 3,000[th] hit—two-and-a-half years after Caminiti's death.

> *Biggio gave a tearful eulogy at Caminiti's funeral but had never really come to peace with the death. Last winter, he asked the family about moving Caminiti's body from its original burial place to the ranch.*
>
> *He pauses and shrugs. There are no words. He may never understand Ken Caminiti's life. He may never stop trying.*
>
> *"People ask me what kind of person he was," Biggio said. "Everyone knows what kind of player he was. He was a warrior. He played in any kind of pain. He had an obligation to the people who depended on him. He was the guy you'd want in your foxhole.*
>
> *"He was a great guy, too. He was one of those people that would give you the last dollar he had. If you needed something, he'd be there for you, no questions asked. I always said that if I was in trouble and had one telephone call, he'd be the one I'd want to call."*

Six years after Caminiti's playoff home run against Atlanta—with Astros baseball, high school football, and even the Houston Livestock Show and Rodeo all distant memories—the Dome experienced one final shining moment. In the aftermath of Hurricane Katrina, thousands of people displaced from their homes in the New Orleans area found shelter and comfort inside the Astrodome. Although the Dome was not officially closed until 2009, when the evacuees departed, the once grand sporting palace seemed to lose the last of its luster.

On the Reliant Park Web site, you'll find a page detailing the most recent master plan for the future of the Astrodome. Three options are presented for public consideration. Two involve retaining at least the outside shell of the stadium. In one rendering, a facsimile of the Dome's famed gondola hangs inside a massive conference hall. The gondola carries a message, "Welcome to the Astrodome Renaissance."

The third option calls for complete removal of the structure once praised as "beyond belief." The plan shows a plaza built on the stadium's footprint. It resembles, in concept, the memorial at Ground Zero in New York City. This option would seem to be the simplest, but it's not. Because of the proximity to Reliant Stadium and the large amounts of asbestos inside, imploding the Astrodome—as has been done to other major stadia—is apparently not an option.

To demolish the Dome, the entire building would have to be torn down in a pain-staking and costly fashion. Estimates for razing the Astrodome in this manner go as high as $80 million.

Houston has failed to preserve many of its architecturally-significant buildings. The legendary Shamrock Hilton was demolished just a few months after I took the Astros job. Great homes and other historical landmarks here have been lost to the ages. Preserving everything is impossible.

Sometimes, progress is about letting go of the past.

In *Moneyball*, as the A's near the American League record for consecutive victories, Brad Pitt's Billy Beane character suggests the significance of the accomplishment will be diminished unless the team can reach and win a World Series. His is an "all-or-nothing" mindset.

"I know these guys," Pitt/Beane says near the end of the movie. "I know the way they think and they will erase us.

"And everything we've done here, none of it will matter."

The future of the Astrodome seems to be a matter of similar concern. Remarkably, despite its architectural significance the Dome has never been nominated for inclusion on the National Register of Historic Places. Someone should look into correcting that oversight.

CHAPTER 19
Turn Out the Lights

When the Harris County Domed Stadium opened in 1965, the newly-christened Astros said goodbye to both their old name, Colt .45s, and their old playing venue, Colt Stadium. From the franchise's inception, the Dome was destined to be the team's permanent home. Colt Stadium was a temporary necessity.

In fact, it was reusable.

Never one to miss a chance at adding to his coffers, team owner Roy Hofheinz not only secured outside funding to erect Colt Stadium—after all a major league team had to have a place to play—but also ensured the facility was his to do with what he wished once it was vacated. So, when the Astrodome opened, he put Colt Stadium up for sale.

The ballpark sat empty for almost five years. Finally, a new owner was found and the stadium was dismantled and shipped to Torreon, Mexico. It was put back together and then taken apart a second time before ending up in Tampico, Mexico. Today it forms the skeleton of a rather attractive and modern-looking soccer stadium.

Technically, Hofheinz never owned the Astrodome. It belonged to the taxpayers of Harris County. He did own the *land* on which both Colt Stadium and the Astrodome were built. He presided over the Houston Sports Authority which, on behalf of the public interest, leased the Dome to his baseball team. Most any way you sliced it, The Judge got a piece of the pie.

Hofheinz did not come from money. His father drove a laundry truck and was killed in an accident when Roy was fifteen. Four years later—while still a teenager—Hofheinz earned his law degree. At twenty-four, he was the youngest person ever elected a Harris County judge. He relished the distinction, enjoyed the power, and the title fit so well—as perfectly as his signature eight-inch cigars—that it stuck with him the rest of his life.

Following World War II, Hofheinz moved naturally from political wunderkind to business tycoon. Like long-time Reds owner Powel Crosley, Hofheinz became a media baron of sorts, purchasing several radio stations. He also supported the development of the FM radio band, and put the nation's first sustaining FM station on the air in 1946.

In 1953, Hofheinz was elected mayor of Houston. One of his greatest political achievements was the desegregation of city-owned buildings. After opening the Houston Public Library to people of all colors, Hofheinz was purportedly admonished by a leading socialite. "I won't let my children sit next to blacks in the library," the woman scolded. "I don't know what they would catch."

Legend has it Hofheinz replied: "Tolerance, I hope."

After his term as mayor ended, The Judge bought Houston's minor league baseball team. He desegregated Buff Stadium by simply painting over the signs which designated the ballpark's restrooms as "Colored" and "White." The move brought surprisingly little reaction from the community.

While he did not own the Dome, the idea of an air-conditioned indoor stadium was *all* his. Every day and night the Astrodome was in use, The Judge indirectly benefitted. So it made perfect sense—in a Hofheinz sort of way—when he added to his holdings by buying a circus.

In 1967, Hofheinz purchased the Ringling Brothers and Barnum and Bailey Circus, dubbed "The Greatest Show on Earth." For The Judge, it was the greatest "toy" on earth, too. With a nearly endless line of credit at the bank he succumbed to his lifelong love of the big top. Extended local runs of his circus helped keep the Astrodome's turnstiles clicking. His ownership, though, lasted but a short time. In 1971, he sold the circus to an actual toy company, Mattel.

Fittingly, the Dome's swan song was played in a somewhat circus-like atmosphere. Although he died in 1982 and probably never imagined his enclosed stadium would eventually fall out of favor, The Judge would have been pleased, I think, with how his visionary dream ended its days in confetti-strewn style.

Bob Dorrill was among those in the sellout crowd on October 3, 1999, as Houston hosted the Dodgers in the Astrodome's final regular season game. Bob is the long-time chair of the Houston Chapter of the Society for American Baseball Research, also known as SABR. A native of New Jersey, Bob settled in Houston with his wife Peggy and spent thirty-five years in the oil business.

"The most exciting game I ever saw at the Astrodome," Bob remembers of the '99 season finale.

"A lot was riding on the outcome of that day's game," Dorrill says. "Houston was just a game ahead of Cincinnati in the NL Central Division. In the NL East, the Mets had the same record as the Reds. If the Astros lost and the Mets and Reds both won, playoff pandemonium would have ensued. Houston and Cincinnati would have played for the NL Central title and then the loser of that game would have faced the Mets for the Wild Card.

"I expected a lengthy pre-game ceremony, but that didn't turn out to be the case. I think the ball club was nervous about the game—given its post-season ramifications—and didn't want too many distractions."

As Bob points out, if the Astros won, they would be outright division champs—for the third year in a row. A win also ensured the game would be my final broadcast in the Dome, as HSE did not hold the rights to post-season play. As much as I'd like to see the Astrodome preserved and eventually put to some functional use, I'd be lying if I said I had anything resembling mixed emotions about the team moving into its new facility. The new ballpark downtown was nearly completed and it was a magnificent palace. Personally, I looked forward to being back out in the proverbial sunshine and fresh air.

Lord knows the skies had been cloudy—at least in a figurative sense—over so much of the Astros' 1999 campaign.

***

"Somebody's down in the Astros' dugout."

I'm not sure who first uttered those words. What I thought I heard through my headset was: "Somebody is down in the Astros bullpen." I initially took that to mean the team had a reliever warming up.

The date was June 13, 1999. There's that number again: 13.

Jeff Bagwell had just stepped to the plate late on a Sunday afternoon with Houston owning a 4-1 lead over San Diego. Derek Bell's sixth-inning grand slam had put the Astros on top and Shane Reynolds had pitched well, scattering six hits over eight innings of work. I looked to the Houston bullpen and saw no one there. Then, Jim Deshaies tapped me on the shoulder and pointed toward the home-team dugout.

By that time, the entire stadium had reacted to the occurrence and an eerie silence had fallen over the building. I could see someone lying on the ground, legs twitching, but couldn't make out who it was. I used my binoculars to get a closer look. Astros trainer Dave Labossiere appeared to be waving people away.

"Stay wide, stay wide!" came the urgent off-air instructions from our producer. "Do not go to a close-up!" Then another voice broke in from the low-first cameraman located next to the Astros dugout.

"It's Dierker," I heard through my headset. Third-year manager Larry Dierker, a former colleague and dear friend, was apparently in trouble.

My heart sank.

"Bill, don't say anything until we get official confirmation," the producer warned. I was helpless, both as a friend and an announcer.

In the ensuing moments, I reported to viewers what was painfully obvious by the shots they were seeing. When we finally received official confirmation, I immediately thought of Larry's wife Judy, wondering if she was at the game or perhaps watching at home. I didn't want to be the one to bring the bad news her way. Fortunately, Judy was at the game and soon at her husband's side. What no one knew at the time, other than Labossiere and assistant trainer Rex Jones, was that Dierker was in the thralls of a grand mal seizure. The Astros' trainers did their best to secure Dierker so that he could not injure himself.

An ambulance was driven onto the field and parked in front of the Astros' dugout. We went to a commercial break. Jim asked if he could leave the booth, but I wanted him to stay. I wasn't sure I could carry the story by myself. I thought of legendary broadcaster Jim McKay and his coverage of the massacre at the 1972 Munich Olympic Games. With my close friend's life potentially in the balance, I knew I couldn't muster up the professionalism McKay displayed when he told the world, "They're all gone."

Finally, Dierker was stabilized and placed into the ambulance. Judy climbed into the back of the emergency vehicle with him. As they left, the entire Astros team huddled in prayer in front of the dugout and the crowd broke into applause offering a heartfelt sendoff. If any solace was to be found that day, it came from the fact the best medical care in the world was only a few miles away at the Texas Medical Center.

The game was suspended in the bottom of the eighth inning. The entire city waited and worried.

By the time the contest was resumed on July 23, the Padres' next trip to town, Dierker was—miraculously—back at the helm of his club. His seizure had been triggered by an arteriovenous malformation of blood vessels in his brain and two days after suffering the attack, doctors performed surgery to repair the condition. Dierk was playing golf within a week and just over a month after the incident he was back at work. He missed only twenty-seven games and bench coach Matt Galante did an unbelievable job in the interim. When the Astros learned Dierker would be returning to the bench, the team promptly went on an eight-game winning streak to welcome him back.

Dierker wrote in great detail about the experience in his fabulous book *This Ain't Brain Surgery: How to Win the Pennant without Losing Your Mind*. What he doesn't reveal in his memoir is the crazy lineup he came up with when the suspended game was resumed.

Two Astros starters in the June contest, Carl Everett and Ricky Gutierrez, had suffered injuries and were on the team's disabled list by late July. While starting pitcher Shane Reynolds had appeared headed toward a complete game in June, when play resumed, Houston would use a reliever to wrap things up.

As it turned out, not one but *two* pitchers were placed into the Astros' revamped lineup and neither one of them would take the mound in the ninth. Billy Wagner had been tabbed to close out the game, so I found it odd that Jose Lima and Scott Elarton had been added to the lineup. Even stranger was the fact that Lima had been placed in the third-baseman's slot, while Elarton was designated as the new center fielder. I caught myself wondering if Dierker had lost his mind, then realized the inappropriate nature of that thought.

"Have you seen this lineup?" I asked when Deshaies walked into the booth in advance of our broadcast. "What's up with this?"

I handed my scorebook to Deshaies who studied it intently.

"My guess is that Dierk wants the flexibility to insert a pinch-hitter in the spots where Everett and Gutierrez were if the team gets that deep into the inning," JD offered. "But he doesn't want to show his hand and waste his reserves. That makes sense. I'm assuming neither Lima nor Elarton will hit or take the field defensively in the ninth."

"So, basically we've got an Abbott and Costello lineup here," I replied, still scratching my head. "'Who's' on first. 'What's' on second. Lima's on third. And Scott Elarton is in centerfield." Dierker also had reserve outfielder Daryle Ward listed as his pitcher.

"That's right," Deshaies said. "If the pitcher's spot comes up, Ward will hit and my guess is he could stay in the game for defensive purposes. See, he's in Everett's spot in the lineup and that's where Wagner will go when he comes in for the ninth.

It was all so very *unclear*.

Bagwell eventually struck out in the re-start to the game and the Astros failed to score in the eighth. When the Houston defense took the field for the top of the ninth, Glenn Barker trotted out to center field instead of the 6'8" Elarton, and Russ Johnson took third in place of Lima. Wagner began the ninth with the 4-1 lead and promptly gave up a leadoff home run to Padre Phil Nevin. Wagner surrendered *another* ninth-inning homer to Rubin Rivera, but in typical feast-or-famine style,

Billy struck out the other three batters he faced, picked up the save, and the Astros ultimately finished with a 4-3 victory.

In the regularly scheduled matchup which followed, Matt Mieske—who had not even been a part of the team in June—hit an eighth-inning grand slam and Houston won again by a score of 7-4. Mieske had been obtained before the trading deadline in a deal with Seattle for minor-league pitcher Kevin Hodges.

Judge Hofheinz really needn't have bothered. Baseball—Astrodome style—was often a circus in its own right.

***

Dierker's seizure and subsequent surgery turned out to be sort of par for the course during the injury- and illness-marred '99 campaign. The team became a veritable M-A-S-H unit that year. Most of you will remember the famed television show *M*A*S*H* and the movie of the same name on which the series was based. The movie was one of two Robert Altman-directed films released in 1970. The other was— drum roll, please—*Brewster McCloud*!

The acronym "M-A-S-H" stands for "Mobile Army Surgical Hospital." I knew of the concept from my days in Vietnam. While accruing interviews for the "Hometown Heroes" project, I'd visited a couple MASH units. The Army deactivated the program in 2006, replacing it with Combat Support Hospitals.

As mentioned, Adam Everett and Richard Hidalgo spent time on the Astros' disabled list in '99 with injuries, as did Ken Caminiti. Catcher Mitch Meluskey lasted three weeks before his season came to an end with shoulder injury. Outfielder Moises Alou missed the entire year after falling off a treadmill in the off-season. Several stories floated as to the real cause of his injury and the Astros hired a private investigator to go to the Dominican Republic and look into the matter, but nothing untoward was ever announced.

May was a particularly bad month for the Astros *coaching* staff. On May 10, Jose Cruz took an extended leave after being diagnosed with an irregular heartbeat. Six days later, Tom McCraw left to begin treatment for prostate cancer. Dierk himself had been complaining of headaches for some time. We all figured those were triggered by the *team's* poor health, never imagining it was symptomatic of a much more serious condition.

Somehow Dierker, his coaching staff, and his players not only survived the collective health crisis, but also managed to thrive. Heading into the last day of the '99 regular season, the team carried a record of 96-65 and was a win away from a division title.

The final day's pitching pairing certainly weighed in the Astros' favor. The Dodgers—long eliminated from post-season contention—trotted journeyman Robinson Checo to the mound. Checo would be making only his second start of the season. Houston countered with ace Mike Hampton. The feisty little lefthander was 21-4 on the year and sported an earned run average which ranked third-best among National League starters.

Ten days earlier, Hampton had been involved in the season's second most-shocking episode. On September 24, Astros right-fielder Bill Spiers was attacked by a fan in Milwaukee. The seemingly deranged man jumped onto the field in the bottom of the sixth, ran up to Spiers, and tried to tackle him to the ground. Pitching that night, Hampton sprinted to his teammate's aid. Entering the melee, Hampton threw caution aside and started kicking the attacker. Soon the man was subdued, handcuffed, and taken to jail.

Spiers suffered from whiplash and a lost contact lens, but otherwise sustained only minor injuries and remained in the game for the rest of the inning. Sadly, his assailant received only a ninety-day jail sentence.

The event certainly seemed to "in-Spier" the Astros. Down 4-2 at the time of the attack, Houston scored three in the eighth and four in the ninth to win the game 9-4.

I saw something similar happen once at a Houston game in Chicago. Cubs' reliever Randy Myers, after giving up a home run to James Mouton, was confronted by a fan near the Wrigley Field mound. How security guards and teammates allowed the individual to get that far was puzzling, but Myers managed to defend himself. An expert in martial arts, Meyers decked the assailant with one blow and shook off the incident to remain in the game. The Cubs won a wild one that afternoon, prevailing 12-11. The contest featured thirty-six hits, not including Myers' two "hits" in the sixth: him hitting his attacker and his attacker hitting the ground.

The Astros-Dodgers '99 season finale fortunately lacked such hysterics, and it didn't take Houston long to take much of the drama out of the game.

After Hampton retired Los Angeles in the first, Checo came on and promptly struck out Astros' leadoff hitter Craig Biggio. That, though, was to be the lone highlight of Checo's day. He walked the next four hitters he faced and then gave up a bases-clearing double by Daryle Ward. After Checo walked the next batter—the eighth Astros hitter of the inning—his afternoon was over.

The Astros scored four in the first, jumped out to a 9-1 lead by the sixth, and won the ball game 9-4.

"First time I'd ever seen what's come to be known as a 'dog pile'," Bob Dorrill says today of the scene which ensued on the field after the final out was recorded. "I'd been to a lot of baseball games, but had never seen players bury a teammate like that."

Given the team's health issues that season, it was fortunate no one—most significantly relief pitcher Jay Powell at the bottom of the celebratory scrum—was injured. While Astros players continued their revelry, confetti began to rain from the roof.

The good times were just beginning.

As the team drifted into the clubhouse for its much-deserved post-game victory party, Astros greats from the past made their way onto the field. All season, fans had voted for an Astros "Team of Honor," and the winners were recognized at the conclusion of the regular-season finale. Three current players were named to the squad and Bagwell, Biggio, and Caminiti came back out of the dugout to a huge ovation from the more than 52,000 fans who crammed into the Dome that day.

After the all-time team was announced, the newly-crowned divisional champions began a spontaneous victory lap around the field, high-fiving fans along the way. Suddenly, the roar of motorcycle engines reverberated throughout the stadium. No one could be sure what that meant until one of the outfield gates opened and Biggio and Caminiti came slowly through riding atop a pair of Harleys. Hampton, who pitched three-hit ball over seven strong innings to get the win that afternoon, sat on the back of Biggio's bike and all three players clenched Roy Hofheinz-sized victory cigars between their teeth.

When it appeared the celebration might never end, stadium public address announcer Bob Ford offered one final surprise. Amidst all the jubilation, few people had taken notice of the bearded man in a cowboy hat who had assumed a spot on the field near home plate. Ford introduced the "special guest" as none other than Willie Nelson.

The crowd went wild.

Quickly, the stadium fell silent as Nelson began singing one of his classics, *"The Party's Over:"*

Turn out the lights, the party's over
They say that all good things must end
Let's call it a night, the party's over
And tomorrow starts the same old thing again

What a crazy, crazy party,
Never seen so many people
Laughin', dancin'
Look at you, you're havin' fun

"We *were* having fun," Dorrill says today. "Even when they literally turned out the lights, no one wanted to go. We knew there was more playoff baseball to come, but this was the storybook ending the franchise had been denied for so many years."

Larry Dierker calls it his "all-time Astros memory."

It certainly was quite a ride.

Bill Brown's All-Time Astrodome Team of Honor—1999

Catcher – Alan Ashby
First Base – Jeff Bagwell
Second Base – Craig Biggio
Shortstop – Craig Reynolds
Third Base – Ken Caminiti
Outfield – Jose Cruz
Outfield – Cesar Cedeno
Outfield – Jimmy Wynn
Starting pitchers- Joe Niekro, J.R. Richard, Nolan Ryan, Mike Scott, Larry Dierker
Relief pitchers - Dave Smith, Billy Wagner, Ken Forsch, Joe Sambito, Fred Gladding
Manager – Bill Virdon

CHAPTER 20
Sidekicks

The days of the great nicknames in sports seem to be a thing of the past. Every baseball fan knows Joe DiMaggio was "The Yankee Clipper." Football enthusiasts remember Red Grange as "The Galloping Ghost." Hockey faithful recognize Bobby Hull as "The Golden Jet." Sportswriters and publicists spent much time coming up with those jewels.

More recently, there's been Magic, Tiger, and The Great One. I'm not sure if I've quite bought into Lebron James as "The King." In my estimation, Elvis Presley will always hold that distinction.

Of course, there's also the matter of Chad Ochocinco and Metta World Peace. The former Chad Johnson wore Number 85 on his football jersey, but in legally changing his last name, shouldn't it have been "*Ochentaycinco*?" As I write that, I suppose not.

As for the basketball player formerly known as Ron Artest, *"Metta"* is said to be a Buddhist word meaning "friendliness toward all." In 2004, Artest charged into the stands during a game to confront an opposing fan. That encounter set off an ugly brawl and Artest ultimately was suspended for almost ninety games. World Peace failed to live up to his name in April 2012, when an elbow to the head of an opponent landed him yet another suspension.

I guess it's true: a zebra can't change its stripes.

Like the entire planet, I got a little caught up in hubbub surrounding New York Knick guard Jeremy Lin. Heck, when Ben & Jerry's names an ice cream flavor for you, as the company did for Lin just two weeks after he took the NBA by storm, you're a pretty big deal. Sadly, Lin's ballyhooed season came to a premature end with a knee injury. He does appear to be the real deal, but one wonders if New York City can survive both "Lin-sanity" *and* "Tebow-mania."

Maybe you've seen Ben & Jerry's "Brownie Batter" flavored-ice cream in your supermarket's dairy case. In baseball circles I'm known as "Brownie," but I don't think my nickname inspired the famous ice cream makers.

Tom Seaver was the first person to call me "Brownie" and I have to say I like the name. Of course, if Seaver had chosen to call me something else, say "What's-Your-Name," or "Hey You," I probably would have tried hard to get one of those monikers to stick. After all, Willie Mays was the "Say Hey Kid."

Seaver was known as "Tom Terrific," and terrific, indeed, he was.

No inductee into the Baseball Hall of Fame has received a higher percentage of votes than Tom Seaver. Members of the Baseball Writers Association of America are notoriously selective with their Hall ballots, particularly in a player's first year of eligibility, or if the candidate was a "son of a gun" with the media, or a bad citizen off the field, or a suspected user of performance-enhancing drugs. Seaver was none of those. He won 311 games in his career, struck out 3,640 hitters, and posted a career earned run average of 2.86. He was the 1967 National League Rookie of the Year and won three Cy Young awards with the New York Mets.

I first met Seaver when I interviewed him as a Met for the *Redscene* pre-game show in Cincinnati. He was gracious and accommodating and even called me by my name. When Seaver was traded from New York to Cincinnati in June 1977, we got better acquainted. Every time I saw Tom around the ballpark, he'd make a point to say hello.

"Hey, Brownie, how's your daughter?" Seaver might ask. "Brownie, the team really picked me up the other night," he might say from the dugout.

"Brownie, did I ever tell you about my time in the Marines?"

Actually, Seaver never did mention his military service, but as he's gotten older—he retains his boyish charm even in his late 60s—he's spoken more publicly of his service experience, a time in his life of which he's obviously proud.

Upon graduation from high school in Fresno, California, Seaver joined the Marine reserves and spent six months on active duty. "I was a mediocre student," Seaver told reporter Christian Red of the *New York Daily News*. "If it didn't have a ball involved, I wasn't much interested.

"The principles that I learned in boot camp were the principles I took to the mound—focus and dedication. I wouldn't have made it (as a ballplayer) without the Marine Corps."

Seaver says he learned one other thing as a Marine which served him well in baseball. "My uniform was always to the nines when I went to the mound," Seaver told Red. "It's a matter of respect."

No question Seaver respected the game. He also respected his talents and the talents of those around him, even a young guy with a microphone. As I think about it today, I'd have to say Tom Seaver was a bit of a hero to me. You could very much also call him a "clean Marine," which was the nickname for another of the heroes from my youth— Astronaut John Glenn.

John Glenn was a military fighter pilot and the first American to orbit the earth from space. So important was his role as an American hero, he was prohibited from going back into space until 1998 when he flew aboard the Space Shuttle at the age of 77. Glenn not only has "the right stuff," but also hero stuff as far as I'm concerned.

As you've guessed, my criteria for heroism are pretty high. Very few athletes make the grade, at least for what they do when playing their game.

Pat Tillman was a standout football player at Arizona State University and with the NFL's Arizona Cardinals. The Cardinals reportedly were prepared to offer him a three-year $3.2 million contract when Tillman retired from football and joined the Army. His enlistment came eight months after 9/11. He was 25-years-old.

Tillman was the only professional athlete to volunteer for service in our country's war against terrorism. That fact alone makes him a hero to me. Tragically, Tillman was killed while on active duty in Afghanistan.

Colonel Mark Tillman is no relation to Pat, but in my mind, he's just as big a hero. Mark Tillman was at the helm of Air Force One on 9/11. His job was to ferry the President of the United States to safety that day.

I first met Mark at an event called "Salute to Our Heroes." I've emceed that banquet several times and it's a privilege to honor men and women serving in the military. Tillman first spoke at the Houston fundraiser several years ago. Since then, we've become friends.

On 9/11, Tillman was among a select group of people charged with making decisions to keep the president safe and America's political leadership intact and functioning in what, for all purposes, was a time of war. He relied that day on instincts more than training and every one of his decisions proved to be the correct one. As he says, he was simply doing his job.

"Flying over the Pentagon (on the way back to Washington, D.C.) kind of brought it all home to me," Mark says of his 9/11 experience. "I could see the destruction. Up to that point, I wasn't really thinking about who had been killed or injured that day. My goal was to keep (the president) safe and to continue on with my job. Not until I landed and went back to my office did I realize exactly what we had done."

Mark's last official act as captain of Air Force One was to fly President George W. Bush home to Texas upon the completion of his stay in the White House. Mark has since retired from military service and today lives in the Phoenix area. We try to get together whenever our schedules permit.

Staff Sgt. Keni Thomas is another former member of the military whom I've come to know through "Salute to Our Heroes." As an Army Ranger, Thomas was involved in the Battle of Mogadishu, made famous by the movie *Black Hawk Down*. In fact, Thomas was a consultant on the 2001 film and actor Tac Fitzgerald played him on screen.

When speaking, Thomas tells his audience, "Use the gifts you have been given. Do what feeds your spirit, because when you do, the world around you becomes a better place."

His message is quite simple: You don't have to attain valor on the battlefield, let alone be a famous athlete or celebrity, to be a hero. An inspiring teacher, an involved parent, someone who gives time and talent for the betterment of others, those people are heroes, too. Heroes come in all shapes and sizes. My friend Zach Hamm—whom you'll meet in Chapter 26—is a hero, too, and he's just 12 years old.

***

Ask around Minute Maid Park for "Sluggo," and fingers in the know will point Larry Dierker's way. Despite the fact he was once a twenty-game winner and twice a National League All-Star, he's also a bit of a clod, but in a friendly, year-old-Labrador-retriever kind of way.

I've kept all my scorebooks through the years. They occupy considerable space in the home I share with Dianne. A few are blotted with coffee stains. After the first half-dozen-or-so times Larry's animated hand gestures or general clumsiness knocked over a cup of coffee in the booth, I tried to build a Great Wall of sorts between our vantage points. But with all the shuffling I did from booth to booth during my first decade with the Astros, I eventually realized trying to preserve order while sitting next to Dierk was an exercise in futility.

In the end, I learned to live with his "idiosyncrasies," just like he tolerated my compulsions. Working together as broadcasters requires the same give-and-take you'll find in a good marriage.

I've been lucky: one great wife for forty-plus years at home, and two fantastic "sidekicks" at the ballpark. All matches made in heaven.

When I arrived in Houston, Larry Dierker was doing radio, television, and writing a column for the *Houston Chronicle.* I instantly took a liking to him—as almost everyone does—and enjoyed working together with him.

Dierker, or "Dierk" as he's more commonly called by friends—we try to keep a lid on the whole "Sluggo" thing as best we can—was the consummate on-air professional. He was a fantastic teacher and like our audience, I learned much from him about the finer points of the game. On the air, he was erudite and insightful. Off the air, Larry liked to have a lot of fun.

Dierker won 139 games during his fourteen seasons as a major league pitcher, yet he's probably better known today for his easy-going sartorial style. No matter the occasion, chances are you'll find Larry comfortably attired in one of his brightly-colored Hawaiian shirts. In fact, I was present the day he gave birth to the trend. He wrote about it in his memoir:

It happened near the end of (a) losing streak, during a game with the Marlins. Florida didn't have a very good team that year but they were making us look like Little Leaguers.

We were way behind, maybe 9-2, in this particular game. Our cameras panned the dugout and it looked like a morgue. "You know what's wrong with this team, Brownie?" I asked my partner Bill Brown.

"Well, we're not hitting," he offered.

"No, it's not that," I said.

"Well then, what is it?"

"Not enough Hawaiian shirts," I said.

"Hawaiian shirts?"

"Yeah, Hawaiian shirts," I repeated. Everyone in that dugout looks like someone in their family has died. You have to have spirit to win games. This team looks dead. Did you ever see someone wearing a Hawaiian shirt that wasn't having a good time?"

"Well, no," he answered. "But where's yours?"

"I'll wear it tomorrow night," I said, not knowing how difficult it would be to find one, even in Miami.

Sure enough, Larry showed up for the next day's broadcast clad in a shirt printed with a pattern of large flowers. He explained it wasn't really a Hawaiian shirt and for the next several broadcasts, Dierker spent considerable time discussing the functionality and practicality of the latest additions to his wardrobe.

I've even acquired a few of these "aloha" shirts through the years, mostly as gifts from people perhaps confusing me with Dierk, difficult to do considering he stands close to a head taller than I. Dierker can pull it off, the shirts I mean. I cannot.

Larry left the broadcast booth before the 1997 season when he was named manager of the Astros. The announcement came as a complete surprise. I don't think Larry had any real aspirations to replace Terry Collins as the team's skipper until Tal Smith approached him about the position.

Hiring Dierker to manage turned out to be one of the best moves in club history. Under his watch, the team won three consecutive division championships in his first three seasons on the bench. The Astros got to the playoffs in four of his five years on the job.

While Dierk's Astros never reached the World Series, he definitely instilled a winning attitude on the club. He did it as a no-nonsense sort of boss. He was also a hands-off manager, much in the style of Sparky Anderson. He didn't have a lot of rules and the rules he did have were flexible, depending on whether or not a player was a star and, if not a star, whether or not the player was dedicated to the game.

A testament to Larry's integrity and class is that he's continued to work for the club even after being fired as manager. There is no doubt in my mind Dierker should have landed another managerial job, but seeing him at the helm of another team would have been an odd sight. Save for his final season as a player in St. Louis, Larry Dierker is first, last, and will always be a Houston Astro.

I now have the privilege of turning over narrative of my baseball journey to my former broadcast partner. It's been a while since we've worked together, but it gives me great pleasure to say: "Here's Larry Dierker."

> *One of the first things Brownie told me after he landed the Astros' job in 1987 was that he felt like he had gotten out of jail. He had been doing sports for a financial news network, so, he hadn't exactly been*

working in his dream job. Plus, he and his family had been living in Canoga Park, California. I grew up near there in the part of town once called "Hollywoodland," so, I knew that wasn't the best of places to be raising a young daughter.

Brownie was in a hurry to stay put as a baseball broadcaster. His time away from the game gave him an appreciation for just how fortunate he had been to land the Reds' job at such a young age. By the time he touched down for spring training, he seemed to have had a full winter's worth of preparation. I didn't know it at the time, but that was just Bill. I remember he tried to get in as many of those facts into the first inning of his first exhibition-game broadcast from Florida. He was something a little different for Houston baseball. No one could say he was unprepared.

One time, that first year, we went out to dinner in San Francisco with our TV director, Joe O'Rourke. Brownie had us laughing with his dry sense of humor. O'Rourke said, "Why don't you talk like this on the air? People would love it." Game by game and year by year, that wry wit leaked into his broadcast work. He still has enough material to last forever when he plops his stuff down in the booth before a game. But no longer does he feel compelled to use it. If something of greater interest comes up, he'll go with it.

I always knew that Brownie had my back. He knew everything, even long lost things. One time in Atlanta, we were talking about nicknames and I mentioned that they used to have some descriptive, if elaborate, monikers. "There was one guy they called, 'Death to Flying Things' because of his prowess as a fielder," I said. "Oh, you're talking about Bob Ferguson," he replied. Ferguson played in the 1880s!

You don't know these things unless you've been a baseball fan from the moment you could read. It's a comfort to have a guy like that working next to you – like having a good catcher. And, I imagine it's a comfort to those folks who are watching the game at home, too.

As a broadcaster, Bill never strays from the reporter's first duty—the facts. As his partner, I was aware of most things that were happening in baseball; Brownie was aware of everything. He bought newspapers from every big league city, every day. He cut out and saved articles he thought could add value to the broadcast. He prepared for every game as if it were "The Iowa Baseball Confederacy," a W.P. Kinsella story about a game that lasted forever. Kinsella also wrote the story on which the film Field of Dreams *was based.*

There are many famous lines in that movie, among them, "Go the distance."

Bill Brown has.

***

I was pleased Larry got the opportunity to manage the club, but sad to see our on-air partnership end. We had good chemistry and I think our listeners and viewers agreed. With Dierk's departure, the team not only began a search to find his replacement, but also decided to make me the full-time TV guy and keep Milo in the radio booth. That move made all the sense in the world to me, but the big news turned out to be the selection of my new partner.

Jim Deshaies also has a little-known nickname: "Ace." Starring for Central High School in his home town of Massena, New York, Deshaies was the ace of his prep squad's pitching staff. From there he attended Lemoyne College and, following his senior year at the small Jesuit school, he was selected in the twenty-first round of the amateur draft by the New York Yankees.

"I was a political science major with bad grades," Deshaies says today. "As far as career choices were concerned, there really wasn't a Plan B after baseball." He received a whopping $1,500 bonus to sign his first professional contract.

JD, as Astros viewers more commonly know him, spent three years in the minors—playing for a time with a young prospect by the name of John Elway—before making his major league debut in pin stripes near the end of the 1984 season. He was shelled in two appearances and then traded to Houston for Joe Niekro—one of the Astros' all-time pitching greats—midway through the 1985 season. By the time of the deal, Niekro was a 40-year-old knuckleballer on the downhill side of his career. At just 25 years of age, Deshaies was about to enter his prime as a big leaguer.

Jim went 12-5 in his rookie season, and helped lead the Astros into the 1986 playoffs. That team—from what I've been told—included quite a cast of characters, Deshaies chief among them. Kevin Bass, Larry Andersen, and Charlie Kerfield also helped to keep things lively in the clubhouse. I missed the fun, arriving in Houston the following year.

In all, Jim spent seven seasons as an Astro, winning—as a member of the team's starting rotation—more than he lost, and usually posting an earned run average in the threes. After leaving the Astros following the 1991 season, he pitched five more years in the majors, playing for four different teams.

After he retired as a player, JD returned to Massena and knocked around for a year. I don't think he'd given broadcasting much of a thought, but when he called to congratulate Dierker on getting the manager's job, Larry encouraged him to think about becoming an announcer. At first Deshaies wasn't interested, but a case of cabin fever prompted him to inquire about the position.

"Initially the Astros weren't all that interested," Deshaies says. "Larry Anderson, a former teammate of mine in Houston, was actually offered the job, but he decided to stay in the Phillies' organization as a minor-league coach. I think the Astros also talked to someone else about their broadcast opening before finally getting around to me."

The 2012 season marks my sixteenth year together with JD, who is a favorite with the fans. I'm not sure we're the kind of duo capable of finishing each other's sentences, but I'm comfortable handing over the keyboard for him to finish this chapter.

"Grinder" is a word that, like so many in the lexicon of sports, gets used and abused. Its use is especially prevalent in baseball. Hitters grind out at bats, and "come to play every day" while pitchers grind out the innings. Grinding best describes those with a workmanlike approach. Not flashy, but steady and always at the ready.

While we tend to ascribe this grinding quality to players, it applies off the field as well. As a matter of fact, I can't think of anyone who personifies this more than Brownie. Bill—and not James Brown (the two are not related to my knowledge)—is the "hardest working man in show business!" I can't tell you how many times through the years I've wondered "Who is this guy?" when some kid from Double A-ball shows up unexpectedly to face the Astros. Brownie, meanwhile, is never caught off guard. "I think I've got a card on him," he'll casually say. And he almost always does.

Bill spends countless hours in the off-season preparing index cards on just about every player in the game. National League, American League, even New York Penn League, he's got it covered. Brownie backing off a little in his preparation would be perfectly understandable. He's been doing this job for so long he could put it on auto-pilot and still be one of the best. But, that's not his style.

If you were to fly with the Astros on an out-of-town trip, you would likely encounter this fairly typical late-night scene: A whole bunch of people twisted up trying to sleep and one lonely light shining down on Brownie's seatback tray table as he fills out his record books and tears stories from the sports pages. Since 9/11, they won't allow him to bring scissors onto the plane.

Baseball is a sport that honors those who are able to answer the bell every day and play through pain. On a Sunday in San Diego a few years back, Brownie went above and beyond.

One of the toughest days in baseball, for players, coaches, and media personnel is the Sunday afternoon game following a Saturday night contest. I'll never forget sitting on the hotel bus in San Diego when Bill struggled aboard. I knew he wasn't feeling very good the night before and I had hoped he'd be able to get a good night's rest. Instead, he looked awful, pasty with deeply-sunken eyes. As he sat down across the aisle from me I told him, "Man, you don't look so good."

"I don't feel so good, either," Brownie replied.

"Maybe you should take a sick day."

He turned and looked at me with his peaked eyes. He nodded his head slightly then settled into his seat and mumbled, "I'll be fine."

At the ballpark, the rest of us were making plans to adjust the radio and television broadcast teams to give Bill the day off. While we were doing so, he found an empty booth, curled up on the floor, and took a short nap. When he returned to the FSH booth, the hair on the side of his head was matted and sticking straight up. Worst case of "rack-head" I'd ever seen. Otherwise, though, he didn't look quite as close to death's door as he had earlier in the morning.

"Feeling better," he said to no one in particular, perhaps trying to convince himself. "Let's do a ballgame."

And so he did. He got the hair fixed in time for the pre-game show and pulled off the rest of the broadcast, too. I know he felt terrible the whole time, but I'm guessing not a soul watching had a clue as to how sick he really was.

I'll always be indebted to Bill for the patience he showed when I first took the job in '97. I'm sure breaking in a new guy after all those years with Larry wasn't easy. Once that first year, I left Brownie hanging in Pittsburgh for four innings. It was the first game after the All-Star break and I was meeting the team after spending the break with my family at our camp in northern New York. I made a big rookie mistake and booked travel for the day of the game. Sure enough, the flight was delayed and I didn't get to the ballpark until the game was almost halfway through. Bill had every right to unload on me, or at least act perturbed, but he rolled right on like nothing happened. Maybe he was thrilled not to have to carry my inexperienced self for a change!

As I'm sure Dierk would tell you, working with Bill is a real treat. He laughs at almost all my one-liners—even the really lame ones. He has that smooth, fluid style that is both easy on the ears as well as the brain. The Astros celebrated Brownie's twenty-five years of service with his own day in 2011. The team also gave him the highest honor which can be bestowed on someone associated with the game. He got his own bobblehead doll. For some reason, they placed a poor representation of me next to his smiling ceramic face.

I have one of those bobbleheads in my office at home and I like to give it a poke every now and then. It reminds me of the time Brownie and I spend together in the booth: Bill chatting away all-knowingly with me at his side, nodding in agreement.

CHAPTER 21
Killer B's

Hockey's Boston Bruins have long been known as the "B's." The logo on the club's sweaters prominently features a capital B representative of the alliterative nature of the team name. During Boston's run to the 2011 Stanley Cup, the Bruins became known as the "Killer B's."

A team in Texas could have taken exception to that.

The Rio Grande Valley Killer Bees—a name derived from the label long associated with the Africanized honey bee—have been a fixture in the Central Hockey League since 2003. In fact, the Killer Bees have twice been honored as the CHL's franchise of the year. The team regularly plays to an enthusiastic crowd in hockey-mad Hidalgo, Texas.

In a way, the Killer Bees are a descendent of the old Cincinnati Stingers of the defunct World Hockey Association. During my broadcast years in Cincinnati, I called a number of Stingers games. Cincinnati's last year in the WHA—the 1978-79 season—was Wayne Gretzky's first in the league. He broke in as a 17-year-old wunderkind with the Indianapolis Racers and recorded his first professional hat trick against the Stingers at Cincinnati's Riverfront Coliseum. After only eight games in Indy, Gretzky was traded to the Edmonton Oilers. The Racers soon folded while Gretzky went on to score forty-three goals that season. His presence was one of the major factors in the National Hockey League's assimilation of four

WHA clubs—most notably Gretzky's Oilers—prior to the 1979-80 season.

The Stingers were not invited to join the NHL and moved to the Central Hockey League. Downsizing to the minors proved fatal and the team ceased operations in mid-season, but not before playing the U.S. Olympic hockey team twice in exhibition games. Team USA won in Cincinnati 3-2 and beat the Stingers again in Minneapolis 6-1. In their final tune-up before the 1980 Olympics, the Americans lost to the Soviet Olympic team at Madison Square Garden 10-3. The Yanks seemed anything but "killer" heading to Lake Placid and any chance of a miracle seemed improbable at best.

We've already covered how that turned out.

The Houston Astros band of Killer B's sprung from the imagination of GM Gerry Hunsicker after he obtained Derek Bell in a trade with San Diego following the 1994 season. With Craig Biggio and Jeff Bagwell already on board, the deal gave Houston a formidable—and alliterative, as Hunsicker pointed out—top of the batting order.

Soon, other additions were made, although first- or last-name initials probably weren't the Astros' highest priority. Still, on April 27, 1997, in a game against the San Francisco Giants, skipper Larry Dierker sent this lineup onto the field:

Craig **Biggio**—2B

Pat Listach—SS (replaced in the ninth inning by **Bill** Spiers)

Jeff **Bagwell**—1B

Derek **Bell**-CF

Luis Gonzalez—LF

Sean **Berry**—3B

Bobby Abreu—RF

Brad Ausmus—C

Darryl Kile—P (relieved in the eighth by **Billy** Wagner)

With the dawn of a new decade, century, and millennium, the Astros got even more mileage from the Killer B's tag when Lance Berkman established himself as a top-tier talent.

Although Bagwell and Biggio are now retired and Berkman has moved on to become a World Series champion in St. Louis, I would submit the "Killer B's" are alive and well, still buzzing about Minute Maid Park. The Fox Sports Houston crew which puts Astros baseball on the air features the likes of Murphy **Brown**, Paul **Byckowski**, Jerry **Blancas**, Robin **Barrow**, Mike **Brady**, and Phil **Boudreaux**. And, Bill **Brown**, come to think of it. Every one of us, whether or not our last name begins with the letter B, takes great pride in our individual and collaborative effort. A baseball team is comprised of twenty-five individuals working together for the good of the whole, and as it turns out, about that same number of people goes into the production of a Major League Baseball telecast.

I've been in TV for a long time and I much prefer my vantage point in the booth to the darkened confines of the production truck located just inside the loading dock at Minute Maid Park. The "truck" is actually a long portable trailer filled with millions of dollars worth of electronic equipment. While my job is reasonably straightforward— simply sitting and talking about a baseball game as it happens—when it comes to weaving together the tapestry that creates the overall television experience, the production truck is the nerve center of the broadcast. There, countless split-second decisions are made to formulate a show. If anyone fails at his or her job—whether I get the pitch count wrong or there's a bad sound mix on a field microphone—the overall telecast is diminished.

Pitching with the winning run on third is certainly a pressure-packed situation, but what the people of FSHouston do to create live television—whether in Houston or any of the other venues where the Astros play—is fraught with equal amounts of tension. Our wins and losses, however, are measured in slightly different terms from the ball club we cover.

David "Wave" Robinson is the towering figure behind Houston Astros telecasts. Standing about 6'7" with a fully-shorn skull, Wave is our lead producer. The nickname dates back to his days in San Antonio where another David Robinson was playing a Hall-of-Fame caliber of professional basketball. While the Spurs center was known as "The Admiral," the team's statistician became "Big Wave Dave," a term of endearment bestowed by a girlfriend at the time. The name stuck and now getting our David to answer to his real name is virtually impossible.

Wave grew up in Milwaukee and became a baseball fanatic at an early age. After high school, he joined the Air Force and was ultimately stationed at Randolph Air Force Base in San Antonio. While still in the service, he talked his way into a job keeping stats at Spurs home games and ultimately became a member of the team's radio and television crew. After leaving the Air Force, he attended Texas State University where he continued his stats work for a variety of outlets—including ESPN. He was ultimately "discovered" by Murphy Brown and Jeff Muckleroy of Fox Sports, who made Wave the associate producer on Astros road telecasts in 2001.

Robinson is well regarded for his work. He commutes to Astros games—about 110 a season—from his home in New Braunfels, Texas. Wave knows his business about as well as anyone, which makes him the ideal tour guide for a behind-the-scenes look at how Astros television comes to life.

I've been asked many times to describe my job as a lead producer. In a real sense, I'm sort of like the head coach of a football team. I create the game-plan for the broadcast and ensure that it's executed to the best of everyone's ability. I line up guests in the booth, time commercial breaks, and call the sequence for instant replays. I'm more a "jack-of-all-trades" than truly the "boss."

Once the game gets underway, the director takes control. He becomes the quarterback of our operation. He calls all the "plays"—shot sequences—and his instructions are carried out by the individual sitting next to him in the truck, the technical director.

The director makes hundreds of decisions over the course of a ballgame, choosing from visuals available to him on dozens of monitors inside the truck. At Minute Maid Park, we try to operate with a minimum of eight cameras. In addition to those live camera shots, the director monitors replay decks, graphic channels, and a multitude of effects and animations to build the live broadcast.

Even though the production team is located beyond the field of play, we're in constant contact with the announcers in the booth. We talk frequently to the announce team via an "IFB" device, the earplug virtually every television figure wears during a broadcast. From the truck, we control how many voices Brownie and JD hear in their heads—usually just the producer, director, statistician, field reporters, and the floor manager in the booth. I hear and can communicate with everyone.

For instance, JD may tell us via his talk-back switch— which kills his on-the-air microphone: "Let's see that play again." In the truck, our record-deck operators will cue the replays and I'll determine the sequence they're shown. Then, when Jim tells viewers, "Looking at that play again, we see..." the sequence of replays magically—or so it would seem—appears.

For me, the single most important rule in televising a baseball game is to never, ever miss a live pitch. And that's not always as easy as it sounds. If I suggest a replay sequence of three different shots, the director has to determine if there is time for three or if only two can be squeezed in before the next pitch. Nothing is more sacred than showing that next pitch as it happens "live," although thanks to the signal delay to prevent any inappropriate sights or sounds from making it into viewer's homes, about thirteen seconds elapse between the live action on the field and what's shown on FSHouston. So, if you want to turn down the sound and try to listen to Milo and the guys on radio, we're going to be messing a little with your mind!

As I've said, we normally use eight camera operators. If you've been to the ballpark, chances are you've noticed most of them, although there is a second crew present shooting in-stadium video, what fans see on the scoreboard's high-definition screen and the public monitors throughout the stadium. Here's our broadcast camera positions:

- **Camera 1—Low Third**: inside the visitor's dugout on the side closest to home plate
- **Camera 2—High Home**: "shags" balls in play and trucks backward in the booth for on-camera shots of Brownie and JD
- **Camera 3—High First**: shags the left field line and is the best look at double plays since it's directly in line with first and second base
- **Camera 4—Center Field**: shows the standard shot of the pitch being thrown to the plate
- **Camera 5—Low First**: inside the home dugout on the side closest to the plate; the camera operator there is within ten feet of Astros manager Brad Mills
- **Camera 6—High Third**: shags the right field line with great looks into the Astros bullpen
- **Camera 7—Left Field** usually behind the Crawford Boxes near the "Astros Live" set
- **Cameras 8 and 9—Robotic cams**: one is on the backstop behind home plate while the other

moves around, sometimes just outside the Astros dugout, sometimes high atop the outfield upper deck. The individual controlling these two cameras sits in a tiny room near the production truck.

In the truck, there are three replay operators, each running two machines. Each operator takes in the feed from multiple cameras and has two outputs. This technology has come a long way over the years. We now use digital recorders, sort of like the DVRs found in many homes. In the old days, when actual videotape was used, a replay operator recorded, then rewound, and then played back the footage. Now one person can do all three of these functions at virtually the same time. The digital recorders allow instant cues and much better replay sequences and highlight packages. Good replay operators frequently anticipate what the producer or announcers want to show which keeps the broadcast flowing smoothly.

Our audio unit includes three people. The "A1" mixes the show from the truck, controlling all the microphones in use, both in the booth and on the field. Two audio assistants, or "A2's", help with the announcer mics and the pre/post game set.

We also have microphones placed in the padding around the field and one which zeroes in on the home plate area. That's the one which gets the crack of the bat or the sound of the ball slamming into the catcher's mitt. If you listen carefully, you'll hear the audio on that mic potted up just as the ball reaches the plate. Our sound elements are part of the reason watching a game at home can be a better experience than being at the ballpark. Interestingly, viewers often notice bad audio more than anything else. Fortunately, our sound people are good at their jobs.

The modern day baseball telecast is greatly enhanced thanks to the abundance of information posted graphically on screen. No broadcaster in the business is better prepared with stats and stories than Bill Brown, but thanks to computer technology, we're able to enhance his observations at the touch of a button.

The graphics department has two people, a coordinator, commonly called the associate producer—which is how I got my start in television—and the graphics machine operator. They pre-build graphics including lineups, defensive positioning, hitting and pitching stats, and divisional standings. FSHouston utilizes Stats, Inc., whose proprietary "Stats Graphics Loader" software features a daily download of at least 5,000 made-for-broadcast graphics. For each batter, there are at least 60 graphics we can call up at a moment's notice.

The truly unique aspect of baseball as compared to almost all other sports is that the scoring is done away from the ball. For instance, the on-air shot sequence for a bases-loaded double might go something like:

- Camera 4 (centerfield) shot of the pitch and the batter making contact, cut to
- Camera 2 (high behind home plate) shot of "shag" of the ball in the outfield, cut to
- Camera 5 (low first) field-level shot of first runner scoring, cut to
- Camera 2 shot of throw from the outfield, cut to
- Camera 5, shot of second and third runners crossing home plate, cut to
- Camera 2, batter sliding into second base, cut to
- Camera 3 (high first) reaction shot of crowd, cut to
- Camera 1 (low third) field-level shot of batter standing on second base, add
- Pre-programmed graphic with pertinent statistical information about the batter, cut to
- Camera 4 dugout shot of high fives...cut to
- Replay sequence.

Immediately after Craig Biggio's 3,000th hit, we aired nine consecutive replays representing angles of the play from every camera in the stadium and reaction shots of his wife and children.

Additional broadcast personnel include a video technician, who ensures the cameras are transmitting a quality video signal; an operator to run the "Fox Box" which provides a constant on-screen readout of score, pitch count, outs and runners on bases; a stage manager who handles copy and controls traffic in the broadcast booth; a statistician to catch anything the announce team might miss; two "utilities" who assist with set-up and tear-down and run errands as needed; and two engineers who make sure the dreaded "Technical Difficulties" slide never appears on one of our telecasts.

Add to that our roving reporters Greg Lucas, Patti Smith, and Bart Enis; our pre- and post-game crew of Kevin Eschenfelder, Art Howe, Steve Sparks, and Mike Stanton; and the people at the network—from executive producer Murphy Brown to the individuals in accounting, traffic, and sales—and you have the FSH Astros lineup. It takes a village—and then some—to bring Houston Astros baseball to our television audience.

***

I learned a long time ago complacency is a killer when it comes to a job well done. One of the big differences between a great ballplayer and an average one—in addition to God-given talent—is the ability to focus and block out distractions. The same holds true for our broadcast crew. I am both privileged and fortunate to be working with an outstanding group of individuals.

Chicago native Paul Byckowski normally occupies the director's chair. He's been a member of the Astros broadcast team since 1985. "To be honest, I wanted to direct live sporting events as a kid," Byckowski says. "Executive producer Roone Arledge with *Wide World of Sports* and director Arnie Harris with WGN were my heroes growing up. Kinda weird, I know.

"What I enjoy most about my job is working with a variety of people in multiple venues. Through the years I've developed some great and lasting relationships and I'd like to think I've played a part in making some pretty good television."

Technical Director Damon McGavock has been with the Astros crew since 1984. He got his start as a tape operator and was promoted into the TD's position in '95. Damon grew up in Louisville and was a big Reds' fan as a kid. He played college basketball at the University of Southern Colorado where he got his degree in TV production. Damon is a man of strong faith and consistently pushes the envelope in creating enhancements to our telecasts.

Emmy-Award winner Kim Elston, who operates the High Third Camera, got his baseball start in Houston working as a batboy at Colt Stadium. In that position, he transitioned into the Dome and before the end of the '60s Kim was an in-stadium camera operator, usually hitching a ride to the ballpark with his father, former Astros broadcaster Gene Elston. Free-lancing as a network cameraman, Kim has worked six All-Star Games and ten World Series.

Frank Trevino also haunted Colt Stadium as a kid. "I remember the mosquito repellant they sold at the park," Frank says. "You lit the end of a green coil and the smoke was supposed to keep the mosquitoes away. It didn't work very well." Trevino has been a part of the Astros crew for more than thirty years, mostly as High First cameraman. Frank attended the University of Texas and says one of his biggest thrills was getting to work UT's 2005 Rose Bowl game for ABC Sports. Trevino also serves as secretary/treasurer for his local chapter of the International Alliance of Theatrical State Employees.

For many years, Frank has been married to Margaret Krausse who operates one of the replay decks on our crew and specializes in building highlight packages. Margaret's father was a member of the U.S. State Department and she moved frequently as a child. She says she was never much of a sports fan growing up and likes to tell the story of how she once met a seemingly anonymous baseball player while she attended an American school in Brazil. The player shook Margaret's hand and autographed a photo, but given her indifference at the time, Margaret passed along the picture to one of her friends. Years later, after she developed an interest in baseball, Margaret realized the player she met in Brazil was none other than the great Roberto Clemente.

A self-proclaimed "computer geek," Cliff Crowley grew up in West Texas. "My biggest baseball thrill as a kid—maybe ever—was getting to see Mickey Mantle play," Crowley says. Married for thirty-four years and a member of the Astros' crew for thirty-three seasons, Cliff—who operates the High Home camera from inside the booth—calls live television a "handmade art."

"My biggest job is to keep the ball in the center of the screen," Crowley jokes. He adds, "Live television requires focus and teamwork. To do the job well, we have to work well together." Like so many members of our Astros broadcast team, Cliff has free-lanced for most of the major networks.

Television comes naturally to Center Field cameraman Jamey Tidwell. "For many years, my dad was the executive producer for a statewide television show about Texas," Tidwell says. "He filmed lots of events in the Astrodome. When I got to come with him, he'd usually drop me off in the press dining room and encourage me to eat to my heart's content. Later, when he gave me career advice, he told me, 'If you want to make lots of money and amount to something, stay out of the business.' The next day he'd ask me to help him on a shoot and I'd always go."

Kevin Allen operates the Left Field camera and has been a member of the Astros broadcast crew since 1999. Kevin grew up in St. Louis during the Cardinals' dynasty of the '60s and remembers fondly his first game at Busch Stadium when Hall-of-Famer Bob Gibson beat the Mets 1-0.

Another St. Louis product is A1/A2 Matt Weaver who began working on Astros telecasts in 1995. Matt comes from a musical background. He's played in bands since he was thirteen and bought his first multi-track recorder while still a teenager. Matt says one of the most interesting things he's *heard* on an Astros broadcast took place when a baby grabbed field reporter Patti Smith's microphone during a between-innings interview and dropped it into a cup of beer.

Matt also speaks to a more personal side of our business. "I've been married to my wonderful wife Julie for sixteen years and we have an amazing six-year-old boy, Matthew. It takes a special family to put up with a work schedule like mine. I typically have to be at the park for set-up six hours before the game and then stay well after the game ends. I work lots of weekends and holidays and sometimes I think to myself, 'It sure would be nice to be that guy sitting in the stands enjoying the game with his wife and son'."

When Jason Martin isn't spending time with his wife Valerie, an emergency center nurse, you'll find him mixing audio on the Astros broadcast. Jason was born in Nashville, but grew up in Houston and received his television degree from the University of Houston. He's been running sound for us for the last fifteen years. He says, "If the viewers enjoy listening to the game and the announcers enjoy broadcasting the game, I've done my job." He does his job very well.

Former Astro Rusty Staub was one of Low Third cameraman Mike Brady's baseball heroes growing up in Montreal. When Staub became an Expo, fans gave him the nickname *"Le Grande Orange"* for his orange-colored hair. Mike's been a camera operator with the Astros crew since the early '90s. He's covered every major sporting event in North America, from the World Series to the Super Bowl, from the Grey Cup to the Stanley Cup. He met his wife Carole working the 1988 Winter Olympic Games in Calgary.

Another of our Killer B's is Robin Barrow, proficient as both a Low First and Low Third camera operator. He's been on the crew a year longer than I, getting his start in 1986. Robin is from Beaumont and a graduate of Lamar University. In life, he's worked as everything from a truck driver and a carpenter to a studio tech and a surgical photographer. "My greatest feeling of satisfaction comes in finding and capturing the play, the reaction, and the emotion of the people and performers in the arena," Robin says. "You have to be able to anticipate, recognize, and react to the events around you, then compose the frame and focus the camera to best capture the moment."

Raising a daughter and two sons helped groom floor manager MaryCarol Hoesel for her job in the booth. She stays busy at the ballpark keeping things flowing smoothly; tending to the surprising number of visitors we have in the booth each game, orchestrating live drop-ins during the broadcast, and ensuring that JD and I have our basket of Cracker Jacks which we toss out of the booth during the seventh-inning stretch. MaryCarol has been with us since 1994, but says her biggest Astros thrill was being on hand—as a spectator—for Mike Scott's 1986 no-hitter.

Phil Boudreaux sits in the seat next to me at Astros home games and has been there since I arrived on the Houston scene. He's a stat guy extraordinaire, a Houston native whose job is to extrapolate storylines of interest via statistical analysis of the game. He's been at his pursuit for so long and is so good at what he does, it's almost a given that any notes he passes my way will make it onto the broadcast. He's also a great husband to his wife Julie and fantastic father to kids Emily and John. Emily has sung the National Anthem at Astros games the last couple of years, a particularly special thrill for Phil. He's a distant relative of Francis Scott Key, the composer of the "Star Spangled Banner."

As you can tell, most of us on the FSHouston crew have worked together for a long time. We consider ourselves a family. We truly care about each other, and I think that enhances the quality of our collective work.

To every lady and gentleman who plays a role in putting Houston Astros baseball on the air, I offer my gratitude and admiration. It is a privilege to work with such an outstanding group of professionals.

CHAPTER 22
Candy Man

One million is a number that gets kicked around a lot in baseball.

Nolan Ryan was baseball's first million-dollar man when he signed a free-agent contract with Houston following the 1979 season. Today, the *average* salary for the *average* player hovers close to $4 million a year. Many managers now get millions for plotting the use of millionaire players. According to Wikipedia, Dodger announcer Vin Scully works under the terms of a multi-million-dollar contract in Los Angeles. Those deals aren't commonplace for the rest of us plying the trade.

Millions of dollars, *lots* of millions, are needed to buy a big league baseball team. In fact, with the sale of the Los Angeles Dodgers in 2012, baseball has moved into *billion-*dollar territory.

Over the course of a season, one million fans are sort of a minimal benchmark for big league teams. Two million is closer to the break-even point for most clubs. Some teams attract three million paying customers over the course of a year. Four clubs have exceeded four million spectators in a single season. The Colorado Rockies drew nearly four-and-a-half million fans in their first year of existence playing games at the old Mile High Stadium—a football venue—in 1993.

At the outset of the 1975 season, Major League Baseball held a promotional campaign to commemorate its one millionth run. The idea was the brainchild of a young man by the name of Mark Sackler, who had spent considerable time as a college student in Boston tallying up all the runs ever scored in professional baseball. In 1974, he decided to extrapolate totals for just the National and American Leagues.

Sackler turned his obsession into a job. On behalf of baseball, he convinced the Tootsie Roll company to sponsor the One Millionth Run contest. Leo Hirschfield, an Austrian immigrant living in New York City, created the confectionary concoction in 1896 and named the chewy chocolate candy for his five-year-old daughter Clara, whom the family called "Tootsie."

According to the Tootsie Roll Industries Web site, the company today manufactures sixty-four million pieces of candy...every day. So, the one-million Tootsie Rolls offered to the player who scored the one-millionth run must have seemed like a drop in the bucket to the promotion's sponsor. To "sweeten" the pot, $10,000 also would be awarded to the player's team. Naturally, the prize would be paid out in pennies—the original cost of a single Tootsie Roll—one million pennies to be exact.

Tote boards were set up in every major league park. As play began on Sunday, May 4, 1975, the milestone was within reach, and as fate would have it, I came within seconds of witnessing the historic event myself.

Online accounts of the contest suggest Dan Ford of the Twins scored baseball's 999,998[th] run in Chicago. Oakland's Claudell Washington crossed the plate with run number 999,999. When the scoreboard in Cleveland clicked down to "1"—meaning the next run would be recognized as the one millionth—Indians outfielder John Lowenstein stood on third base. Aware he was a mere ninety feet from a permanent place in the annals of the game, he pondered the possibilities.

"I thought about trying to steal home," Lowenstein remembered years later, "but we were behind by so much (8-

1) that I figured if I didn't make it, I might as well just keep on running." He knew his rookie skipper Frank Robinson—already a no-nonsense, by-the-book sort of guy—was under the microscope as baseball's first African-American manager.

Boog Powell, one of Robinson's former teammates in Baltimore, was also in his first year in Cleveland as a player. He left Lowenstein forever stranded at third striking out to end the fateful inning.

Some two hundred fifty miles away in Cincinnati, the scoreboard at Riverfront Stadium also displayed a "1." When Davey Concepción stepped to the plate with none on and two out in the Reds' half of the fifth inning, he knew what was on the line. Concepción already had scored a run in the game on an RBI single by Johnny Bench in the first. As he hit in the fifth, a sellout crowd of 51,000 cheered wildly. While not the home-run threat of a Bench, Concepción had the ability to go yard. Facing Braves knuckleballer Phil Niekro played to his advantage.

I watched the moment unfold from the back row of the Channel Five television booth. During the pregame show that afternoon, I had speculated about the millionth run. An hour and a half later, a Reds' player appeared to have a shot at achieving the milestone. With plenty of games underway elsewhere around baseball, it behooved Concepción to try to get the feat done in a hurry.

At nearly the exact same moment Concepción dug in to face Niekro, Bob Watson was taking his lead off second base at San Francisco's Candlestick Park. The Astros first baseman had drawn a second-inning walk off Giants pitcher John Montefusco and then surprised everyone by stealing second. "Bull" as the stocky Watson was called, was not the speediest of runners. His stolen base that day would be one of only three he would record during the '75 season. Under normal circumstances, Watson told me more than thirty-five years later, he probably wouldn't have attempted the steal.

264

"Like everybody else, I was watching the scoreboard," Bob said. "That steal put me in scoring position."

Another base on balls brought Houston catcher Milt May to the plate. The Giants starting pitcher was struggling with his control.

"Montefusco couldn't throw a strike. He walked me on four pitches and he walked Cruz on four pitches. He went two-and-oh to May before he finally grooved one down the middle."

May hit the pitch out of the park.

As the blast cleared the fence, instinct took over and Watson started jogging casually for home. Quickly, teammates in the Astros' bullpen implored for him—in a moment worthy of the movie *Forrest Gump*—to pick up the pace.

"Run, Bull, run!"

Nearing third base Watson suddenly took off as fast as he could.

Meanwhile, in Cincinnati, Concepción had also homered and was tearing around the bases in a sprint worthy of a track star.

Pandemonium broke loose in both cities as fans beseeched the two players to circle the bases as fast as they could. In its own peculiar way, the moment seemed worthy of the Sport of Kings.

"And down the stretch they come!"

Paired in a footrace, Watson would have been no match for the speedy Concepción, but the Astro had what proved to be an insurmountable lead. At 12:32:30 PDT, Watson touched home plate in San Francisco as Concepción rounded third in Cincinnati. The One Millionth Run contest was over.

Earning the honor cost Bob Watson a decent pair of shoes.

After the game at Candlestick Park—the first of a doubleheader there that day—officials from the Baseball Hall of Fame dug up home plate. They also claimed both May's bat and Watson's cleats for enshrinement.

"I really didn't want them to take my shoes," Watson recalls. "In those days you took a long time to break in your spikes. They weren't like the shoes players have today where you can wear them right out of the box. We were three weeks into the season and I had just gotten my shoes broken in and then they took them."

The Astros put up a five-spot in the inning in which Watson scored his historic run, but couldn't hold the lead, losing to the Giants 8-6. The setback was one of the ninety-seven the team suffered that season under manager Preston Gomez. Houston actually won the nightcap of the Sunday twin bill against the Giants, topping San Francisco 12-8.

Watson did not play in that second game for want of a pair of good shoes.

As it turned out, the Tootsie Roll candy was of little use to Watson. His children were allergic to chocolate. Bull donated his prize to both the Boy Scouts and Girl Scouts—he had been a Boy Scout as a kid—and dentists throughout the Houston area rejoiced.

The Astros purportedly invested its million pennies in the organization's minor-league system, perhaps helping to pave the way for the club's first playoff appearance five years later.

***

Robert Jose Watson was originally signed by Houston as a catcher in the club's last days as the Colt .45s. Before then, he was a Pathfinder, one of a seemingly countless number of graduates to reach the big leagues out of Fremont High School in Los Angeles. Hall-of-Famer Bobby Doerr attended Fremont, as did Gene Mauch, Bobby Tolan, George Hendrick, Eric Davis, and others.

In its prime, Fremont was one of the Los Angeles Unified School District's largest schools. The racial make-up of the school has changed through the years. In Watson's time, the school was predominantly black. Today, the student body is nearly ninety percent Latino.

Integration didn't come to Los Angeles schools until the late 1970's, in part because it wasn't a pressing priority. Southern California was far more of a melting pot than other sections of the country. Watson grew up in South Central L.A., raised by grandparents who instilled in him both a sound moral foundation and a sense of fairness. He also learned never to back down from intimidation. That determination served Watson well when Houston assigned him to its Class A team in the Western Carolina League. The racial prejudices he found south of the Mason-Dixon Line would have driven a lesser man from the game. Bull persevered, paid his dues— and then some—and after five years became a regular in the Astros' lineup.

He took to heart his being a Pathfinder.

Watson spent fourteen seasons in a Houston uniform. He was the Astros' lone representative to the 1975 All-Star Game, an honor he earned him twice in his career. After scoring the one-millionth run that season, he went on to hit .324 for the year with an OPS of .870. Later in his career, he played for the Red Sox, Yankees, and Braves, and retired at the end of the 1984 season. Over the course of his nineteen years in the big leagues, Bob carried a career average of .295. He came within shouting distance of 2,000 career hits and 1,000 RBI.

A few years after the ballyhooed Tootsie Roll contest, Sackler's calculations came under scrutiny. Sabermetricians determined Watson had not scored the actual one-millionth run, and, in fact, no one really knew who did. But Watson got the candy, the pennies, a watch, and eventually a new pair of spiked shoes for earning the distinction.

Some things they can't take away from you.

Following his retirement as a player, Watson moved back to California where he was a coach and hitting instructor for the Oakland A's. He returned to Houston as assistant general manager following the 1988 season, one in which Watson and the Athletics reached the World Series.

Bull lived up to his nickname working under Astros GM Bill Wood. Watson was tireless in the execution of his duties and quickly earned the respect of everyone in the organization. When the team was purchased by Drayton McLane in 1993, Bob was charged with helping the new owner get a feel for the game.

"He called me after he bought the club," Watson reflects, "and told me he'd been to only five baseball games in his life. He didn't know how to read a box score except for the attendance figure and final score. He said it was my job to teach him the game. We flew all over the country in his private airplane so I could show him what baseball was all about."

McLane apparently learned quickly because after one year he fired both Wood and the team's manager Art Howe. He didn't have to look far for his front-office replacement.

On October 5, 1993—and true to his roots as a Fremont Pathfinder—Bob Watson became the first African-American to hold the title of general manager for a major league team. Bill Lucas—Hank Aaron's brother-in-law—ran the Braves in the late '70s, but he was officially vice president of player personnel. Atlanta owner Ted Turner chose not to hire anyone for the GM's job, perhaps hoping he could figure out a way to assume that title himself. Nonetheless, a decade and a half passed between Lucas' unexpected death from a cerebral hemorrhage in 1979 and Watson being named general manager of the Astros.

Houston was barely a fortnight into its first season under Watson's watch, when Bull suffered his own health scare. Shortly after his forty-eighth birthday, Watson was diagnosed with prostate cancer. Ultimately he beat the disease and didn't let the illness sidetrack him from his baseball duties. His staunch advocacy for prostate-cancer screening has undoubtedly saved many lives in subsequent years.

After only two seasons as the GM in Houston, Watson accepted the same position with the New York Yankees in 1995. One of his first moves in the new job was to recommend and hire Joe Torre as manager of the club. That move brought a long-needed sense of stability to the New York organization and under Watson and Torre, the Yankees thrived, winning the 1996 World Series.

In gratitude, Yankees owner George Steinbrenner fired Bull a year and a half later. When asked by reporters to speculate on whom within the New York organization might have influenced Steinbrenner's decision to dismiss him, Watson said, "Little people that run around in his head are the baseball people he listens to."

After working a dozen years in the executive offices for Major League Baseball, Bob Watson officially retired from the game in 2010. He remains active in assisting MLB's Urban Youth Academy program, one of several initiatives to encourage African-American youths to take up the game. As a baseball pathfinder himself, he's a fitting role model.

Today Watson thrives in a mostly stress-free retirement. Gone are the one-hundred-hour work weeks he was known for as a big league executive. He's in good health and spends much of his time at his Houston home working on wife Carol's "honey-do" lists. He says she's not quite the taskmaster that Steinbrenner was. He also helps daughter Kelley in her budding entrepreneurial venture.

Fittingly, she's started a candy company.

CHAPTER 23
Blind Faith

"The Lord has done this, and it is marvelous in our eyes."

Matthew 21:42 (NIV)

Bob Aspromonte stepped out of his cap and gown after graduating from Lafayette High School in Brooklyn, New York, and into the uniform of his beloved hometown Dodgers. The year was 1956 and as a newly-signed 17-year-old, Aspromonte was introduced as the club's most recently signed amateur free agent prior to a workout at Ebbets Field.

Fielding grounders alongside the likes of Jackie Robinson and Pee Wee Reese, Aspromonte was a bundle of nerves, misplaying ball after ball. Finally, Robinson walked over and asked to see the rookie's glove. "It's too large for a shortstop," Robinson said. "Here, try mine." For the rest of the workout Aspromonte's defensive play was flawless. When the Dodgers concluded practice that day, Aspromonte handed the glove back to Robinson. At least he tried.

"Keep it, it's yours," the future Hall of Famer said.

As a hometown boy, the Dodgers had a strong desire to see Aspromonte succeed. He was sent to the team's Class A farm club in Macon, Georgia, but played just thirteen games there. He got the call to the parent club in September, and made his Brooklyn debut on September 19. In a pinch-hitting role, Aspromonte struck out swinging—his only big league at-bat of the season and, ultimately, his only appearance as a Brooklyn Dodger. He did not get called up again until after the team had moved to Los Angeles. Aspromonte played sparingly on the West Coast for two seasons.

While publicly the Dodgers still considered Bob a player with promise, the team did not protect him in the 1961 expansion draft. Subsequently, he was selected by the newly formed Houston Colt .45s. He quickly found a spot in the fledgling club's starting lineup.

The Colts, as fans quickly began calling them—"Colt .45s" was a bit of a tongue twister—made their major league debut at home on April 10, 1962. Bob Aspromonte was the first Colt player to bat, hit safely, and score a run in a regular-season game. He went three for four in the opener as Houston pounded the Cubs 11-2. The Colts swept their three-game series with Chicago and despite losing ninety-six games their first year, finished eighth in the ten-team National League standings, seven games ahead of the Cubs, and twenty-five-and-a-half games up on their expansion brethren, the New York Mets.

Aspromonte hit a respectable .266 in his first year as a Houston starter. He also set a National League record in the field that season, playing fifty-seven straight games without committing an error at third.

The Colts' presence in the National League brought a welcome change of scenery to fans throughout the Southwest. In El Dorado, Arkansas, nine-year-old Billy Bradley took early note of the Texas club. With its Old-West nickname and the promise of a space-age ballpark, Houston had a unique allure to a youngster like Billy.

No real surprise then that Billy hitched his wagon to the Colts' star. He quickly found the nearest radio affiliate and spent nights listening to broadcasts of the team's games. Early in that inaugural season, Billy's Colts flirted with respectability.

But, Billy wasn't just a fan. He was a player, too, and a good one at that. His age-group team began practices while school was still in session with workouts set for Friday afternoons after class. A summer's worth of games would soon be at hand to compete with Billy's newfound affection for the Colts.

Springtime in Arkansas also meant weather warnings and advisories, but those were of little concern to boys like Billy. The tandem of lightning and thunder was thrilling to see and hear and few things beat the pleasure of getting drenched in a downpour.

On the Friday afternoon of April 27, 1962, as Billy and his teammates went through their drills on a ball diamond in a quiet El Dorado neighborhood, the wind suddenly picked up from the west. Soon the sky turned gray and in the distance came the rumbling sound of thunder. A light drizzle began to fall and then, with the first flash of lightning, the deluge came. Shrieks of boyish delight filled the air as the storm settled in. Billy's coach called his team off the field and told them to find cover under the canopy of a large old maple tree which stood just a few yards behind the backstop.

The boys raced toward the shelter of the tree. A cast-iron water fountain nearby offered the chance to slake parched young throats. Fastest among his peers, Billy arrived first. As he leaned over the fountain to get a drink, a bolt of lightning hit the tree under which the team had gathered. Because Billy was touching metal, the charge found its way to and through him on its path toward the ground.

***

"It basically killed me," Bill Bradley told reporter Marlon Morgan of the Memphis *Commercial Appeal* newspaper in a story which ran in 2008. Fortunately, none of the other boys were seriously injured and Billy's coach knew CPR. After a time, he was able to get Billy breathing again. A half century ago, people didn't realize a tree was the last place one wanted to be in the event of a thunderstorm.

Unconscious for hours, Billy woke up in a local hospital the next morning. Miraculously he had survived the strike, but it had extracted a heavy toll.

Billy was blind.

"The electricity fried the lens of my eyes, melted a big glob of my hair, and punctured my right ear drum," Bradley recounted to Morgan in an interview which ran in advance of an episode about Billy in the Fox Sports series *Amazing Sport Stories.*

Local doctors told Billy's parents the loss of sight was permanent. Not satisfied with the diagnosis, the family reached out to Dr. Louis Girard, chairman of ophthalmology at Baylor University College of Medicine in Houston. Girard believed Billy's vision could be restored, at least partially. The first of a series of surgical procedures was scheduled for late July.

As Billy recovered from his other injuries, he faithfully followed the Colts' fortunes from afar, careful to keep the radio close to his left ear. The team slowly lagged in the standings, but the club's young third baseman, Bob Aspromonte, went on a tear. Hitting just .197 at the end of April, Aspromonte raised his average to .290 by mid-July, leaving a big impression on one particular young boy in Arkansas. Billy had been looking for a Colt to call his own. Aspromonte turned out to be the man.

With the time for Billy's surgery growing near, Billy became more and more despondent. His concerns had little to do with the procedure which might help him regain his eyesight. He was disappointed in the fact his trip to Houston would not include a chance to see his favorite team play. Of course, Billy couldn't see anything, but he had no trouble imagining what the experience might be like.

Billy's story—his survival from the lightning strike and the ensuing blindness—traveled far and wide. Word got around in Houston. Most likely Dr. Girard or another member of the Baylor staff alerted the Colt .45s' organization that one of their biggest fans was coming to town.

As I've grown to know Bob Aspromonte, I can easily imagine how willing he might have been to go out of his way to offer support to an impressionable young boy and his heartsick parents. When told about Billy's plight—and the fact he was the boy's favorite player—Bob readily agreed to call on the Bradleys once they arrived in town. And when the time came, he wasn't unprepared. In visiting Billy's hospital room, he brought along two of his teammates, an autographed baseball, a pair of Colt pajamas, *and* a transistor radio on which Billy could listen to games while he recovered from surgery.

Close your eyes and imagine what it might have been like when Bob Aspromonte walked into that hospital room on the afternoon of July 25, 1962. Imagine the doctor saying, "Billy, there is someone here to see you," then another voice adding, "Hi, Billy. I'm Bob Aspromonte."

Imagine you were that excited little boy.

No doubt, Billy's parents beamed with delight and appreciation that a big league baseball player—let alone their son's favorite—had taken the time to pay them a visit. As Aspromonte recalls the visit, no one else could get a word in edgewise. Billy talked non-stop about such things as the size of Aspromonte's hands, the fortunes of his own team back home, and the weather outlook for that night's Colts game.

The forecast called for clear skies and high humidity.

Over and over Billy kept saying, "I can't believe you're here." Not once, did he talk about the accident or his loss of sight.

When the time finally came for Aspromonte and his teammates to go, Billy had one final request of the Houston third baseman.

"Could you hit a home run for me tonight?"

***

To a little boy who couldn't see, Bob Aspromonte was larger than life, but in real life, the Colt third-baseman wasn't considered a power hitter. In his two years as a part-time player in Los Angeles, Aspromonte had hit one home run. As a regular with the Colts, he didn't hit his first home run until the team's twentieth game of their inaugural season, but entrenched as a starter, he became more productive offensively. Not only had he raised his batting average more than one hundred points, he'd also hit nine more home runs by the time he met Billy. Ten might seem like a lot to a young boy, but surely Aspromonte knew better than to make a promise he didn't think he could keep.

But, Aspromonte couldn't take it upon himself to tell Billy no.

Billy's powers of persuasion were in further evidence after Aspromonte left. After much bargaining, pleading, and cajoling, he convinced his parents and his doctor to allow him to go to the game. His insistence was compelling and a compromise was reached. He could go, but he couldn't stay for the whole game. He had to be back early to get a good night's sleep before his surgical procedure the next day.

The next time you're at the ballpark, close your eyes and experience what that Colt game might have been like for Billy. Without the sense of sight, sounds and smells become abundant and wonderfully varied. Listen for the crack of the bat and the roar of the crowd. Smell the variety of aromas emanating from concession venues. Taste the savory goodness of a freshly-cooked hot dog. Hold a souvenir

Bill Brown

baseball or felt pennant in your hands, and experience their texture with your fingertips.

Seated between his parents and a representative from the hospital, Billy squealed with excitement when the public address announcer introduced Aspromonte's at-bat in the bottom of the first. He groaned in disappointment along with the rest of the Colt Stadium crowd as San Francisco pitcher Billy O'Dell struck out his hero. O'Dell retired Aspromonte again in the third on a ground ball back to the mound.

"Just one more inning, just one more," Billy pleaded with his parents after five frames. *"Please???"* This time there was no compromise and the Bradleys headed back to the hospital to put Billy to bed.

By the time they had settled their son for the night, a new agreement had been reached. Billy could stay up and listen to the end of the game on the new transistor radio Aspromonte had given him. Clad in his team pajamas and clutching the autographed baseball, Billy listened intently as the Colts, trailing 3-1, loaded the bases in the bottom of the seventh. Don Larsen—of World Series perfect-game fame—relieved O'Dell and squelched the Houston rally, getting Jim Pendleton to fly out to end the inning.

Aspromonte had been the on-deck hitter.

Was Bob nervous that night? "More than you could even imagine," he revealed years later. "By the time I got to the ballpark that afternoon, I was really kicking myself for not doing a better job deflecting Billy's request. I could have offered to get him a hit or knock in a run. Honestly, I'd never been in that situation before and I just didn't know what to say or do."

The Giants went down in order in the eighth as Billy's parents did everything in their power to convince their son to turn the radio off and go to sleep. Fortunately, they failed.

Stu Miller took the mound for San Francisco to face the Colts in the bottom of the eighth inning. Miller achieved a

276

certain degree of infamy in one of the two All-Star games played in 1961. A gust of wind at Candlestick Park blew him off the mound on his home field and caused him to commit a balk. Otherwise, he was typically a tough customer. In 1963, he would lead the American League in appearances and saves after a trade to the Orioles.

Unlike closers today, Miller was not a power pitcher. In fact, his big roundhouse curve was once clocked at a pedestrian fifty-three miles per hour. If Mariano Rivera is the greatest reliever of all time, consider that he has given up 0.5 home runs per nine innings in his career. In 1962, despite his lack of heat, Miller's home run rate was an impressive 0.7.

As Billy listened from his hospital room he found it increasingly difficult to stay awake after the second most eventful day of his young life. Billy's head nodded and his father reached to pry the radio from his hand. "Bob Aspromonte will lead off the eighth for the Colts," Gene Elston proclaimed and with the sound of his hero's name, Billy again was wide awake. At Colt Stadium, Aspromonte stepped in to the batter's box for his fourth and final plate appearance of the night. Telling the story later, he said he had only one thought on his mind in that moment. He really wanted to hit a homer for that kid from Arkansas.

And he did.

And the little boy in the hospital room in the Texas Medical Center went absolutely crazy.

The home run wasn't enough for the Colts and the Giants held on for a 3-2 win. Aspromonte had sworn the teammates who had joined him for the hospital visit to tell no one about Billy's request. He figured there was no way he could make the little boy's wish come true and he didn't want anyone to know that he had failed.

But he didn't fail.

Bob Aspromonte also didn't hit another home run the rest of the season.

***

Girard's plan was to perform three surgeries on each of Billy's eyes. Bolstered by the success of the first procedure, the next round of treatments was scheduled for the following year. Attitude plays a large part in the healing process and one can imagine that Aspromonte's home run bolstered Billy's spirits. Billy may have even willed himself to heal with the hope he would someday get to *see* his hero play.

Billy returned to Houston in June 1963 with a very small amount of vision in both eyes. The world was a blur and his eyesight wasn't enhanced much by the thick glasses he wore, but when he met Aspromonte again, he could at least make out the facial features of his handsome hero, so long as the Colt leaned in close. Close enough to touch. Close enough to whisper to.

"Could you hit another home run for me tonight?"

Most other ballplayers would have chuckled and mumbled something like, "Kid, you're killing me." Aspromonte said he couldn't promise anything, but that if he did happen to hit another home run, it would definitely be for Billy.

On Tuesday night, June 11, 1963, Aspromonte failed to homer against the Cubs—through nine innings of regulation play. In the bottom of the tenth, with the score tied 2-2 and the bases loaded, Aspromonte hit a walk-off grand slam against Lindy McDaniel giving the Colts a 6-2 victory.

The homer was just his third of the year, but for Billy Bradley, Aspromonte was an astounding two for two.

Six weeks later—almost exactly one year to the day from the first of his "miracle" shots—and with Billy again in town for his final round of surgeries, the young boy from Arkansas and the ballplayer from Brooklyn struck another of their cosmically-inspired deals. Billy asked for a homer. Aspromonte again said he would try.

Carrying just a .200 average and dropped to sixth in the Colts' batting order, Aspromonte stepped to the plate in the first inning of a game against the Mets with the bases loaded. Incredibly, he hit another grand slam home run. This time, Billy's eyesight had been sufficiently restored and the home run hit early enough for the youngster to witness the amazing moment in person.

By then, word had spread about the magical bond between Billy and Bob. Gene Elston's call of the home run included, "Another one for you, Bill Bradley!" Fans surrounding Billy and his parents and throughout the stadium gave the boy—and the player—a standing ovation. Rounding third and approaching home, Aspromonte's eyes filled with tears and he was mobbed by teammates as if he had just won the seventh game of the World Series. Later, he called the blow "divine intervention."

Bruce Nash began work on his *Amazing Sports Stories* series in 2007. His company, Nash Entertainment, produced a total of thirteen episodes for broadcast on the Fox Sports Networks. Four were nominated for Emmy Awards, including Episode 109, entitled "Bob Aspromonte: Blind Faith," which first aired in June 2008.

Billy's eyesight was completely restored. He returned to little league play and threw a no-hitter. When the local paper found out about the achievement, they interviewed Billy for a story. He told the reporter he wanted to dedicate his gem to Aspromonte for all the Houston ballplayer had done for him. Billy sent a clipping of the story to Aspromonte. The two have remained in contact through the years.

Aspromonte played thirteen years in the big leagues, seven in Houston. In more than 4,300 career at bats, he hit just sixty home runs. He held the Astros' club record for grand slams in a career with six until it was broken in 2011 by

Carlos Lee. Two of those bases-loaded blasts were hit for Billy Bradley. And consider that he was one batter away from coming up with the bases loaded before he hit the first home run for his young friend. Divine intervention.

***

A few years after retirement, Bob Aspromonte was helping jump start a friend's car when one of the batteries blew up in his face. He was struck by debris and blinded in one eye.

In advance of his own surgery, Aspromonte was asked to remain on his back and virtually motionless for several days as doctors tried to alleviate the pressure of swelling around the eye. At his darkest moment, he got a call. It was Bill Bradley—by then a young adult—offering reassurance.

"You're in good hands," Bradley reminded Aspromonte. Dr. Girard would be his surgeon, too.

Girard was only able to restore partial vision to Aspromonte's left eye, but the former Colt and Astro is grateful for the vision he has. Now in his mid-70s, Aspromonte is as dashing as in the days of his youth. After retirement as a player, Bob chose to move back to Houston, where he's made his home ever since.

"Sight into Sound" is a Houston-based non-profit organization which "enriches the lives of individuals with visual, physical, and learning disabilities...through Radio Reading, Custom Recording, and Audio Description services." I do volunteer reading there and Bob often speaks on behalf of the agency. We both try to play in their annual charity golf tournament.

When I shared this chapter with Bob to confirm its accuracy and get his approval, he responded with this e-mail:

MY EYE INJURY HAS MOTIVATED ME TO HELP OTHERS YOUNG AND OLD TO BE MORE AWARE OF THE PRESERVATION OF SIGHT. TELLING THE "BLIND FAITH" STORY AND TALKING ABOUT INCREDIBLE PROGRAMS LIKE SIGHT INTO SOUND, THE LIONS FOUNDATON FOR SIGHT, AND THE HOUSTON EYE ASSOCIATES, GIVES ME THE OPPORTUNITY TO INCREASE PUBLIC AWARENESS TO SOME OF THE CAUSES OF BLINDNESS AND INFORM THE COMMUNITY ABOUT WHAT'S BEING DONE TO RESTORE SIGHT AND TO GIVE PEOPLE HOPE.

He signed his message, *"ASPRO THE ASTRO."*

CHAPTER 24
Grave Circumstances

"You've got to be kidding."

I stood at the breakfast table, coffee mug in hand, peering down at the front page of the *Houston Chronicle's* sports section. An illustration of a tombstone proclaimed the Astros' 2005 season already dead. Just fifty-one games into the year—on June 1—the local newspaper seemed to be giving up on the hometown team. The club *was* already fourteen games out of first place.

"What is it, dear?" Dianne asked, as she brought over the coffee pot to freshen my cup.

"Look at this," I told her pointing at the grave marker.

"Oh, my! Did someone die?"

"The paper says the Astros are dead, no chance of reaching the playoffs. I think that's a little extreme this early in the season."

Once Dianne took a closer look at the illustration she mused, "Well, that *does* seem a little harsh." Still standing, I was intently reading the story, figuring it would create a topic for discussion with Jim Deshaies on that night's telecast. Dianne shrugged her shoulders and walked away.

My wife does not share my passion for sports, but she's picked up a thing or two in our time together. She has a sixth sense about a ballplayer's character and she knows the baseball season is a long and drawn out affair.

The article, written by Jose de Jesus Ortiz—a good young reporter who remains with the paper—suggested the '05 Astros were in unchartered waters. Only one team ever, Ortiz wrote, had rallied from a larger June 1 deficit to reach the playoffs: Art Howe's 2001 Oakland A's, the year before the club's *Moneyball* season.

With the *Chronicle* story top of mind, I walked into Astros manager Phil Garner's office later that afternoon. His club was set to face the Reds in the rubber game of a three-game series. Garner greeted me warmly, as he always did. Phil's a great guy.

"Feeling 'funereal'?" I asked, referencing that morning's newspaper. He laughed. The two of us had talked at length about the club's slow start a couple weeks earlier. Both Jeff Kent and Carlos Beltran had left the team via free agency following the 2004 season, a year in which the club had come within one game of reaching the World Series. Nagging shoulder problems had shelved Jeff Bagwell less than a month into the '05 campaign. The injury effectively ended his Hall-of-Fame-worthy career.

The team also began the year without another star, Lance Berkman. Playing in an off-season flag-football game, Berkman had hurt a knee and underwent surgery. Risking injury might have seemed like a knucklehead thing for Berkman to do, but to his credit, he was trying to stay in shape. Lance had been oft-criticized for showing up to spring training and beginning the regular season a little "soft around the middle."

Garner had predicted his team would be slow to gel. "We'll be fine in the long term," the Astros' skipper assured. "Remember, we don't have to do it all with our offense."

The team had proven resilient in 2004. With starting pitchers Roger Clemens and Roy Oswalt the best one-two punch in the National League and with closer Brad Lidge in possession of one of the most lethal pitches in baseball—his slider—Houston had put together a deep and capable pitching staff. After Phil Garner adopted his own "Captain Hook" approach with his bullpen, things fell into place for the '04 team.

Garner took over the Astros the day after the 2004 All-Star game, played in Houston. He replaced Jimy Williams, who in his two-and-a-half years at the helm of the club never caught the imagination of the city's fans or even his own team. With the Astros' record hovering at .500 at the mid-season point, speculation had run rampant the team would make a change.

News of the move was not released until the day after the All-Star Game. Williams was one of the coaches on the National League All-Star team and when he was introduced to the home crowd, the response was definitely mixed.

By the time Garner took over, the Astros were ten-and-a-half-games behind St. Louis in the NL Central Division. Second-guessers had a field day with the hire. Under the former Astro second baseman, the club immediately lost four of five. A month later, things weren't much improved. Houston appeared to be no better than a win-one-lose-one kind of team and a loss in Montreal on August 14 dropped them to nineteen-and-a-half games behind the Cardinals. Division title hopes for the 2004 season were certainly bleak.

Just days before, I decided to keep a diary of the remainder of the 2004 season. I was perplexed the team hadn't lived up to its potential and was curious whether a day-by-day analysis might reveal idiosyncrasies affecting play. Or maybe I was just bored.

Here's what I wrote on the team's flight from Montreal to Philadelphia:

> The Expos were going for a sweep of the three-game weekend series in Montreal. The Astros, losers of eight of their last eleven games, had sagged to a 56-60 record. They were seven games behind the Chicago

Cubs in the Wild Card Race, tied for seventh place. The Expos' Livan Hernandez took a 4-2 lead to the ninth. As the league leader in innings pitched and complete games, he needed three outs to secure his tenth win. He got one. Luis Ayala came in with two on and one out. Jason Lane singled in one run. Jose Vizcaino's ground out tied the game, 4-4. Orlando Palmeiro's two-out pinch single gave the Astros an improbable 5-4 win, snapping the Expos' seven-game winning streak.

The Astros then swept three games from the Phillies, but my journal entry on the flight home for a weekend series against the Cubs was revealing.

Garner and (general manager Gerry) Hunsicker had lunch this week (in Philadelphia). Garner told Gerry that the team wasn't responding for whatever reason and if it were his team, he'd blow them up. "I'd trade guys and I'd get myself a pile of cash and I'd start all over the next year," Garner told Hunsicker. Gerry's reply: 'I want to give these guys every chance I can.'

Garner's words seemed prophetic as his team lost two of three to the Cubs. The Wild Card deficit stood at seven-and-a-half games. The club was going nowhere.

And then, for the next seventeen games, the Houston Astros almost forgot how to lose.

***

Without question, the finish to the 2004 regular season was one of the most exciting stretches of baseball I've ever seen played. In the last week alone, each game seemed to be a do-or-die situation and with each win, a different hero emerged. When I go back and reread my journal entries, it's almost like being at the ballpark again.

After dropping a Sunday afternoon game to the Cubs on August 22, the Astros won fifteen of their next sixteen outings.

In St. Louis, the Cardinals were playing magnificent baseball themselves, but in Houston—where the season had appeared a lost cause—the city suddenly had a case of playoff fever.

The Astros began the final week of the season bunched with the Cubs, Giants, and Padres in the Wild Card standings. Houston finished its year with six games at home—and won all six, sweeping the Cardinals and the Rockies. On the last day of the season, starter Brandon Backe led a seven-pitcher parade as the Astros prevailed 5-3 to claim the 2004 National League Wild Card by a one-game margin over San Francisco.

Over the course of the last six weeks of the season, Houston won eighteen consecutive games at home and thirty-six of its last forty-six games overall. For the entire year, Houston pitchers threw only *two* complete games.

"When I took over the team," Garner said, "I thought there was a bit of uneasiness in the bullpen. I came in and the first thing I did was to say, 'Look, we're just gonna run Lidge out there and he's gonna be the guy. I'm gonna use the bullpen frantically. When a guy starts to go into a tailspin, I'm gonna get him out and run another one in'."

Garner's faith in his bullpen was rewarded, but at the cost of some individual tension.

"After (Hunsicker) told me he was going to stay the course with our roster," Garner said, "he encouraged me to do anything I thought might help the club to win. Brad Ausmus and Adam Everett were two of the best defensive players at their positions, but in tight contests with every game critical in the standings, 'good-field, no-hit' guys will only get you so far. I made the decision to pinch-hit for both of them earlier than we had been doing.

"I remember the first time I did it with Brad. When I told him in the dugout I was taking him out of the game, he wasn't very happy. If looks could kill, I would have been dead. I used Mike Lamb and he got a bases-loaded double and we wound up winning the game.

"I give Brad an awful lot of credit for the success we had that season," Garner continued. "He was one of the veterans on the club and the message I was trying to send to everyone—to use every player on our roster to win—could have rubbed him the wrong way. If a guy like him doesn't buy into what a manager is trying to do, that attitude could very well derail the entire team."

The winning continued into the postseason as Houston finally got the playoff monkey off its back. In the decisive fifth game of the National League Divisional Series, Carlos Beltran went four for five with two home runs and five RBI and six Houston pitchers kept the Atlanta Braves' bats in check. The visiting Astros' 12-3 win gave the franchise its first-ever playoff series victory. And, the club came close to another win—and the team's first trip to the World Series—when it extended the Cardinals to seven dramatic games in the NL Championship Series. In the end, Houston fell just short, but if the 2004 season stood for anything, it was that you can never count a good team out regardless of how improbable a comeback seems.

***

In sports, anything in print—and more recently online—which calls into question a team's reputation or heart, whether individually or collectively, is said to be "bulletin-board material." A derogatory story, whether a reporter's opinion or reports of what an opposing player has told the press, often motivates performance. In football, that provocation counts for a lot. Getting a team to an emotional peak is key to success in the sport. Baseball is different. The season is long and less dependent on emotional highs and lows.

The *Chronicle's* "tombstone story"—as it came to be known—did become a regular topic of conversation among

Houston fans and national media as the dramatic 2005 season neared its end. The story probably helped sell newspapers, but whether it inspired victories is open to debate. The team did go out and beat the Reds the night the story broke, but that's probably the extent of the impact the article had on the club. Houston lost two of its following three games at home to the Cardinals.

What happened next, though, reveals much about the nature of the game.

From the World Cup of international soccer to the Super Bowl of endless hype, from the college hoopla of the Final Four to the travesty of the BCS National Championship game, many of the biggest events in the world of sports are title matchups which are "one-and-done" affairs. That's good when you're trying to rake in the largest television audience possible, but baseball is different, more "pastoral" as comedian George Carlin once said. "In baseball," the late funnyman offered in one of his most well-known bits, "the object is to go home! And to be safe!

"In football," Carlin continued in a much more somber tone, "there's unnecessary roughness and *sudden death!*"

Although a season is one hundred sixty-two games long, baseball people in the know think of it in much smaller increments. The '05 Astros, once Berkman got healthy and the rest of the team settled into its roles and responsibilities, began moving in the right direction one series at a time. From June 7 to July 10, the Astros won nine series in a row, sweeping two games from the same team, or winning at least two out of three against an opponent. Steady improvement elevated Houston from a 21-34 record to a 44-43 mark. In fact, with a loss in St. Louis in the team's first outing after the All-Star Game, Houston had *exactly* the same record after eighty-eight games in 2005 as it had in 2004. The "dead" had been reborn. The hunt for an October playoff berth was alive.

Remarkably, the second half of the '05 season played out in much the same fashion as the year before. Beginning on July 18, a month before the team's torrid late-season run of '04, Houston put together six- and seven-game winning streaks and at one point captured fifteen of seventeen games. With a win over the Mets on July 30, the '05 Astros had the third best record in the National League.

By season's end, the Astros were still the third-best team in the NL and won the 2005 Wild Card by six games over the Marlins and Mets.

For the second year in a row, Roy Oswalt won twenty games as the ace of the Astros' staff. Andy Pettitte shook off his injury-marred 2004 campaign to win seventeen games. Roger Clemens, the '04 NL Cy Young winner, managed a seemingly paltry 13-8 record, but the mark was deceiving. During one five-game stretch, Clemens averaged seven-plus innings per start, while his teammates scored a *total* of four runs.

Offensively, the club ranked thirteenth of the sixteen National League teams in cumulative batting average and eleventh in runs scored. As good a job as Garner had done with the club in '04, his work in '05 was even better. And yet, he managed but a third-place finish for NL Manager of the Year. Just like his ball club, he finished behind Bobby Cox of the Braves and Tony LaRussa of the Cardinals.

And as had been the case in 2004, Houston's playoff road was headed once again through the cities of Atlanta and St. Louis.

***

So, how does an idled broadcaster pass the time when rights restrictions keep him from occupying a seat in front of a live microphone during postseason play? Since Fox Sports Houston does not broadcast games beyond the regular season,

I've seen the Astros' playoff runs more from the perspective of a fan than an announcer. In 2004 and 2005, I did appear on the occasional local postgame show and was interviewed from time to time by out-of-market radio stations, but my perspective on the game changes slightly when I'm no longer behind a microphone.

Although I didn't call the contest, I can't argue against Game Four of the 2005 Astros-Braves National League Division Series as the greatest game in Houston history. I was at the ballpark that afternoon and although seated in the press box, I definitely had a rooting—if silent—interest in the outcome of the game.

I also had dinner plans with Dianne that evening, but I would have to call and cancel those.

At eighteen innings and five hours and fifty minutes, that Astros-Braves game remains the longest postseason contest ever. Houston has become notorious for its baseball marathons. But, as everyone knows, everything is bigger in Texas.

If I've used that line before, it certainly bears repeating in the context of the "Miracle at Minute Maid."

Having defeated the Braves in the NLDS the year before, Houston stood toe-to-toe with an Atlanta ball club which had reached the postseason as a division champion for the fourteenth time in fifteen years. The Astros drew first blood in the series in Atlanta thanks to none other than Brad Ausmus and Adam Everett. Those light-hitting defensive specialists ignited a five-run eighth-inning rally which broke open Game One and helped give Houston a 10-5 win. Atlanta bounced back behind John Smoltz to win Game Two, 7-1.

In Game Three, a four-run seventh broke open a tight contest and Houston went on to claim a 7-3 win at home. Game Four of the best-of-five series, also at Minute Maid, loomed large. While Houston had lost Game Four the year before but won the deciding game in Atlanta, a visiting team playing a winner-take-all contest at Turner Field was always a tough assignment.

The Braves seemed well on their way to pushing the series back to the Deep South when Adam LaRoche clubbed a third-inning grand slam off Brandon Backe. By the eighth, Atlanta's lead had grown to 6-1.

Braves starter Tim Hudson had been dominant through seven innings of work, but in the home half of the eighth, he allowed the Astros' first two hitters to reach base. At that point, Cox called for his closer Kyle Farnsworth, hoping to seal the win. Farnsworth had been obtained from Detroit at the mid-summer trading deadline and immediately bolstered the Atlanta bullpen. The team had run through two mostly ineffectual closers before Farnsworth's arrival. After joining the club, Farnsworth converted ten of ten save opportunities.

Pitching against the heart of the Astros' lineup, Farnsworth got Biggio to ground into a fielder's choice. With Luke Scott at the plate, the Astros pulled a nothing-to-lose double steal and then on a 3-2 pitch, Farnsworth succumbed to the mounting pressure by walking Scott. The last thing he had wanted to do was face the on-deck hitter with the bases loaded.

Up to plate stepped switch-hitting Lance Berkman.

Although Farnsworth had joined the Braves from Detroit, he had spent most of his big league career pitching for the Chicago Cubs and Berkman had Farnsworth's historical number. In twelve previous career at-bats versus the Braves' right-hander, Berkman had eight hits for a .667 average. Berkman also was facing Farnsworth hitting left-handed. Throughout his career, The Big Puma has been a much greater threat to go deep batting left-handed. In every way, the showdown favored the Astros' outfielder.

Berkman hit one two rows deep into the Crawford Boxes to pull Houston to within a run.

Farnsworth stayed in the game and got another chance to close out the Astros in the bottom of the ninth. He retired Jason Lane and Jose Vizcaino quickly. Ausmus came to the plate, the last hope for Houston. The year before against Atlanta, the Astros catcher had acquitted himself admirably, hitting for a .333 average in the NLDS against the Braves.

Speculation in the press box was that Garner might bring Bagwell into the game. After rejoining the team in September, the veteran first baseman saw only pinch-hitting duties the remainder of the season. Garner, though, went with Ausmus instead, and the Houston catcher clubbed the game-tying home run to left-center field.

I can still remember watching that blast from Writer's Row of the press box. As the ball jumped off Ausmus' bat, the entire crowd rose in unison. As the ball landed beyond the left-centerfield fence, the stadium erupted. The game had been tied by one of the most unlikely of sources, but one couldn't help but feel good for the hero of the moment. Ausmus had battled hard to regain his manager's faith.

If looks could thrill.

Once the contest went into extra innings, the game became a war of attrition as both managers cautiously played the percentages.

Atlanta mounted a serious threat in the fourteenth, loading the bases with one out against Houston reliever Dan Wheeler. The Astros' season-long set-up man pitched out of the jam and got through a reasonably drama-free fifteenth. He was the team's seventh pitcher of the game. Phil Garner had completely depleted his bullpen.

The Astros did have an eager volunteer ready to give it a go if needed. Granted, a 42-year-old father who had spent part of his Sunday playing ball with his son is not usually considered an ideal candidate to come to the aid of a big league ball club. But this was no ordinary spectator.

"Skip, I've got my spikes on," Roger Clemens told Garner.

"I'm not worried about your feet," Garner replied. "How's your arm?"

"Skip, I'll do whatever it takes."

Clemens had pitched five innings three days earlier in Game Two. He gave up five runs and was tagged with the loss versus Smoltz. While his competitive spirit was willing, what he failed to tell Garner was that he had already thrown for a half hour in one of the team's indoor batting cages earlier in the day. Obsessive with his workout regimen, Clemens held firm to a strict routine which included a grueling throwing session between starts. Son Koby, recently signed by the team in the amateur draft, stood in at the plate with bat in hand, symbolic of a real hitter and a part of the intricacy which Clemens employed to enhance his focus on the practice mound.

When Wheeler got into his fourteenth-inning fix—and knowing the team was out of relievers—I was curious as to what Garner might do next. As Clemens began warming up in the bullpen, I said to myself, "Garner is playing this game as a must-win situation."

Both teams had played too long to give this one away.

Clemens actually entered Game Four in the bottom of the fifteenth as a pinch hitter. After Biggio singled, Clemens laid down a successful sacrifice bunt. Chris Burke, who had taken Berkman's place in the batting order in the thirteenth, walked, but then Braves pitcher Jim Brower induced Morgan Ensberg to hit into an inning-ending double play.

When Garner tabbed Clemens to pinch-hit, Astros pitching coach Jim Hickey told no one in particular. "Here comes The Rocket. He's going to hit a home run for us to win the game and tomorrow he'll save a small country."

After laying down the bunt, Clemens returned to the Houston dugout. "You're on the mound next inning," Garner told him. "Give us what you can."

Clemens threw three shutout innings, striking out four and giving up just one hit. He hit for the second time in the game when he led off the bottom of the eighteenth.

Burke was in the on-deck circle.

"People thought Rocket was gonna win the game for us," said Burke, "I remember when he struck out (in the eighteenth), there was kind of a lull in the stadium. I came up to bat and I remember thinking, 'We've been out here for six hours. Chipper Jones has played this entire game. He has to be half asleep right now. Maybe I can sneak a bunt, steal second base, somebody gets a single and we win this thing.'"

Braves reliever Joey Devine missed the strike zone with his first pitch to Burke. The next pitch was well inside, putting the Astro up in the count 2-0.

"So on the 2-0 pitch my eyes had kinda been moved toward the inside corner of the plate," Burke said in the days following the game. "He runs (throwing inside) a 2-0 pitch and really, if you look at the replay, it speaks to what I'm saying because really that's not a pitch you usually get. Really, it's like right on the black at about ninety-four (miles per hour). But I've always been able to pull the ball and my eyes were looking in and man, he threw the pitch right where my eyes were and I got the barrel right there and the rest is history."

Burke swung and lifted a drive toward left field. The Crawford Boxes there make Minute Maid Park one of the friendliest home run havens in the big leagues. After all those years in the cavernous Astrodome, when the team moved into its new stadium team management was determined to get in on the power parade which baseball in the Steroid Era had become. In fact, so cozy were the Minute Maid confines in left field, they benefited everyone, including hitters like Burke. In 318 at-bats during the regular season—despite his self-proclaimed ability to turn on the inside pitch—Burke had hit just five home runs.

Brad Ausmus's regular season tally had been just three.

When Burke's line drive landed two rows deep into the Crawford Boxes—in fact, the same fan who caught Berkman's grand slam, Shaun Dean, also corralled Burke's home run— the restless crowd exploded and Houston fans finally got what they had come for: a playoff-series-clinching victory at home, a first for the franchise. Burke was mobbed at the plate and a celebration unlike any other in Astros history—to commemorate a game unlike any other—was underway.

Burke's home run, the sixth-ever to end a playoff series, came on the 553rd pitch of the contest. The win propelled Houston into a National League Championship Series rematch with St. Louis. The most memorable moment of that series was Albert Pujols's two-out, three-run homer off Brad Lidge in the ninth inning of Game Five. The Cardinals' own Miracle at Minute Maid staved off elimination for a night and sent the series back to St. Louis. In 2004, the Redbirds had won the last two games at home to claim the NL pennant, but in 2005, destiny was on the side of the the team which had been left for dead.

Roy Oswalt's dominant pitching performance at Busch Stadium II highlighted the Astros' 5-1 Game Six victory. With the win, Houston was champion of the National League for the first time ever.

The first World Series game played in Texas went fourteen innings at Minute Maid Park. Not surprisingly, that tied a World Series record. Former Astro Geoff Blum led off the fourteenth with a solo home run and the Chicago White Sox went on to post a 7-5 victory. After losing the first two games of the Series at U.S. Cellular Field, Houston found itself in a deep hole.

No more miracles were in the offing.

Chicago completed the four-game sweep the next night as yet another former Astro, pitcher Freddie Garcia, threw seven shutout innings. Jermaine Dye's eighth-inning RBI single off Lidge accounted for the only run of the game. While Houston had waited forty-four seasons to play in its first Fall Classic, Chicago's World Series triumph ended *eighty-eight* years of championship futility. Back in the Windy City, White Sox fans celebrated with great gusto, all through the night and into the days to come.

***

When the Astros defeated the Cardinals in St. Louis to win their first National League title, a celebration of sizable proportions broke out in downtown Houston even though the home team was nowhere to be found. Somewhat uncharacteristically, I decided to join the revelers out that night.

While watching Oswalt's dominant Game Six pitching performance at home, it occurred to me that what I was seeing was indeed history in the making. I had spent nearly twenty years associated with the ball club and the team's victory—in a sense—also felt like a small personal triumph of my own. When the final out was recorded in St. Louis, I told Dianne I wanted to see how our adopted hometown would make merry with its very first league championship. I urged her to join me. Her look not only said "no," but also told me she thought I might be a little off my rocker. "You go and have fun," she answered with a knowing smile.

Some five months after being given up for dead, the Houston Astros were again front-page news as 2005 National League Champions. This time, the stories in the *Chronicle* were a little more upbeat. Reporters Ruth Rendon and Dale Lezon described the downtown celebration.

Nearly 2,500 fans watched Wednesday's playoff game projected on the side of the Binz building at Main and

Prairie. Several hundred others watched the game in bars along Main.

When the Astros won, the party began. The crowd took to the streets and sidewalks, screaming, chanting, and laughing.

Cars packed with Astros fans clogged downtown streets soon after the game. Drivers inched forward and held their hands out their windows, high-fiving pedestrians milling in the streets. People stood up through the sunroofs and hung out the side windows of their vehicles, waving Astros banners, flags, towels, and the occasional brassiere as others marched on the sidewalks chanting "Astros, Astros, Astros!"

More than 150 police officers, including at least 20 officers on horseback patrolled the crowd. Despite the crowd and slow parade, officers reported no problems, saying people were rowdy, but well-behaved.

Early the next season, the Astros' organization presented both players and front-office staff with NL Championship rings. I wear that ring to this day, not all the time, but on special occasions. A baseball *team* is more than the sum of its parts and a baseball organization is made up of many people who perform a wide variety of functions and services. Everyone contributes.

I also received a ring from the Reds when Cincinnati won its 1976 World Series title.

The rings today are bigger than the ones of a generation or two before. The symbolism, though, remains the same. For one incredible season, a group of talented young men achieved uncommon excellence and set themselves apart from their peers. The success, though, is fleeting. Players move on. Things change.

As of the beginning of the 2012 season, only one Astros player, Wandy Rodriguez, has a ring just like mine.

CHAPTER 25
Blown Off Course

Baseball strives to be a game of order. There's the batting order, retiring the side in order, and a "beer and a dog" order at the concession stand.

In nature, the opposite of order is chaos and as any fan knows, there's plenty of that in baseball, too. From bad-hop groundballs to fly balls lost in the sun, from blown calls at second base to botched calls to the bullpen, from Billy Goats to Rally Squirrels, Yogi Berra was exactly right.

"It ain't over 'til it's over."

In other words, the natural order of the world is chaos, not calm. So said Victor Davis Hanson, a senior fellow at the Hoover Institute, albeit he was writing about "America's Nervous Breakdown" in an article for the *National Review*, not about the national pastime.

Still, he has a point.

Chaos theory is the mathematical study of how small variances in initial condition can lead to major differences in what might be called random outcome. This is also called "The Butterfly Effect," which suggests the flap of a butterfly's wing can have a major impact on weather half a world away.

Whether or not butterflies had anything to do with the chaos that resulted from Hurricane Ike in 2008, the destruction was very real. The storm slammed into the Texas Gulf Coast in the early morning hours of Saturday, September

13, and by the time it crossed the Canadian border late the next day, Ike had caused nearly $38 billion in damages and claimed nearly 200 lives.

The storm also blew that year's Astros season off course. Arguably, the club still suffers from the series of turbulent events which Ike set into motion four years ago.

Hurricane Ike's brief existence was a classic example of the principles of chaos theory. According to Wikipedia, the weather system which ultimately became the devastating hurricane got its start as a wave—an unorganized mass of thunderstorms—in the heart of the African continent. Once the system moved into the warm waters of the Atlantic Ocean, it increased in size. From that point though, tracking its exact path would have been an impossibility.

At about the same time summer showers pelted the Sudan, the Houston Astros were making few waves of their own in the National League standings. Following an August 26 loss to the Reds, Houston's record was a mediocre 66-66. The team was sixteen games out of first in the Central Division and eleven games back in the NL Wild Card standings.

Not unfamiliar territory for the never-say-die Astros.

Just two weeks later, Houston had surged into contention, winning fourteen of fifteen games. Meanwhile, the African low-pressure system had traversed the Atlantic and become Hurricane Ike. After hammering the island of Cuba, Ike moved into the Gulf of Mexico and as it spun its way westward, forecasters predicted its enormous force could affect those living in the coastal areas of either Texas or Louisiana.

By the time Roy Oswalt put the finishing touches on his three-hit shutout of the Pirates the night of Thursday, September 11, the Astros were just three games out in the Wild Card standings and Ike was just four hundred miles from shore. The closer Ike came to making landfall, the more certain was its path. Forecasters put the Houston metro area directly in the middle of the cone of probability.

That led baseball officials to postpone the first two games of the Astros' weekend series at home against the division-leading Cubs. Everyone living in Houston—Astros and non-Astros alike--did their best to batten down the hatches. While those living near coastal areas were issued mandatory orders to evacuate, many stayed.

No one wanted a repeat of the panic-induced mass exodus which had taken place in Houston just three years before.

***

The tragedy which befell New Orleans in the aftermath of Hurricane Katrina was an overwhelming blow to the American psyche. A false façade of invincibility was stripped from the nation's consciousness by both the unyielding power of Mother Nature and the failure of the Crescent City's infrastructure to protect its citizenry in the summer of 2005.

The heartbreaking images of destruction and death in New Orleans were still top of mind one month later when Hurricane Rita came barreling out of the sea. Rita was a large storm, bigger than Katrina. Forecasts were especially grim. Speculation ran rampant as to whether Rita might bring another major American city—Houston—to its knees.

As all of this unfolded, I could only watch helplessly from afar. I was out of town and my wife back home appeared to be in great peril. As the Astros played a four-game series in Pittsburgh it was difficult for the team—and its broadcasters—to stay focused on business. The phone calls with loved ones and the stories we saw on television combined to paint a surreal picture.

Everyone was leaving town.

More than three million people evacuated the Houston area in the days before Rita made landfall. Gridlock became pandemic as families literally ran for their lives. When Dianne asked me what I thought she should do, my gut told me she should stay. Many of our neighbors came to the same conclusion. Could the storm be any worse than the unimaginable chaos on the roadways?

Ultimately, Rita twisted its way east of Houston and nary a raindrop fell in the part of town where Dianne and I live. Meanwhile, dozens died in the evacuation. Although the scope of human loss was nothing compared to New Orleans, both events were tragedies of unprecedented scale.

Three years later, as Ike made a direct hit on Houston, the Browns were ready to make their stand. Dianne took charge of hurricane preparedness.

I had never been through a hurricane. When Hurricane Rita missed us, I realized I needed to be better prepared.

By the time Ike came ashore, we had battery-operated lanterns, a battery-operated fan, and even a battery-operated television. And I made sure we had plenty of batteries to operate all those devices. I also stocked up on bottled water and non-perishable foods. I even filled up both bathtubs in our home. For people unfamiliar with the rigors of hurricane season, bath water becomes vital to keeping toilets functional in case water service is interrupted.

Hurricane Ike hit our part of town in the middle of the night. Bill and I heard lots of wind, but neither one of us got out of bed to check things out. We just sort of hunkered down and hung on to each other. We quickly lost power and from the sound of things outside, we both anticipated a worst-case scenario. When the storm finally passed, we looked out our front windows and saw our lawn littered with debris. We were in the dark, save for our lanterns, but we both felt fortunate that our home had survived the storm.

Later that morning, after cleaning up the front yard, Bill discovered the wood fences in our backyard had been blown to the ground. That turned out to be the only significant damage we sustained, although we were without electricity for several days.

In fact, it was just about the time we were breathing our collective sigh of relief that Major League Baseball yanked the rug right out from beneath us.

Dianne is a little biased—that's one of the reasons I love her so—but the "fix" baseball put into place to get the Astros season back on track was anything but ideal.

***

Dianne and I are no strangers to natural disasters. We grew up in western Missouri on the periphery of "Tornado Alley." At some point every spring, both of our families would huddle up in the corner of our homes when a tornado was spotted nearby. In 1977, years after Dianne and I had married and moved to Cincinnati, a tornado demolished the Sedalia Country Club where my mother had won many of her golf championships. Another major twister hit Sedalia in the spring of 2011, at about the same time as the terrible tornado outbreak which caused ruin in nearby Joplin.

We've also been through an earthquake. Two of them, in fact. The Astros were playing a four-game weekend series against the Dodgers in the summer of '92 and Dianne and Allison were with me on one of the team's "family get-aways." Each year, the ball club offers an opportunity for family members to go on a road trip and the '92 excursion took us to Cincinnati and Los Angeles, both cities we once had called home.

We were sleeping comfortably in the team hotel the final morning of the trip—Sunday, June 28—when we were awaked by a loud rumble. At first Dianne thought an intruder was outside our door.

"Bill, wake up! Someone's trying to get into the room!" she said. I was already awake.

"I don't think that's what you hear," I replied. "This may be 'The Big One'."

Anyone who has spent time on the West Coast knows "The Big One" is the earthquake yet-to-come which will send all of California crashing into the sea. During our nearly two-year stay in L.A., we had managed to miss seismic activity of any consequence.

As our hotel room continued to tremble, toiletries came crashing down onto the bathroom floor. The time was just before five in the morning.

"Grab some clothes and let's get out of here," I ordered. Allison wanted to wash her hair, but there was no time for that. We scrambled down the stairway and were directed outside, joining hundreds of other guests—including the entire Astros team—in the parking lot. By the time we reached safety, all grew quiet—eerily so—and soon we were given an "all-clear" announcement and allowed to go back to our rooms.

Relieved, Allison and I went back to sleep, but not Dianne. She stood sentry until I awoke again a couple hours later. As daylight broke, Dianne relaxed. While I went downstairs for breakfast, she tried to go back to sleep. As I was enjoying a cup of coffee and the morning paper, the restaurant started shaking again. The hotel's emergency notification system again requested that everyone vacate the premises. I hurried up the stairs, but met the girls before reaching the room. While outside, a majority of the Houston contingent decided to get the heck out of there and everyone scrambled to check out of our rooms early. We spent the rest of the morning at Chavez Ravine in advance of that afternoon's game.

In researching this book, I've made numerous discoveries. Things aren't always as one remembers or as they may have seemed. I always assumed that second temblor in Los Angeles was an aftershock, but it turned out to be the only time in recorded history that two major earthquakes struck virtually the same place at roughly the same time. The first quake—and the stronger of the two we experienced— was centered near Landers, California, in the Mojave Desert. That event measured 7.3 on the Richter scale. Three hours later, the second quake—a 6.3 jolt—occurred with an epicenter near the city of Big Bear Lake, an hour west of Landers. Los Angeles was spared serious damage as both quakes were located a considerable distance from the city, but not so far that they didn't create quite a stir for the Browns.

Tornadoes, earthquakes, and hurricanes: I've seen them all. But no calamity equals traveling twelve hundred miles to play a "home" baseball game. That turned out to be a disaster of epic proportions.

***

As close as Landers is to Big Bear Lake—about 55 miles—so, too, is Milwaukee to Chicago. Technically, it's about ninety miles from Wrigley Field to Miller Park, but Milwaukee is a heck of a long way from Houston. Yet, after Ike ravaged the Texas Gulf Coast, baseball's decision-makers opted for the Astros to resume their season with a home game in Wisconsin, less than forty-eight hours after one of the most traumatic experiences imaginable.

When the Loma Prieta earthquake struck the San Francisco area two hours before Game Three of the 1989 World Series, play wasn't resumed for ten days. Astros players could have used at least that much time to get their personal lives back in order after Ike. The devastation from the storm was considerable and the weeks-long power outage in many parts of town added to the misery.

From a practical perspective, the Astros couldn't sit idly by while the rest of baseball went about the business of completing the season. When the announcement was made that the Houston-Chicago series would shift from Minute Maid Park to Milwaukee, the Astros' organization was not pleased. The move made sense—but for all the wrong reasons.

Milwaukee seemed to be a suspect choice for two reasons. The city was an easy two-hour drive from Chicago, thus making it a *de facto* home game for the Cubs. Secondly, the Astros' best chance at reaching the playoffs meant catching the Brewers. As hot as Houston had been prior to Ike, Milwaukee had gone equally cold, losing seven of ten games before dropping all four outings in a series at Philadelphia the weekend of the Houston hurricane. Milwaukee's Wild-Card edge over the Astros had been cut to a scant two-and-a-half games. With the Astros forced to play a home game at Miller Park, Brewer fans had a unique opportunity to root against their nearest rival in a game in which their team wasn't even involved.

No one in Houston was pleased with the decision.

"I'm definitely not happy with it," Houston manager Cecil Cooper told Alyson Footer in a story on MLB.com. Speaking from his Katy home where power would not be restored for another week, Cooper added, "It's a bit of a disadvantage. You want to play in your home ballpark."

He added pragmatically, "It's bigger than me."

I got the call about the Chicago trip late Saturday afternoon. The team met at Minute Maid Park early the next morning—a few players had been living in the luxury suites there—and then headed by bus to Bush Intercontinental Airport where we would catch our charter flight. Ours was the *only* plane on the tarmac at the entire airport. A TSA detail had been arranged to screen us for boarding, but otherwise the airport was completely shut down. No one—neither security screeners nor ballplayers—really wanted to be there that morning. Many of the Astros could have passed for "the walking dead" in a zombie flick.

By the time we arrived at our hotel in Milwaukee, there was little time to unwind and relax. I was so exhausted from the events of the weekend that I feared if I tried to catch a catnap, I might not wake up until Monday morning. With nothing else to do, I decided to head to the ballpark. Outside the hotel, pitcher Randy Wolf asked if I wanted to share a cab.

Talk in the backseat of the taxi quickly turned to Ike. Wolf had been a mid-season acquisition from San Diego and was living in a downtown Houston hotel. With no power to run the elevators in his building that morning, he had been forced to feel his way down fourteen flights of stairs in a darkened fire escape, exactly what you *don't* want your starting pitcher to do on the day he's scheduled to work one of the biggest games of the year. As tired as I felt, Wolf looked worse.

After we got to the park, Wolf caught up with me in the locker room. "Bill, do you remember the name of the cab company we used to get here?" he asked. "Why?" I replied, "Did you leave your cell phone in the back seat?" My comment was a feeble attempt at humor, but I had inadvertently hit the nail on the head. At a time when Wolf desperately needed to stay in close contact with family and friends, he had lost his connection to the outside world.

In all my years covering baseball, I've never seen a team as drained of emotion and energy as was the Houston club that night. Wolf gave up a leadoff home run to Chicago's Alfonso Soriano. The Astros' lefty failed to make it out of the third inning as the Cubs jumped on him for a quick 5-0 lead. From that point, the game was as close a thing to *Dawn of the Dead* as you'll ever likely to find on a ball field.

Small wonder Chicago ace Carlos Zambrano threw the Cubs first no-hitter in thirty-six years that night. After Wolf departed, Chicago managed just one more hit the rest of the game. Both teams played like I felt, physically and emotionally spent.

The Astros lost the Monday game in Milwaukee, too, and then flew to Florida where they lost all three games of their series against the Marlins. Back in Houston, recovery efforts moved at a snail's pace as sizable parts of the coastal region were heavily damaged. If ever a team could be forgiven for taking its collective eye off the ball, the 2008 Astros were that team over the course of the last two weeks of the season.

***

The circumstances surrounding Carlos Zambrano's no-hitter over the Astros certainly were unusual, but no hitless game ever was quite like the Astros' gem against the New York Yankees in 2003.

Don Nottebart threw Houston's first no-hitter in 1963. Don Wilson threw two no-hitters in the late '60s. Larry Dierker threw one for the club on July 9, 1976, against the Expos. Colt Ken Johnson was the first pitcher to *lose* a no-hitter as he fell to the Reds 1-0 on April 23, 1964. Ken Forsch's no-hit win on April 7, 1979, was the earliest no-hitter ever until the mark was broken in 2001.

Nolan Ryan threw one of his record seven no-hitters in an Astros' uniform. Mike Scott's no-hitter on September 25, 1986, clinched a division championship. Darryl Kile did not give up a hit and allowed only one batter to reach base in a 7-1 win against the Mets on September 8, 1993. I got to call the middle three innings of that game on radio. There was no television that night.

Scott came within one out of a second career no-hitter in 1988. During that broadcast—one in which Milo and I alternated between television and radio audiences—I had kept my viewers and listeners dutifully informed of the unfolding drama. In the ninth, Scott started the inning by getting Atlanta pinch-hitter Ken Griffey, Sr. to ground out. Albert Hall also grounded out weakly. Ken Oberkfell then lined the first pitch he saw into right field for a no-doubt-about-it single, ending the no-hit bid. Scott retired the next hitter, Gerald Perry, to conclude the 5-0 Astros victory.

Before the next day's broadcast, my boss at the time Jamie Hildreth stopped by the booth for a chat.

"Bill, do you think a no-hitter can be jinxed?" Hildreth asked. Immediately, I knew why he had posed the question. I frequently had mentioned variations of the phrase "no hits" on the air during Scott's outing, a definite no-no on the field when a pitcher flirts with a no-hitter. *But*, since a broadcaster is nowhere near the dugout and a pitcher is certainly not listening to the game, holding an announcer to the same standards of bewitchment always seemed a tad ludicrous to me.

"No, Jamie, I don't believe in that stuff."

Hildreth frequently monitored both radio and television broadcasts, so, I suspect he may have heard me fail to honor the code. Perhaps a disgruntled fan could have called. Hildreth hinted—in a not-so-subtle fashion—that it might be good for me to play ("-by-play"?) by the "rules." In his sixty-plus years behind the microphone, Milo has figured out a million ways around the term "no-hitter." I figured it was in my best interest to follow in his lead to avoid putting the kibosh on any future no-hit bids.

So, after five innings of Houston's game against the New York Yankees on June 11, 2003, I recapped the home team's showing this way:

"The New York Yankees have zero, zero, zero and the Astros lead it 4-0." During Zambrano's no-hitter five years later, I talked about the matter all the time, hoping to jinx

Houston to at least a couple hits. No such "luck" and proof—at least as far as I'm concerned—how preposterous superstitions can be.

Six Houston pitchers combined to hold New York hitless in the second game of the Astros' inaugural series at Yankee Stadium. That set a record and marked the first time in nearly seven-thousand games the Bombers had been on the losing end of a no-hitter.

Six pitchers. And Phil Garner had yet to be named Astros manager. Jimy Williams pulled the strings masterfully that memorable night. Less memorably, he said after the game, ""It just happened." Yankee manager Joe Torre offered a conflicting opinion: "The whole game stunk."

Here's a rundown of the Astros' hurlers who made history in the Bronx that night:

> **Pitcher One**: Roy Oswalt. He lasted one pitch into the second inning before re-injuring a groin muscle which had put him on the disabled list the month before.
>
> **Pitcher Two**: Pete Munro. A native New Yorker, Munro pitched two-and-two-thirds innings, walking three. He pitched around a walk, an error, and a hit batsman to get out of a bases-loaded jam in the third.
>
> **Pitcher Three**: Kirk Saarloos. He was a spot-starter in 2003 and pitched one-and-a-third innings against the Yankees, giving up one walk.
>
> **Pitcher Four**: Brad Lidge. Baseball's all-time leader in strikeouts per nine innings, Lidge was the Astros' first-round draft pick in 1998. He served as a set-up man on the 2003 team and was given the closer's role beginning in 2004 after Houston traded away both Billy Wagner and Octavio Dotel. He threw the sixth and seventh innings against the Yankees and got the win in the game.

Pitcher Five: Octavio Dotel. Dotel set a National League record with the Astros in 2000 making sixteen starts and saving sixteen games. In the eighth inning against the Yankees, he tied another record striking out four batters in one inning. Alfonso Soriano struck out swinging but reached first when Dotel's pitch got away from catcher Brad Ausmus.

Pitcher Six: Billy Wagner. With the Astros sporting an 8-0 lead, Wagner entered the game in a situation he would not normally have faced. Williams brought his closer in to preserve the no-hitter. Wagner struck out the first two batters he faced before inducing Hideki Matsui to hit a routine grounder to Jeff Bagwell who flipped to Wagner at first to end the game.

"First appearance in Yankee Stadium for most of us," Wagner said after the game. "What better place could there be (to throw a no-hitter)? This is like the history book."

The closest New York came to a hit was in the fifth when Soriano sent a looping liner into short left field. Lance Berkman—who hit a two-run homer in the game and was traded to the Yankees to end his stellar Houston career midway through the 2010 season—made a tumbling catch to retire Soriano.

"It probably looked more spectacular than it was," the self-effacing Berkman told reporters after the game.

In the Houston clubhouse after the game, each of the six pitchers who participated in the record-setting night found a bottle of champagne in front of his locker. "That's how the Yankees are," Wagner said. "Pretty classy."

***

At the close of the 2008 season, Milwaukee earned the National League Wild Card title with a record of 90-72. The Astros finished third in the Wild Card race, three-and-a-half games behind the Brewers. Milwaukee won six of its final seven games to reach the playoffs.

To their credit, the Astros battled the Brewers to the end. Houston won each of its final three series of the season, but the five-game losing streak after Hurricane Ike proved to be the difference in the end.

In 2009, the Astros finished fifth in the six-team NL Central. Cecil Cooper was fired as manager as the team ended the year fourteen games below .500. Brad Mills took the managerial reigns in 2010 and the club ended up fourth in the standings and ten games under the .500 mark. In 2011, the wheels came off completely.

Had a solitary butterfly not flapped its wings somewhere, had the rains in Africa dissipated before reaching the ocean, had Ike opted for another port of call, one can't help but wonder what might have been for the Astros of 2008. And, had that team reached the playoffs, what impact would that success have had the next season, and the next, and the next one after that.

Three years after Ike, billboards around the Houston area still urged victims of the storm to seek legal counsel to ensure a fair insurance settlement in the aftermath of the hurricane. No such restitution was ever made available to the Astros.

CHAPTER 26
Don't Sweat It

The baseball season precludes me from making too many appearances on the golf course. I enjoy golf, having taken up the sport after my knees got a little too creaky to play tennis as much as I wanted. I play in a few charity golf tournaments as my time and schedule allow. During the off-season, especially living in a place like Houston where winters are a lot like spring in many other parts of the country, I get out and play golf once every couple of weeks.

Golf is a very popular pursuit among professional athletes. Toward the end of their careers, former NBA greats Michael Jordan and Charles Barkley were almost as well known for their golfing exploits as they were for their basketball skills. The more years of service a ballplayer has in the big leagues, the more likely he is to bring his golf clubs to Florida or Arizona for spring training.

Astros who have held their own on a golf course include Mike Scott, Enos Cabell, and the aforementioned Jeff Bagwell, he of hole-in-one fame.

Larry Dierker is another former Astro who is also a competent and avid golfer. Dierk has dragged me to the course—although "dragged" doesn't accurately reflect his powers of persuasion and my eagerness to accept his invitations—a number of times through the years. Larry believes in the sport's therapeutic powers, particularly for a ballplayer.

As manager of the Astros, Dierker once told Darryl Kile one of the best ways for him to improve as a pitcher during the off season was to play a lot of golf. Dierker reasoned golf tested and shaped an individual's mental toughness. "You can't let one bad hole or one bad inning beat you," Dierker viewed. "In golf, you need power off the tee. That's your fastball. You need accuracy to reach the green. That's your control. You need mental toughness to maintain your concentration for eighteen holes. That's about four hours' worth of play.

"A baseball game typically takes three hours or less."

After heeding Dierker's advice, Kile went from being a middle of the rotation hurler to becoming ace of the Houston staff.

Those of you in business—particularly if sales is your game—know golf is a great way to enhance a relationship with a client. There's nothing like spending four or five hours together and making sure your game—at least for that one day—is as bad as or worse than your customer's. Given the nature of the sport, golf is also a popular way for charities to raise money. After all, what's better than spending a day on the golf course while helping a worthy cause?

Which brings me to the "Don't Sweat It Golf Classic."

Of all the names of all the golf tournaments anywhere in the world, the "Don't Sweat It Classic" has to be one of the best. For starters, as Larry Dierker and most any psychologists worth their $200-an-hour fee would tell you, that's a great mindset to have, both in sports and in life. But, in the case of the Houston-area golf tournament bearing that name, the label carries a deeper and more significant meaning.

For some, the inability to sweat is a life-threatening condition.

As you read at the beginning of this book, my friend Zach Hamm started the "Don't Sweat It Golf Classic." That's Zach on both the front and back covers of this book. His 2012 golf tournament marks the event's fourth year, which means Zach founded the fund-raiser at the ripe old age of nine. If you're skeptical of a nine-year-old being able to pull off such a feat, you don't know Zach.

He's been exceeding expectations since the time he was born.

Zach suffers from a disorder known as ectodermal dysplasia—a birth defect which manifests itself in a wide range of symptoms and syndromes. In the vast majority of cases, the condition is not a developmental disability. Zach is one of the brightest kids you'll ever meet. In most respects, he's pretty much a normal boy, but he's had to work awfully hard to get where he is today.

***

On the way to see her obstetrician for a scheduled examination during the second trimester of her pregnancy, Susan Hamm had little to worry about. She and her husband Paul discovered they were going to have a baby while on a vacation trip to Florida in the latter half of 1999. Their news ramped up the joy and excitement of their holidays. Susan was vice president of operations for a small natural gas producer. Paul worked as director of sales for a medical research equipment company. The couple had much to be thankful for and knew they were blessed.

Susan and Paul were dutiful and responsible parents-to-be. After learning their child would be a boy, the Hamm's were always excited to see their doctor and get another look, via ultrasound, at their future son growing inside Susan's womb. Paul had played baseball at the University of Houston and had visions of grooming a future Hall of Famer.

"That's strange," Susan's doctor said as she stared intensely at the ultrasound monitor. For the first time in their joyous shared experience, the Hamm's looked nervously at one another. "What is it?" Susan asked.

"I'm not sure," the doctor replied moving the probe slowly to get a better look at the fetal image.

"I don't want to alarm you," the doctor finally said, "but I'm not seeing all of your son's toes. I've never seen anything quite like this." She referred Susan and Paul to a specialist.

On their way home after receiving the troubling news, the Hamms did their best to encourage one another. "Let's work toward getting an answer before we rush to any conclusions," Paul suggested. Once they got to their house, Susan logged onto the computer and began to search for clues.

Answers, unfortunately, would be a long time coming.

Even the specialist was puzzled after he had run his own series of tests. "There's definitely a problem," he concluded. "Since we don't really understand what we're dealing with, let's explore our options."

The doctor counseled the Hamms on the challenges of raising a child with disabilities. He also suggested that Susan, four months into her pregnancy, might want to consider not carrying the child to full term. That elicited a strong response from Paul. "No sir!" he exclaimed looking at Susan, "that's our son!"

Zachary William Hamm was born in Houston on April 25, 2000. On his right foot he was missing three toes. On his left foot, four toes were absent. He also had significant finger and rib anomalies and troublesome internal issues. Doctors still were unable to determine exactly what was wrong with Zach, and thus, no one could offer a long-term prognosis. "We don't know what's wrong" became the common refrain from the medical community for the next three years.

"The fear, stress, and anxiety were constant and almost overwhelming," Paul Hamm says today. "My heart broke for

Susan after Zach was born, but she never came close to losing faith. She's a former teacher and a driven individual and she was determined to find out exactly what we were dealing with."

Zach underwent several surgeries to correct what modern medicine could fix. These procedures offered him the best chance to live as normal a life as possible. Early tests revealed that his cognitive function was good, in fact well above average. He was—and is—an exceptionally smart, sensitive, and happy child. Uncertain how long Zach's life expectancy might be with his undiagnosed condition, Paul and Susan did their best to see each day as an extraordinary blessing from God.

"I was anxious, scared, and nervous about this new life I was responsible for," Susan Hamm says of her earliest days as a mother. "At eight months, doctors performed corrective surgery on Zach's feet and left hand. Afterwards, he had a cast on each foot and one on his arm. Those got a lot of looks from strangers.

"Having a child with birth defects made me extra sensitive and protective," Susan adds, "like a mother lion with her cub."

In August of 2003, more bad news came the Hamms' way. X-rays taken by a pediatric dentist revealed Zach was missing several permanent teeth. For the little guy and his parents, life kept delivering one blow after another. The new diagnoses made for more sleepless nights, particularly for Susan. She had returned to work under the stipulation that Zach would constantly be at her side. Her value to her company was such that her employer eagerly agreed to the terms. Zach loved the attention he received from Susan's co-workers and his presence actually seemed to boost office morale.

A few days after the dentist's appointment, Susan realized the information about Zach's missing teeth could prove significant. When she did an online search combining the phrases "missing teeth" and "missing toes," a brand new listing popped up on her computer screen: the National Foundation for Ectodermal Dysplasias. The information she found on the organization's Web site offered new hope.

The next day, Susan called the NFED offices in the Illinois suburbs of the Greater St. Louis area. She asked for and reached Mary Kaye Richter, the organization's founder and executive director. Mary Kaye was a warm and compassionate woman who listened to Susan's story. When it was time for her to respond, she spoke from a place of understanding.

"Mom, he's going to be okay."

Like Susan and Paul Hamm, Mary Kaye also has a son with a form of ectodermal dysplasia. In her quest to seek the best for her child, Mary Kaye started the NFED foundation in 1981. Her personal story and expert advice lifted Susan's heart in a way that only her love for Zach had been able to do before. Mary Kaye pointed out that despite its many guises, ectodermal dysplasia can be managed. Individuals with the condition can and do live long and productive lives.

According to the NFED Web site, ectodermal dysplasia is not a single disorder. It's a group of heritable syndromes deriving from abnormalities of the ectodermal structures of the human body. "Ectoderm" is defined as the outermost layer of the cells which make up the early embryo. Ectodermal dysplasias present along the body's outer layer, most commonly affecting hair, nails, skin, teeth, and sweat glands. In many cases, individuals affected with ectodermal dysplasias are unable to perspire normally. Zach falls into that category.

That's why Zach's "Don't Sweat It Golf Classic" is so aptly named. Some of us spend too much time sweating the "small stuff." Zach's struggles, thanks to his disorder—he chooses not to call it a "disease"—to sweat at all.

Which can be a problem when you live in a place like Houston.

***

For many teams, over the course of many years, beating the Astros with a Biggio on board was no easy task. Imagine, then, trying to beat a team with three Biggios in uniform.

Such was the plight of opponents playing against the St. Thomas High School baseball team during the 2010 and 2011 seasons. With standouts Conor and Cavan Biggio leading the way, and their dad Craig coaching the team, the Eagles won back-to-back 5A TAPPS state championships. Upon graduation, Conor earned a scholarship to play second base at Notre Dame. Cavan is a corner infielder and two years younger than his brother. He's also a top college prospect as a wide receiver on the St. Thomas football team.

Many big league managers employ a bench coach as their right-hand man, someone with whom to talk strategy and lean on in the decision-making process. Craig Biggio has one on his club. He's a little shorter—and younger—than you might expect, but Zach Hamm is an important part of the St. Thomas baseball team.

I'm constantly amazed at the baseball knowledge Zach possesses. Given his age, he looks like he could be a bat boy or perhaps the team mascot. He sort of assumes the latter role, but what he specializes in is offering wisdom beyond his years, plus advice and encouragement which lifts the spirits of everyone on the Eagle team. Craig Biggio will tell you Zach was an instrumental part of St. Thomas's back-to-back state-championship runs.

"You don't have to be around Zach for very long to know he's a winner," Biggio says. "Given everything he's been through in his life, he's also an inspiration.

"In his own way, Zach commands respect. When he offers advice to our guys, they listen. He offers me suggestions from time to time and, you know, sometimes his way of thinking about baseball makes a lot of sense."

Biggio and his Eagles also keep an eye on Zach. Like a lot of 12-year-old boys, Zach can get a little carried away at times. Because he doesn't sweat normally, he can easily overheat if those around him aren't careful and dutiful. Occasionally one of the St. Thomas coaches or players offers Zach advice, too.

"Cool it, Rookie!" one of the Eagles will say with a smile, to which Zach always responds with an appreciative nod.

Given Paul Hamm's love of the game, the fact that Zach has been playing baseball himself since he was five is no surprise. In his six seasons with the Farm League Mudcats, Zach has played on four championship teams. He's also developing into a capable pitcher who wins games more with guile than overpowering stuff. Think of him as a Greg Maddox type.

In the last couple years, Zach also has become a bit of a fixture around Minute Maid Park. I've had him up to the booth on occasion. He's thrown out a first pitch to promote his golf tournament. He's given Jim Deshaies baseball pointers and he's collected a slew of autographs. The fact that he never seems to meet a stranger plays to his advantage. Truth be told, he sort of talked his way onto Biggio's coaching staff.

Zach's true love, athletically, is golf. I first met Paul Hamm on a golf course. After telling me about his son, I was eager to meet the young man. Paul spends a lot more time detailing Zach's achievements than he does recounting his son's challenges. Dianne and I are fortunate to call each of the Hamms our friends.

Despite his disabilities, Zach more than holds his own on the golf course. He's played competitive golf on the South Texas PGA Little Linkster Tour since 2008. He won his first tournament that year and has gone on to win another nine times at last count. He even has a hole in one! His father almost always caddies for him, not only to make sure Zach takes the occasional break to cool off with a wet towel, but also to offer advice on club selection and distance to the pin.

Zach is *also* well on his way to becoming an Eagle Scout. He's a gifted singer *and* a member of his junior high school's drama team. And when he's not the hardest-working young man in show business, Zach still spends more time with doctors than any kid his age—with his outlook on life—should have to do.

The better I've come to know Zach and his parents, the more I realize the value which could be derived if each one of us had a chance to spend just one day walking in Zach's shoes. What would that be like?

"It's cool to be me," Zach says. "Sure, I have a rare syndrome and in a way I'm different from other kids. If someone asks what's wrong with me, I just tell them, 'Nothing. This is how God made me.'

"I'm thankful for having a great family that takes care of me, and for having so many other people who understand and support me. Nothing really slows me down, and nothing ever will."

Earlier this year, Zach visited another of the many physicians in his life—an orthopedic pediatrician—to have the alignment of his chest cavity examined. The cause for concern turned out to be minor, just an indicator that Zach is a growing boy. However, the examination revealed that Zach has a mild case of scoliosis of the spine. The good news is that the condition is nothing serious for now, but it is one more thing that heavies the hearts of Zach and his parents.

Susan Hamm remembers the drive home from the doctor's office.

"We had been in the car for a while and Zach was being unusually quiet," Susan says. "Paul, Zach, and I once drove all the way back to Houston from visiting my parents in Florida and Zach literally talked the entire time. So, when he's quiet, I know there's something wrong.

"When I looked over at him, I saw his little blue eyes well up with tears like they have so many times before. He finally asked, 'So, is there something *else* wrong with me?' As a mother, my heart ached for the emotional pain he was experiencing. I feel so helpless sometimes. I wish it were me going through all of this instead of him."

Paul Hamm reacted in much the same way when he learned—away on a business trip—that his son faced yet one more future uncertainty.

"I got the news from Susan while sitting in a rental car in Lubbock," Paul says. "I've prayed to God many times, 'Make it me instead of him,' but then I always realize that's not the way God works.

"Susan and I are grateful for the many blessings which have come our way through Zach's life. While the struggles also are many, he never gives up. In fact, it seems each time he faces adversity; he comes through it better than before. He's just a remarkable boy.

"I'm really glad our son is a lot stronger than I am."

CHAPTER 27
Opening Day

At just after 6 p.m. on a picturesque Friday night in downtown Houston, the red tally light came on to mark a new season of baseball.

> Bill Brown (BB): *"The stadium is sold out, festively adorned as usual, great pregame ceremonies. Bill Brown and Jim Deshaies back with you for the 2012 season. New ownership group for the Astros, new general manager, a lot of new faces on the ball club."*
>
> Jim Deshaies (JD): *"I don't know where all you folks have been. Brownie and I have been here for the last six months just waiting for this thing to get started. The beer is cold. The hot dogs are hot. We're headed in a new direction. It should be a lot of fun."*
>
> BB: *"We hope you'll stay tuned because that first pitch is just a moment away. It's Astros baseball against the Colorado Rockies right after this."*

For twenty-six years now, I've had a difficult time sleeping the night before Opening Day, imagining the feeling I'll have when I go live again for the first time. At the dawn of the Astros' 2012 campaign—April 6—I was wide awake at 5 a.m. Jumping out of bed I felt like a five-year-old on Christmas morning. It's the only day of the season I get this excited. Over the course of my morning ritual—reading the newspaper, reviewing my note cards, and making sure the latch on my leather messenger bag is unlocked and in working order—I begin to sense a familiar and welcome feeling in the pit of my stomach.

Butterflies—and no longer the ones that create chaos.

As a younger broadcaster I did my best to combat nerves before a game. Getting too keyed up sometimes prevented me from being able to focus on my job—and my work suffered as a result. Now I welcome the jitters because I get them so rarely. I've learned to channel emotions—in the same way players do—and harness them in a positive manner.

The year 2011 marked two milestones in my professional life. I celebrated not only twenty-five years with the Astros, but also forty years as a sportscaster. In that time, I've seen a lot of change.

During my stint in the Reds' broadcast booth, Cincinnati—as home to baseball's first professional team— was annually the site of the traditional season opener. In 2012, the inaugural matchup for America's national pastime wasn't even held in America. Seattle topped Oakland 4-1 in Tokyo as Mariner Ichiro Suzuki returned to his homeland with a four-hit Opening Day performance and Major League Baseball broadened its international appeal.

What else has changed in the last twenty-five years?

In 1987, a former actor occupied the Oval Office. Today an African-American is our commander-in-chief. The Dow Jones Industrial Average in the summer of 2012 hovers well above the 12,000 mark. Twenty-five years ago, the stock market posted a record high of 2,500. Apple rolled out its one millionth Macintosh computer in 1987. The company took three years to reach that milestone. When Apple launched its iPad 3 in March 2012, first week sales averaged more than a million units *per day*.

Among those things which haven't changed: *The Simpsons* remain a comedy staple on television, Meryl Streep keeps winning Oscars, and political tensions remain high in the Middle East.

Several athletes born in 1987 already have achieved greatness: hockey player Sidney Crosby, soccer superstar Lionel Messi, snowboarder Hannah Teter, and tennis champions Maria Sharapova and Novak Djokovic.

Youth also was served with the Astros' 2012 Opening Day starting lineup:

Player	Pos.	Age
Jordan Schafer	CF	25
Jose Altuve	2B	21
J.D. Martinez	LF	24
Carlos Lee	1B	35
Brian Bogusevic	RF	28
Chris Johnson	3B	27
Jason Castro	C	24
Marwin Gonzalez	SS	23
Wandy Rodriguez	P	33

If you take veterans Lee and Rodriguez out of the equation, the Astros' Opening Day starters averaged 24.5 years of age. Five of those players had yet to be *born* when I began my career in Houston.

I guess that means I've been around for a while.

In his research for the book, Tim Gregg discovered something of which I was unaware. As far as consecutive seasons with one team, at the time of this writing I am the third longest-tenured television play-by-play man in the big leagues. Vin Scully has been doing Dodger games since TV was invented—at least it seems that way. Dick Bremer has been with the Twins since 1983. Remember, he was the guy who got the Minneapolis job I had applied for after being let go as the Reds' announcer.

Next in order of continuing service: yours truly.

Radio announcers tend to stay much longer in their jobs, maybe because—unlike television guys—they don't have to worry about maintaining a "youthful appearance" in front of a high-definition camera. Milo Hamilton has now joined Scully in the "sixty-years-in-the-business club," and in Milo's case, the fact he's never lost his enthusiasm for the game has helped keep him going strong. The same probably holds true for the rest of us "veterans." Who can grow old when you spend all your time around a kid's game?

I'm frequently asked what it takes to be a top-notch sportscaster. Whenever Deshaies is around, he'll chip in, "If you find one, let us know." Such a comedian.

When I was hired in Cincinnati I was told that even though booth announcing was my main job three days a week and sportscasting only two days, the station had been looking for someone who "lived and breathed sports." Most of us in the business do just that. We're died-in-the-wool fans first, last, and always. I have a tendency, even as a grandfather, to still eat and drink the stuff. If you're a woman involved with a man who possesses these tendencies, then you know what a saint Dianne has been to put up with me for such a long time.

Although we've been married for forty-four years, my wife still jokes that we've only been a real couple for half that time since baseball steals me away for six months every season. I remind her I'm no different from any other husband who works for a living, at which point she usually rolls her eyes and gives me an, "Oh, Bill," before changing the subject.

I was thrilled when the Astros honored me in 2011 for my twenty-five years behind the mic. Dianne was, too. I was excited that Allison and her family were able to join us for the on-field ceremony. Owner Drayton McLane gave me a shadow box filled with photos commemorating my years with the club. Steve McNair, general manager for Fox Sports Houston, presented me with a crystal microphone. After the pre-game festivities, the Astros hosted our contingent—which also included about fifty of our friends from church—in one of the luxury suites at Minute Maid Park.

Usually, Opening Day—or "Night," as the case may be—is the one game each year Dianne attends. Since I get to the ballpark about four hours before the first pitch, Dianne traditionally asks our friend Ann Nance to join her for her pilgrimage to the ball park. They try to get downtown early and usually grab a bite to eat at Irma's—one of Houston's best Tex-Mex restaurants—located just a few blocks from the ballpark.

Zach Hamm has told me I have the best seat in the house to watch a baseball game and he's right about that. Zach and his dad missed the Astros' 2012 opener working on three different Boy Scout merit badges. I understand it is technically possible for Zach to become an Eagle Scout at twelve years and five months of age. None of us will be surprised if—*and when*—he achieves that honor.

The beginning of a new baseball season rekindles relationships which lay dormant over the winter months. There is a fraternal feeling among media veterans in the press box and it's always good to see those familiar faces. On Opening Day I'll spend a little more time mixing and mingling than I would otherwise. Eventually though, the time always comes to get down to business.

I spend the hours leading up to game time getting my mind right and my things situated in the three or so feet of booth space that is exclusively mine. Managing that space is a challenge at times. This year, I've added an iPad—a Christmas present from Dianne—to the mix of informational resources I use during a broadcast. The tablet is much smaller than my laptop and works perfectly as a means to access data from the Internet. However, most of the pertinent details I try to incorporate into a broadcast still come the old-fashioned way: from the hand-crafted index cards which have yet to fail me in my vocation.

As Colorado hit in the top of the first of the 2012 opener in Houston, the Rockies faced Astros lefty Wandy Rodriguez. After the leadoff batter was retired, up stepped Colorado's number-two hitter in the lineup.

> Bill Brown: *"Dexter Fowler is an interesting player. The Rockies think this could be a breakout season for him. Switch-hitter with speed, he covers a lot of ground in center field. He drove in forty-five last year and he just turned 27. After the All-Star break last year he really got rolling. He hit .288 after the break. He had the third most extra-base hits in the National League after the All-Star break last year."*

All of that information came from one of the dozens of note cards I use over the course of a broadcast. Gleaning those facts and transcribing them into functional form makes up the bulk of my time as a broadcaster. Just as a baseball player may spend countless time in the batting cage or a golfer hours on the driving range, prepping and maintaining my note cards is the "toil and trouble" which enables me to do my job the way I believe it should be done.

I think of it as my on-going homework assignment.

***

During the baseball season, my game-day routine begins at breakfast as I pour through the local newspaper wherever I happen to be. Going through the box scores, I take notes, lots of notes. These entries are first made into an old-fashioned spiral notebook and include all pitchers used, home runs hit, and anything else of significance from any game involving a team the Astros will play. The information will be used later for research in preparing index cards in advance of Houston's first game against each of the teams on the schedule.

My note-taking also involves a substantial amount of time on the Internet. I try to stick to facts and figures as much as possible, as the Web also is a source of limitless opinion. I have to be careful not to get swallowed up in this subjective world. Unless it's a big story—and I don't mean to seem rude—I don't pay too much attention to what the "experts" think. I'm interested in the opinions of those directly involved in the game: players, managers, coaches, and scouts.

By mid-morning—in advance of a night game—I try to hit the gym, both for the sake of my mental health as well as my physical well-being. I belong to a fitness facility in Houston and all of the hotels in which the team stays on the road have quality exercise venues. After my workout and a shower, typically it's time for lunch. During the baseball season, this meal is the only one during which I'm not immersed in my craft. If the team has a day game, my routine is significantly compressed and my workout might not come until the evening, if at all.

In advance of heading to the ballpark, I fill out my scorebook with detailed information about the game's pitching pairing. There is a specific place on my score sheet for every piece of statistical information I might need. As time permits, I also might file newspaper and magazine clippings in a set of old-fashioned manila folders I keep for every Astros opponent. Then about 2 p.m. for a home night game, I give Dianne a kiss goodbye—if she's not out and about—and leave the house for the forty-five minute drive to the ballpark. On the road, the team bus typically leaves the hotel at 4 p.m. for a 7:05 contest.

After squaring things away in the TV booth—a sense of order I share with Tom Seaver thanks to my time in the military—I head to the Astros' clubhouse to get the starting lineups for both teams. While there, I try to listen in on the manager's chat with the media. I usually don't ask many questions myself as I like to get a feel for what other reporters are thinking about the team. As time permits, I try to talk to at least a couple of players to keep my finger on the pulse of the club. During my time in Cincinnati, the batting cage was a swarm of activity in advance of a game, but you rarely see reporters lingering around for an on-field chat. Today's players aren't really wired that way and I don't blame them. As focused as I try to be in advance of a broadcast, players try to do the same. That concentration means keeping distractions to a minimum.

About ninety minutes before the first pitch, I head back to the press box and grab a quick dinner. Usually, I eat in the booth while reviewing game notes provided by the home team's media information department. With the starting lineups in hand, I finish filling out my scorebook. Frequently, I'll meet with one of the opposing team's announcers and we'll exchange observations and trends. A few of my counterparts—but not too many—forego this "fraternization."

An hour before game time, JD and I have a final in-booth meeting with our producer and then I take a few moments to establish my composure for the broadcast. Our pregame "hit"—on-air appearance—is usually done live at 6:35 for a 7 p.m. game. Once we've gotten that behind us, we record our on-camera open for the broadcast to avoid overlap with the National Anthem. About four or five times a year, particularly if someone of note is performing, we try to incorporate the "Star Spangled Banner" into the beginning of our telecasts. I like that. A show of flags on Opening Day, coupled with the red, white, and blue bunting featured around the stadium, fill me with a sense of patriotic pride.

Before every game, I make sure to take care of "business"—if you know what I mean—well in advance of air time. JD is free to leave the booth to manage "necessities" as needed, but I'm locked into my seat for the duration. And, no, I've never heard of a broadcaster taking an "astronaut's" approach to bladder control. If anyone ever experiments in that fashion, it probably will be one of the "young" guys in Houston.

If you're young and sportscasting sounds like an intriguing way to spend your time, then my advice is simple: follow your dream. Chances are someone along the way will say you're wasting your time. I've gotten that same advice from a few people—not as much recently—but don't mistake pessimism for good intentions. Putting a Plan B in place is always a good idea and your fallback position should include getting a college degree.

To be honest, journalism is much more about practical experience than classroom instruction. Not to say you don't need a high level of skill and training to be a good broadcaster, but the best way to get better at what you want to do is by doing it in the real world. If that means a stint doing Kewpie games or even just sitting in front of a television with a microphone in hand, Chris Lincoln and I are living testimony that practice makes perfect. Actually, nobody is perfect, but practice—like boot camp—enables you to be the best you can be.

My other piece of advice for budding broadcasters: Try to get acquainted with one of "us"—those already in the business. If baseball is your thing and you live in a big league city, get involved with your local SABR chapter. Chances are good a few professional journalists are going to be members, too, because just like you, we're fans at heart.

***

BB: *"It's one to nothing, Astros lead it, bottom of the second inning, and we're pleased to be joined by new owner Jim Crane who was among the owners who threw out first balls and you were right in the strike zone, just as you were at Central Missouri. You struck out eighteen in a playoff game there and that had to be probably one of those butterfly type days. How did today compare to that, Jim?"*

Jim Crane (JC): *"Well, this is a little bigger than that, but you don't strike out eighteen too many times, even in little league, so, that was a big night."*

BB: *"You played catch the other night with a fan and got him to renew his tickets and that personal touch can go a long way. You've enjoyed getting that input from the fans, haven't you?"*

JC: *"Well, I think you've got to listen. They're your customers and they're paying the bills so you'd better listen to them or you'll be in trouble. If I could play catch with 10,000 more, I'd do it and get this place filled every night."*

Opening Night 2012 featured a standing-room-only crowd at Minute Maid with over 43,000 fans in attendance. The Astros took the early lead when Carlos Lee singled home Jose Altuve in the first. Then, after Jim Crane joined us on the broadcast, Colorado bounced back to score three times in the third. All three runs were unearned. Crane knows respectability will come slowly for his young team, but throughout his business life, he has devoted himself to achieving success. He will hold the Astros' organization to those same standards.

Admittedly, there were a couple moments of awkward silence in the booth as Crane watched the Rockies capitalize on a Wandy Rodriguez throwing error. The damage could have been worse as Colorado had the bases loaded looking for more.

JD: *"They're you go, Jim, welcome to the rollercoaster. Club had an early lead, now they've given up a three-spot."*

JC: *"Well, we need to get out of here. The game's early."*

BB: *"Thrilling comeback win on Opening Day would work. (Colorado's Chris Nelson then hit a hard ground ball up the middle, seemingly headed to center for another hit.) Diving play by Altuve! Shoveling to Gonzalez! Spectacular effort for the force to end it! The Rockies getting three runs and we thank Jim Crane for joining us. Jim, all the best to you this season."*

JC: *"Thank you guys. Thanks for your hard work and thanks to the fans for coming out tonight. We'll have a great year. Thanks."*

Before the next half inning started, Fox Sports Houston's roving reporter Patti Smith caught up with ex-president George H. W. Bush, a loyal fan of the club. "I understand we've got a good, young ball club," he told Smith. "If they get going together, it will give them some zip. I'm a great believer in the team and I think if they come together, I think they'll do well."

Back-to-back home runs off the bats of Lee and Bogusevic in the fourth knotted the score at 3-3. That's where things stood until the eighth when another Houston error put the Rockies back on top. Colorado's Troy Tulowitzki homered in the top of the ninth, but the Astros did not go quietly into the night on Opening Day. In the bottom of the ninth inning Houston put runners at first and second with two out. Pinch hitter Matt Downs stepped to the plate as the potential game-winning run against Rockies closer Rafael Betancourt:

BB: *"If you watched Astros baseball last year you remember Downs providing some big moments. He led the majors last year with fifteen RBIs as a pinch hitter. He led the majors, had a .462 on base average, hit three home runs including a very big one against the Texas Rangers in Arlington. Did not have the kind of spring he wanted but he made the club because he had that solid year last year."*

JD: *"He will not get cheated."*

BB: *"Fouled back, strike one. Outstanding fastball hitter Matt Downs, 28 years old from Tuscaloosa, Alabama. With Gonzalez leaving the game, the Astros, if they go to extra innings, could put Bixler at shortstop and Downs at third. Breaking pitch in the dirt, good stop by Rosario."*

JD: *"The Rockies are very high on Rosario but they signed Hernandez to a two-year deal.*

BB: *"Downs with fifteen pinch RBI, atop the leader board last year. (Downs swings and misses.) One and two."*

JD: *"It's not like he's throwing a lot of breaking balls to get the hitters off that fastball either."*

BB: *"Downs hit .156 in spring training. Takes that one up and it's two-two. (Archived footage from 2011 appears on screen) Let's flash back to August 22 when Downs got into one, a long ball. If he does it right here this place will EXPLODE."*

But, in a scene reminiscent of *Casey at the Bat*, Matt Downs swings through a fastball to end the game.

BB: *"The Rockies win it as Betancourt, on a high fastball, strikes out Downs. For the Astros it's no runs on a hit, two men stranded and here's that final pitch."*

JD: (Voicing over replays) *"Downs was trying to get extended on that high fastball but couldn't get the bat to the ball."*

BB: *"Final score: 5-3, Colorado. "*

And thus, a new baseball season had begun.

One of the Texas Gulf Coast's architectural gems is the Fred Hartman Bridge which crosses the Houston Ship Channel between Baytown and La Porte. Its two massive pylons tower more than four-hundred feet into the sky, creating a span of some 1,250 feet, making it one of the longest cable-stayed bridges in the country. Even if you live in Houston, chances are you may never have actually seen the bridge in person since it's a little off the beaten path. The drive out the Pasadena Freeway to take in its visual splendor is well worth the trip.

Fred Hartman was the long-time editor and publisher of the *Baytown Sun* newspaper. He started out as a sportswriter and never lost his love of sports. He became publisher of the *Sun* in 1950, and helped start the local chapter of the Baseball Writers Association of America. That group hands out an award in Hartman's honor each year for "long and meritorious service to baseball." I had the good fortune to be presented the Fred Hartman Award at the 2012 Houston Baseball Dinner.

While twenty-five years went into earning that honor, I only took about three hours to shatter it—literally. I dropped the beautiful crystal obelisk while removing it from the back seat of the car the night Dianne and I got home from the banquet. Fortunately, the Astros in Action Foundation—which underwrites both the banquet and the Hartman Award—was able to make me a replacement, although at first I was hesitant about asking them to do so, not wanting to admit to what a klutz I can be at times.

I can already hear Larry Dierker laughing out loud as he reads about this.

I feel certain I was more sure-handed as a younger man, but I don't think I was a better broadcaster. Experience counts for something in a business like mine and I've seen a lot of games. Despite the excitement contained within a well-contested contest, the routine of a season can get monotonous and the travel can take a toll. The grind is capable of tearing apart even the best of relationships.

A baseball journey is not for the faint of heart.

Yet, I recognize what a blessed existence I've had. I've lived out my boyhood dream and with the beginning of each new season, I succumb again to the game and all its charms. I moved my family to Houston in pursuit of a job. In staying here for more than twenty-five years, my wife, daughter, and I made countless friends and we finally found a home, in the deepest and richest sense of the word.

As much as it might seem I'm thrust into the spotlight, baseball is both a vocation and avocation which will always be about those who play the game. A sportscaster is merely an intermediary between the team and its fans. In my job, I'm as much a salesman as a journalist. I recognize far better now than I did as a younger man that every individual on the payroll of a baseball team has one fundamental responsibility: to get people to come to the ballpark and make sure they have a good time. It's as simple as that.

Others among my peers may have lived more exciting, compelling, and interesting lives. Others might have chosen to tell their stories in a more flamboyant or entertaining fashion. I learned a long time ago not to try to be like anyone else, but to stay true to the person I call "me."

I honored my parents, studied hard, served my country, paid my dues, held my tongue—when absolutely necessary—and loved my wife and daughter. I can look back and say, for the most part, I did my best.

I also sought guidance, purpose, and refuge in the Good Book—and I hope you find this to have been a "good book," too—and I encourage you to do the same.

Bill Brown

Bill Brown and his family celebrate his twenty-five years as an Astros broadcaster during pre-game ceremonies at Minute Maid Park on June 11, 2011

***

For more photos, index, and other special features relating to this book, please visit the Web site: www.mybaseballjourney.com

Produced and designed by

TURN-KEY ENTERPRISES

tkvw.com

NATIONAL FOUNDATION FOR ECTODERMAL DYSPLASIAS

Being diagnosed with a rare genetic condition like ectodermal dysplasia can make a family feel isolated and alone. The National Foundation for Ectodermal Dysplasias (NFED) assures them that someone cares. The NFED is the leading charity in the world serving individuals affected by ectodermal dysplasias, their families, and care providers. Its mission is to empower and connect people touched by ectodermal dysplasias through education, support and research.

The ectodermal dysplasias involve defects in the hair, teeth, nails and sweat glands. Other body parts may be affected such as the skin, eye, parts of the ear, and limbs. The 150+ types are identified by the combination of physical features an affected person has and the way they are inherited. Symptoms can range from mild to severe. Hypohidrotic ectodermal dysplasia (HED) is the most common syndrome and features multiple, malformed and missing teeth, the inability to perspire, and sparse hair. Only in rare cases do ectodermal dysplasias affect lifespan and very few types involve learning difficulties. The ectodermal dysplasias affect men, women, and children of all races and ethnic groups. As few as one or as many as 7 in 10,000 babies are born affected by ectodermal dysplasias.

Proceeds from this book will underwrite the NFED's support, treatment, and research programs. The Foundation publishes high-quality information to empower families with knowledge that their doctors often cannot give. Family Conferences give families the opportunity to network with other affected families, develop mutual support systems, and learn from experienced doctors and dentists. Affected children and their siblings attend Kids Camp where they participate in educational and social activities with other children like them.

When you are missing some or all of your teeth, smiling, eating and talking are not easy. The NFED believes every person deserves a smile. The Foundation works with families to help them understand their treatment choices and get financial help for care. The NFED developed a network of Dental Treatment Centers that offer affordable care from experienced dentists. The Foundation has helped 300+ people with $1.3 million in life-changing care.

Founded by a farmwife with an affected son, the NFED has achieved great strides in research in three short decades. Little to nothing was known about HED in 1981. Today, researchers are testing a treatment that, if successful, will eradicate the symptoms of the condition in newborn males. The NFED has been the catalyst for this research and is excited about the possibilities and hope it holds for families for generations to come.

Treatment and research advancements are critical. Yet, the NFED's biggest accomplishment is simply its existence. The NFED stands with open arms to welcome the family who's just been diagnosed, to answer their questions, and to allay their fears. The Foundation educates families that anything is possible for the person who is affected by ectodermal dysplasia. The conditions come with challenges, but with support and encouragement from the NFED, families can expect a bright future.

To learn more or to donate, visit the NFED's Web site at www.NFED.org.

ACKNOWLEDGEMENTS

Remember that movie version of my life which begins with a game of Wiffleball in Middletown, America? Well, what if it won the Oscar for "Best Picture." I mean, if *Moneyball* can get a nomination, why not this story?

Here then, is my acceptance speech.

In place of "thanking the academy," I'd like to thank the Houston Astros Baseball Club, Inc. If you've ever been a part of the organization, from owner to usher from locker-room to parking-lot attendant, you've been a part of my baseball journey. I've been honored to share this adventure with you.

To the thousands of men whom I've watched play the national pastime, I salute you for your dedication, determination, and devotion to excellence. If you're fortunate enough to still be playing the game, remember, you have a responsibility to those who played before you, those who pay to watch you play, and to the future of the great game of baseball.

To the men and women of our military—past, present, and future—thank you for your sacrifice and service to our country.

For those of you with whom I've shared the pleasure of working at Home Sports Entertainment, Prime Sports, Fox Sports Southwest, and Fox Sports Houston, I'm deeply indebted. My job is a cinch compared to what many of you do day-in and night-out. If you're on the current crew and I wasn't able to track you down for mention in Chapter 21, my humble apologies. Let's grab a cup of coffee sometime soon. I'm buying.

To Larry Dierker and Jim Deshaies, my deepest gratitude for the baseball—and life—lessons you've taught me, and for the friendships we've formed. You guys both mean the world to me.

I was about seventy pages into "The Evolution of Broadcasting Technology" when Tim Gregg suggested I write about something I knew something about. I wasn't sure what that might be until he suggested I tell my own story. Tim, I told you I had little understanding of how this process worked, but thanks to your vision, talents, and patience, I think I get it now. I believed we could whiz through this thing in a matter of weeks, but you insisted we spend a little more time—and effort—than that. You were right and I am grateful for the finished product you helped me put together.

Over the course of writing this book, I've officially adopted a new family. Paul and Susan Hamm, you are an inspiration in so many ways. Your enthusiasm for and support and participation in the process of creating this book have been extremely valuable. And to Zach Hamm, let me say this: Each time I ran into an obstacle within the pages of this book, I'd take a moment and reflect on your personal encouragement and can-do attitude. I've done my best to channel your wonderful spirit.

Valuable contributions to the book came from Judy Dierker, Jonnie Smith, Christi Ensberg, Jennifer Everett, and Wave Robinson. Thank you for your involvement.

Stephen O'Brien took the front and back cover shots. There's a good reason he's the Astros' official team photographer.

Thanks to Pat Getter, Kathy Wagner, Julie Weaver and Marilyn Turner for editing support, to Jessica Swaim and Carol Eubanks for editorial assistance, and to Daisy Durham for coming to our rescue in the layout and formatting of this book. Sumner Hunnewell provided the online indexing for the book.

Several people took the time to read early drafts of the manuscript. That's the mark of a true friend. Thank you for your kindness and suggestions. Hopefully, you'll see a little of your handiwork in the completed product.

If you've finished reading this book and now find yourself here at the end, thank you for investing your time in my story. If you've purchased the book you're holding in your hands, thank you for supporting the National Foundation for Ectodermal Dysplasias. Judy Woodruff, Jodi Edgar Reinhardt and the entire NFED staff do extraordinary work for a courageous group of people.

Finally, to Dianne, Allison, Alan, Luke, Emma, and CC, a special thank you. My baseball journey has required each of you to make compromises and sacrifices. The rigors of my job have often taken a greater toll on you than you deserved. Yet, you've stood by me unflinchingly and with unconditional love. I thank the Lord for the great blessings which you continually bring to my life.

ABOUT THE AUTHORS

Bill Brown is the long-time television voice of the Houston Astros. Bill has worked as a television sportscaster for more than forty years and has won several awards and honors, including the Fred Hartman Award from the Houston chapter of the Baseball Writers Association of America. Bill and his wife Dianne live in Houston. This is his first book.

Tim Gregg is a former radio sportscaster and public relations director on the women's tennis tour. A native Oklahoman, Tim lives in Houston where he owns a video production and Web design company. He has previously collaborated on *Moon Shots: Reflections of a Baseball Life* and *Dear Jay, Love Dad: Bud Wilkinson's Letters to His Son.*

Both Bill and Tim are members of the Larry Dierker Chapter of the Society for American Baseball Research.

Made in the USA
Charleston, SC
07 June 2012